# Neighbours and the Law

# Neighbours and the Law

By

## Tadgh Kelly

CLARUS
PRESS

**Published by**
Clarus Press Ltd,
Griffith Campus,
South Circular Road,
Dublin 8.

**Typeset by**
Deanta Global Publishing Services

**Printed by**
CPI Group (UK) Ltd, Croydon, CR0 4YY

**ISBN**
978-1-905536-48-1

To Michael and Johanna

# Preface

Too often people perceive the law as facilitating disputes in relation to valuable assets and large scale commercial disputes whilst providing no remedies for neighbourly disputes of a more modest nature where the emotional and psychological toll may far outweigh the financial worth of the dispute. Whilst other jurisdictions such as England and Wales and indeed further afield in the United States have a wealth of publications in the area of neighbourhood law, there was no such publication in the Irish context.

This book aims to remedy this situation providing legal practitioners, but also the lay reader, with a simple explanatory guide to the variety legal disputes and issues that arise between adjoining land owners thereafter providing the various statutory and civil remedies available to disputants. Emphasises is given of the need for disputants and their advisors to consider the increasingly important role that Alternative Dispute Resolution (ADR) plays in providing neighbours with a more appropriate forum for the resolution of disputes: especially where the protagonists must continue their daily lives in close proximity after the dispute has been determined.

The book also comes in the wake of the coming into law of Chapter 3 of the Land and Conveyancing Law Reform Act 2009 (the 2009 Act) pertaining to *party structures*, which is the first attempt by the Houses of the Oireachtais to codify and bring clarity to the extent one may carry out of a myriad of works at and on the boundary of their property from the lopping of trees or building of extensions to the their home, to name but two.

This book also deals with the abolition by the 2009 Act of the old methods of acquiring *easements*, such as rights of way, through prescription and details the interaction of the old common law and the new statutory framework along with advising in relation to the options available in relation to protecting the rights they may have acquired over the lands of adjoining land owners. This area of the law does not lend itself to simple explanation but there is hopefully ample clarity provided in order to allow the lay reader to grasp the key concepts in order to have an informed discussion with their solicitor in order to secure their proprietary rights going forward.

Whilst new developments are obviously dealt with in detail, equal emphasis is given to the time honoured sources of dispute between neighbours: noise pollution, dangerous dogs, liability for escaping livestock, roots, overhanging branches, backyard burning, unauthorised developments, planning objections and planning appeals.

There are a number of acknowledgements that I wish to make. Firstly, to all my colleagues in Pearts Solicitors for their assistance and advices and in particular Monica Rowley for her clinical analysis of the nature and extent of occupiers' liability; to David McCartney of Clarus Press for his guidance and support; to Caroline Wade for her seemingly effortless skills in converting the written word to the diagrammatic; to John O'Hara of Laois County Council for his knowledge on the workings of local government; to Shelly Browne for her unwavering support. Sincere gratitude to Brendan Savage BL for sacrificing long hours editing as well as providing critical analysis and advices.

Finally to Valerie Peart and Gerard Wade of Pearts Solicitors for opening a door to the law and for ongoing support and professional guidance from that moment to the ongoing present.

Tadgh Kelly,
August 2012

# Contents

*Preface* ............................................................................................................ vii
*Table of Cases* ................................................................................................. xi
*Table of Legislation* ...................................................................................... xv

1. Boundary Disputes ...................................................................................1
2. Carrying Out Works on a Shared Boundary.......................................21
3. Easements and Profits à Prendre ...........................................................53
4. Adverse Possession and Squatters' Rights...........................................71
5. Trees, Hedges and Roots..........................................................................79
6. Planning, Exempted Development and Unauthorised
   Development............................................................................................95
7. Planning Objections and Appeals .......................................................119
8. Derelict Sites, Dangerous Structures and Unsanitary Sites .............133
9. Noisy Neighbours...................................................................................145
10. Occupiers' Liability................................................................................167
11. Criminal Law (Defence and the Dwelling) Act 2011 .......................181
12. Animals and the Law .............................................................................185
13. Backyard Burning of Waste ..................................................................203
14. Low Flying Aircraft ...............................................................................209
15. Civil Remedies........................................................................................217
16. Alternative Dispute Resolution ...........................................................233

*Index* ..............................................................................................................245

# Table of Cases

*AGS (ROI) Pension Nominees Ltd v Madison Estates Ltd*
Unreported, Supreme Court, 23 October 2003 .......................................62
*Alan Wibberley Building Ltd v Insley* [1999] 2 AII ER 897 ..............................2
*Ali v Lane* [2006] EWCA Civ 1532 ................................................................ 2n

*Bullie Coal Mining Co v Osbourne* [1899] AC 351 ................................... 219n
*Burnie Port Authority v General Jones Pty Ltd* [1996] 4 LRC 605 ............. 221n
*Browne v Flower* [1911] 1 Ch 219 ................................................................ 63n

*Cambridge Water Co v Eastern Counties Leather plc,* [1994] AC 264 ...........222
*Campus Oil Ltd v Minister for Energy* (No 2) [1983] IEHC 4 ......................226
*Carminer v Northern & London Investment Trust Ltd* [1951] AC 88 ..... 85n 87
*Carroll v Sheridan* [1984] ILRM 451.................................................................55
*Chasemore v Richards* (1895) 7 HLC 349 ....................................................... 58n
*Charleton v Kenny* (2006) No 4266P .................................................................233
*Christie v Davey* [1893] 1 Ch D 316 .................................................................218
*Colls v Home and Colonial Stores Ltd* [1904] AC 179 ................................30, 57
*Cook v JD Wetherspoon plc* [2009] EWCA Civ 330....................................... 18
*Cowhurst v Amersham Burial Board* (1878)IV Ex D5....................................88

*Daly v Quigley* [1960] Ir. Jur. 1....................................................................... 10n
*Dunne v Iarnród Éireann* [2007] IEHC 314 ...........................................72, 73 75
*Dyce v Hay* (1852) 1 Macq. 305....................................................................... 61n

*Eircell Ltd v Bernstoff,* Unreported, High Court.............................................55
*Erskine v Adeane* (1873) LR 8 Ch App 756 ......................................................88

*Gillen v Fair* (1956) 90 ILTR 119 ......................................................... 85, 86n, 87
*Glasgow Corporation v Muir* [1943] 2 All ER 44 ...................................... 220n
*Glencar Explorations v Mayo County Council* [2002] 1 ILRM 481 (SC) ......220
*Grainger v Finlay* (1858) 7 ICLR 417, 3 Ir Jur N.S. 175...............................190
*Greatrex v Hayward* (1853) 8 Exch. 291 ........................................................ 60n

*Handel v St Stephen's Close* [1994] 1 EGLR 70............................................. 61n
*Hanley v Shannon* (1834) Hay & Jon. 645 ........................................................ 6n
*Hanna v Pollock* [1900] 2 IR 664 ................................................................... 65n

*Hanrahan v Merck Sharp and Dohme (Ireland) Ltd* [1988] IESC 1;
   [1988] ILRM 629 ................................................................................. 217n
*Heatherington v Gault* (1905) 7 F. 708 ........................................................ 79n
*Heaves v Westmeath County Council* (20 ILT) (Circuit Ct,
   Mullingar, 17 October 2001) ..................................................................... 173
*Home Brewery v William Davies & Co* [1987] 1 AII ER 637 ........................ 59n
*Howley v Jebb* (1859) 8 ICLR 435 ................................................................ 60n

*JA Pye (Oxford) Ltd v United Kingdom* [2005] ECHR 921 ............................. 73
*Jones v Read* (1876) IR 10 CL 315 ............................................................... 22n

*Kelk v Pearson* (1871) LR 6 Ch 809 ............................................................. 57n
*Kelsen v Imperial Tobacco Co* [1957] 2 QB 334 ......................................... 219n
*Kirby v Burke* [1994] Ir 207 ....................................................................... 178n

*Lemmon v Webb* [1891-94] All ER Rep 749 ................................... 79, 80, 81n
*Lynch v Hetherton* [1991] 2 IR 405 ................................................................ 86

*McCoy v McGill* [2008] IEHC 301 ............................................................. 15, 18
*Matts v Hanley* (1813) 5 Taunt. 20 ................................................................ 8n
*Masserine v Murphy* [1931] NI 192 ............................................................. 58n
*Mills v Brooker* [1919] 1 KB 555 ................................................................... 83

*O'Reilly v Lavelle* [1990] 2 Ir 372 ............................................................... 194
*O'Shea v Anhold*, Unreported, Supreme Court, 23 October 1996 ............ 195
*O'Sullivan v O'Connor* (1980) 114 ILTR 63 ................................................. 61n

*Patrick v Colerick* (1838) 3 M. & W. 483 ..................................................... 83n
*Pennock v Hodgson* [2010] EWCA Civ 873 ................................................. 237
*Perry v Woodfarm Home Ltd* [1975] IR 104 .................................................. 77
*Phibbs v Pears* [1965] 1 QB 76 .................................................................... 63n
*Potts v Smith* (1868) LR 6 Eq 311 ............................................................... 56n
*Property Point Ltd v Kirri* [2009] EWHC 2958 (Ch) ..................................... 62

*Quinn v Scott* [1965] 1 WLR 1004 ............................................................... 87n

*R v Inland Revenue Commissioners, Ex parte National Federation
   of Self Employed and Small Businesses Ltd* [1982] AC 617 .................. 223n
*Robinson v Kilvert* (1889) 41 Ch D 88 ........................................................ 217
*Royal Dublin Society v Yates* [1997] IEHC 144 ............................... 217n, 219n
*Rudd v Rea* [1921] 1 IR 223 .......................................................................... 55

*Rylands v Fletcher* (1868) LR 3 HL 330; (1866) LR 1 Ex 265 .........89, 221, 222

*Scott v Pape* (1886) 31 Ch D 554.................................................... 57n
*Searle v Wallbank* [1947] AC 341................................................ 194n
*Steadman v Smith* (1858) 8 EI & BL 1 .......................................... 22n
*Sturges v Bridgman* (1879) 11 Ch D 852..........................................218

*Thomas v Thomas* (1835) 2 CM & R 34 .......................................... 59n
*Tomlinson v Congleton B.C.* [2003] 1 AC 46...................................170
*Transco v Stockport MBC* [2004] 4 LRC 314........................................ 222n, 223

*Vawles v Miller* (1810) 3 Taunt 137 ............................................... 10n

*Weir Rodgers v SF Trust* [2005] 1 ILRM 471 ....................................169
*Wheeldon v Burrows* (1879) LR 12 Ch D 31.................................... 68n

# Table of Legislation

## Statutes

Acquisitions of Land (Assessment of Compensation) Act 1919 .. 136, 141n
Air Navigation and Transport (Amendment) Act 1998 ...................... 209n
Air Pollution Act 1987 ...............................................................................204
    s 4..................................................................................................................204
    s 24(2) ..................................................................................................... 204n
    s 53..............................................................................................................204
Animals Act 1985 ........................................................................................194
    s 2..................................................................................................194, 195, 196
Arbitration Act 1954 ................................................................................ 240n
Arbitration Act 1980 ................................................................................ 240n
Arbitration Act 2010 ...................................................................................240
Arbitration (International Commercial) Act 1998 ................................ 240n
Aviation Act 2006........................................................................................ 209n
    s 2(c)(i)..................................................................................................... 210n
Aviation Regulation Act 2001 ................................................................. 209n

Capital Acquisitions Tax Consolidation Act 2003
    s 62..................................................................................................................76
Civil Law (Miscellaneous Provisions) Act 2011
    Pt 12........................................................................................................... 67
    s 37....................................................................................................... 30n, 64
    s 38....................................................................................................... 66, 67n
    s 39............................................................................................................68
    s 41........................................................................................................... 64n
Civil Liability and Courts Act 2004
    s 45(2)(b) ................................................................................................ 4n
Control of Dogs Act 1986-2010....................................................................153
Control of Dogs Act 1986 ................................................................185, 198
    s 11................................................................................................................190
    s 12................................................................................................................191
    s 21................................................................................................................186
    s 21(1) ........................................................................................................187
    s 21(2)........................................................................................................187
    s 21(3) ........................................................................................................186
    s 22................................................................................................188, 189

s 22(1)(a).................................................................................................198
s 23..........................................................................................................188
s 25...............................................................................................191, 192
s 25(2)....................................................................................................200
s 26..........................................................................................................189
Control of Horses Act 1996................................................................193
s 18......................................................................................................193n
s 20..........................................................................................................193
s 34..........................................................................................................193
s 37..........................................................................................................193
s 40..........................................................................................................194
Courts Act 1964
s 7(3)................................................................................................163,
s 7(6)......................................................................................................165
Courts Act 1981
s 2(1)(d)................................................................................................. 4n
Courts (Supplement Provisions) Act 1961
Third Schedule.................................................................................... 4n
Communications Regulations Act 2002
s 58(1)......................................................................................................91
s 58(2)................................................................................................... 91n
s 58(3)................................................................................................... 91n
s 58(4)................................................................................................... 91n
s 58(5)................................................................................................... 91n
s 58(6)................................................................................................... 92n
Conveyancing Act 1881
s 6......................................................................................................... 53n
Criminal Justice (Public Order) Act 1994
s 8............................................................................................................151
s 19C(1)...................................................................................................69
Criminal Law (Defence and Dwelling) Act 2011...........................181, 184
s 2............................................................................................................181
s 2(3)......................................................................................................183
s 2(a)................................................................................................... 182n
s 2(b)................................................................................................... 182n
s 2(b)(i)..................................................................................................182
s 2(b)(ii)................................................................................................182
s 2(4)......................................................................................................182

s 2(5) ............................................................................................ 182n
s 2(6) ............................................................................................ 182n
s 2(7) ............................................................................................ 182n
s 2(8) .............................................................................................. 183
s 3(2) ............................................................................................ 172n
s 5 .................................................................................................... 183

Defamation Act 2009 ........................................................................... 1
s 6 ...................................................................................................... 1n
s 6(2) ................................................................................... 1n, 119n
s 42 .................................................................................................... 1
s 42(1)(a)-(c) ..................................................................................... 1n
s 42(2)(a) .......................................................................................... 2n
s 42(2)(b) .......................................................................................... 2n
Derelict Sites Act 1961 ................................................................. 133n
Derelict Sites Act 1990 ........................................................... 133, 142
s 3 .................................................................................................... 133
s 8 .................................................................................................... 134
s 8(2) ............................................................................................... 134
s 9 .................................................................................................... 133
s 10 ................................................................................................ 134n
s 11(4) ............................................................................................ 135n
s 12 ................................................................................................ 134n
s 14 ................................................................................................. 135
s 16(3) ............................................................................................ 131n
s 17 ................................................................................................. 136
s 18(2) ............................................................................................ 136n
s 19(2) ............................................................................................ 136n
s 19(3) ............................................................................................ 136n
s 20 ................................................................................................ 136n
s 28 ................................................................................................. 135
s 31 ................................................................................................ 136n
Dublin Corporation Act 1890 ............................................. 33, 34, 35

Electricity Regulation Act 1999
s 45 .................................................................................................. 90n
s 37 .................................................................................................. 90n
s 49 .................................................................................................. 90n

Electricity (Supply) Act 1927
  s 37.................................................................................................... 90n
  s 53(1) ...................................................................................................90
  s 53(3) .................................................................................................. 90n
  s 98(1) ..............................................................................................90, 91
  s 98(2) ...................................................................................................91
  s 98(3) ...................................................................................................91
Environmental Protection Agency Act 1992 ...........................................161
  s 8(1) ....................................................................................................151
  s 9(1)(a)............................................................................................. 151n
  s 11(1) ................................................................................................ 151n
  s 11(2) ................................................................................................ 151n
  s 106....................................................................................................145
  s 108...................................................................................... 145, 146, 149
    ...........................................................................................150, 191, 212
  s 108(2) .............................................................................................. 151n
  s 113 .................................................................................................. 141n

Forestry Act 1946
  s 37......................................................................................................89
  s 37(3) ..................................................................................................90
  s 39......................................................................................................90
Forestry Act 1988
  s 6(3) .................................................................................................. 90n

Housing (Miscellaneous Provisions) Act 2002
  s 24......................................................................................................69

Irish Aviation Act 1993
  s 3...................................................................................................... 210n
Irish Aviation Authority Act 1993 .......................................................209, 214
  s 3...................................................................................................... 210n
  s 74(2) .................................................................................................210
  s 74(3) ................................................................................................ 210n
  s 74(5) .................................................................................................211
  s 74(6) .................................................................................................210

Land and Conveyancing Law Reform Act 2009...................1, 28, 30, 32, 33,
  ...........................................................................................52, 64, 67, 70

s 11(1)(d)(i) ........................................................................... 27n, 83n
s 11(1)(d)(ii) .......................................................................... 27n, 83n
s 33 ................................................................................................ 60n, 64
s 34 ..................................................................... 29, 30n, 63, 64n
s 35 .................................................................... 30n, 64n, 67
s 35(4) ...............................................................................................64
s 36 ............................................................................................... 64n
s 37 ............................................................................................... 64n
s 38 ............................................................................................... 64n
s 38(b) ..................................................................................... 66, 67n
s 39 ....................................................................................................68
s 40(1) ........................................................................................ 68n
s 40(2) ...............................................................................................68
s 43 ....................................................................................25, 39, 82
s 44 .................................................................27, 31, 46, 96
s 44(1) ...............................................................................................27
s 44(1)(b) .................................................................................... 96n
s 44(1)(d) ...........................................................................27, 83, 84
s 44(2) ........................................................................................ 26, 31n
s 44(2)(a) ...........................................................................................45
s 44(2)(b)(i) .......................................................................... 32n, 85n
s 44(2)(b)(ii) ............................................................................ 26, 32n
s 44(3) ...................................................................... 26, 29n, 31n
s 44(4) ...............................................................................................32
s 44(4)(a) ..................................................................................... 33n, 40
s 44 (4)(i) ...........................................................................................45
s 44(4)(a)(ii) ....................................................................................40
s 44(4)(b) ................................................................................... 33n, 40
s 45 ...................................................................24, 25,34, 35, 42,
................................................................46, 81, 82, 84, 93, 96, 97, 125, 176
s 45(1) ...............................................................................................39
s 46 ...............................................................................................27, 97
s 46(1) ....................................................................... 28n, 47, 48, 176n
s 46(2)(a) ..................................................................................... 28n
s 46(2)(b) .................................................................................... 28n, 176n
s 47 ....................................................................... 33n, 39, 43
s 98(1) ..........................................................................................49, 51
s 98(2) ..........................................................................................40, 51

s 100...................................................................................................................52

s 132................................................................................................................ 25n

Pt 4

    Schedule 2 .................................................................53n, 56n, 66n

Pt 8

    Chapter 1 ............................................................................63, 65, 67

Litter Pollution Act 1997

    s 22....................................................................................................192

Local Government (Sanitary Services) Act 1964.......................137, 140, 142

    s 1......................................................................................................140

    s 3......................................................................................................140

    s 3(1)(a)............................................................................................ 140n

    s 3(2)(a)............................................................................................ 140n

    s 11(1) .............................................................................................. 137n

    s 17....................................................................................................138

Local Government (Planning and Development) Act 1976.....................125

National Assessment Management Agency Act 2009

    s 2(b)(viii)....................................................................................... 137n

Occupier's Liability Act 1995................................................................36, 167

    s 1.......................................................................................... 171, 173n

    s 1(1) ..............................................................................167n, 168n, 169n

    s 3.....................................................................................................172

    s 3(1) ................................................................................................ 174n

    s 3(2) ................................................................................................ 172n

    s 4.....................................................................................................170

    s 3(2) ................................................................................................ 172n

    s 4(a) ................................................................................................ 172n

    s 4(1) ................................................................................................ 169n

    s 4(2) ................................................................................................169

    s 4(2)(g) ........................................................................................... 171n

    s 4(3)(a)................................................................................... 178n, 183

    s 4(3)(b) ........................................................................................... 178n

    s 5.................................................................................................... 174n

    s 5(2)(b) ...........................................................................................174n

    s 5(2)(c) ............................................................................................174n

    s 5(5) ................................................................................................175

    s 6(2) ................................................................................................ 175n

    s 7.......................................................................................... 174, 176n

Ombudsman Act 1980

s 4(2)(b) ................................................................................... 229n

s 5 .............................................................................................. 229n

s 5(f) ......................................................................................... 229n

s 5(g) ........................................................................................ 229n

s 6(1) ........................................................................................ 229n

s 7(1)(a) ............................................................................. 228, 230n

Petty Sessions (Ireland) Act 1851

s 10(4) ...................................................................................... 210n

Planning and Development Acts 2000-2011 ....................... 95, 125

Planning and Development Act 2000 .................................. 95, 155

First Schedule ........................................................................ 156

Pt V .......................................................................................... 115

Pt VIII ...................................................................................... 100

s.3 ............................................................................................... 95

s 4(2)(2) ..................................................................................... 96

s 5 ...................................................................................... 96, 97, 98

s 5(4) ......................................................................................... 98n

s 9 ............................................................................................. 157

s 21 ........................................................................................... 139n

s 22 ........................................................................................... 139n

s 23 ........................................................................................... 139n

s 24 ........................................................................................... 139n

s 34 ........................................................................................... 155

s 34(4)(c)(i) ............................................................................. 155n

s 34(4)(q) ................................................................................. 155n

s 34(4)(i) .................................................................................. 138

s 34(4)(g) ................................................................................. 139n

s 34(12) .................................................................................... 105n

s 37 ........................................................................................... 125

s 37(6)(a) ................................................................................. 127

s 37(6)(7) ................................................................................. 128n

s 40 ........................................................................................... 106n

s 42 ........................................................................................... 106n

s 50(2)(a)(i) ............................................................................. 132n

s 63 ........................................................................................... 157n

s 126 ......................................................................................... 129n

s 130.................................................................................................... 129n
s 130(3)(c)............................................................................................ 129n
s 134(1) ................................................................................................ 129n
s 138(1)(a)(i)......................................................................................... 130n
s 138(1)(a)(ii)........................................................................................ 130n
s 138(2) ................................................................................................ 130n
s 138(3) ................................................................................................ 130n
s 152(3) ................................................................................................ 101n
s 152(3)(e) ............................................................................................ 101n
s 152(4)(b) ........................................................................................... 103n
s 153(1) ................................................................................................ 101n
s 153(2)(b) ........................................................................................... 101n
s 154(2) ................................................................................................ 102n
s 154(5) .................................................................................................102
s 154(5)(b) .............................................................................................103
s 154(6) ................................................................................................ 103n
s 154(9) ................................................................................................ 102n
s 155..................................................................................................... 103n
s 156..................................................................................................... 103n
s 156(1)(b) ................................................................................... 89n, 103n
s 156(2)(b) ........................................................................................... 103n
s 157(5) .................................................................................................106
s 160............................................................................................103, 106, 156
s 160(1) .................................................................................................104
s 160(1)(A) ........................................................................................... 104n
s 160(1)(B) ........................................................................................... 104n
s 160(1)(C)............................................................................................ 104n
s 160(2) ................................................................................................ 104n
s 162(3) ..........................................................................................105, 106
s 162(6)(a)............................................................................................. 106n
s 180..............................................................................................138, 139
s 180(1) ................................................................................................ 138n
s 180(2) .................................................................................................138
s 205................................................................................................89, 92
s 214..................................................................................................... 135n
Planning and Development (Amendment) Act 2010
s 23...................................................................................................... 105n
s 46(a) ........................................................................................... 89n, 103n

s 46(b) .................................................................................... 103n

s 59 .................................................................................. 138n, 139

s 162(3) ................................................................................. 105n

Prescriptions Act 1832 ...................................................... 56, 65, 66

s 2 ........................................................................................... 66n

s 3 ......................................................................... 30n, 56, 57, 66n

s 4 ............................................................................................ 56

Prescriptions Ireland Act 1858 ...................................... 56n, 66n

Private Residential Tenancies Act 2004

s 15 ......................................................................................... 152

Pt VI ....................................................................................... 152

s 103 ...................................................................................... 152n

Protection of the Environment Act 2003 ................................. 156

s 10 .............................................................................. 151n, 157

s 83(1) .................................................................................... 156n

s 106 ...................................................................................... 156n

s 107 ................................................................................ 156, 157

s 107(5) .................................................................................. 156n

Registration of Deeds and Title Act 2006 ............................... 11n

s 50 .......................................................................................... 77

Pt 3 ......................................................................................... 14n

Registration of Title Act 1964 ................................................... 13

s 3(4) ...................................................................................... 141

s 6 ........................................................................................... 141

s 8(b)(i) ................................................................................... 64n

s 9 ........................................................................................... 141

s 19(1) ...................................................................................... 77

s 49 ............................................................ 6n, 65n, 75,76, 77

s 49A ........................................................... 64, 65n, 67, 69

s 49A(1) .................................................................................. 64n

s 69(1) ..................................................................................... 65n

s 69(1)(h) ................................................................................. 67

s 69(1)(jj) ................................................................................. 64n

s 82 ......................................................................................... 64n

s 84 ......................................................................................... 12n

s 85 ......................................................................................... 14n

Residential Tenancies Act 2004

s 15(1) ..................................................................................... 148n

s 77(3) ........................................................................................ 148n
Roads Act 1993
   s 11 ............................................................................................... 138

Statute of Limitations 1957
   s 7 ................................................................................................. 73
   s 13(2) ................................................................................. 5, 71, 74
   s 49 .............................................................................................. 73n
Successions Act 1965 ..................................................................... 8
   s 13(1)(a) ..................................................................................... 71n
   s 13(1)(b) ..................................................................................... 71n
   s 13(1)(c) ..................................................................................... 71n
   s 66 ............................................................................................... 8n
   s 126 .............................................................................................. 71

Waste Management Act 1996 to 2008
   s 7 ............................................................................................... 204
   s 18 .............................................................................................. 204
   s 39 .............................................................................................. 204
Waste Management Act 1996
   Pt IV ........................................................................................... 204
Wildlife Act 1976
   s 40 .............................................................................................. 92
   s 40(2)(a) ..................................................................................... 92n
   s 40(2)(b) ..................................................................................... 92n
Wildlife (Amendment) Act 2000
   s 46 .............................................................................................. 92
   s 46(a) ......................................................................................... 92n
   s 68 .............................................................................................. 93n
Wildlife (Amendment) Act 2010
   s 7 ............................................................................................... 93n

## Statutory Instruments

Control of Dogs Regulations 1998 (SI No 442 of 1998) .................... 188, 192

District Court (Land and Conveyancing Law Reform Act 2009) Rules 2010
   (SI No 162 of 2010) ........................................................ 25n, 35, 39
District Court Rules 1997 (SI No 93 of 1997) ....................................... 39, 40
   Order 93A ................................................................................ 39, 52

Derelict Site Regulations 2000 (SI No 455 of 2000)............................... 135n

Environmental Protection Agency Act (Noise) Regulations 1994
    (SI No 179 of 1994) ....................................................... 145, 149n, 155, 156
Environmental Noise Regulations 2006 (SI No 140 of 2006)...................153
    Art 3(1).................................................................................................153
    Art 5(b)............................................................................................... 154n
    Art 6..................................................................................................... 154n
    Art 7..................................................................................................... 154n
    Art 7(b)(iii)........................................................................................... 154n
    Art 12................................................................................................... 154n

Irish Aviation Authority (Rules of the Air) Order
    2004 (SI No 72 of 2004) ...........................................................................214
    Rule 3 ..................................................................................................210
    Rule 3(2)(b).......................................................................................... 211n

Land and Conveyancing Law Reform Act 2009
    (Commencement) Order (SI No 356 of 2009)..................................... 25n

Planning and Development Regulations 2001, (SI No 600 of 2001)
    ................................................................95, 96, 107, 120n, 121n, 125n, 212
    Art 6.................................................................................................96, 98
    Sch 2
        Pt 1................................................................................................96

Registration of Title Act 1964 (Compulsory Registration of Ownership)
    (Cork and Dublin) Order 2010 (SI No 516 of 2010)........................... 11n
Registration of Deeds Rules 2008 (SI No 52 of 2008) ..................... 14n, 15n
Rules of the Superior Courts (SI No 15 of 1986)
    Ord 84, rr 18-27................................................................................ 223n
    Ord 84, r 20(1) .................................................................................. 223n
    Ord 84 r 21(1) ................................................................................... 224n
Rules of the Superior Courts (Judicial Review) 2011
(SI No 691 of 2011) ................................................................................ 224n

Waste Management (Prohibition of Waste Disposal by Burning)
    Regulations 2009 (SI No 286 of 2009) ...........................................204, 206
    Reg 3................................................................................................. 205n
    Reg 4................................................................................................. 205n

Reg 4(1) ............................................................................................. 205n
Reg 5 ................................................................................................... 205n
Reg 5(1)(a) ................................................................................. 205n, 207
Reg 5(1)(d) .......................................................................................... 205n
Reg 5(1)(e) ........................................................................................... 205n

## UK Legislation

Anti-Social Behaviour Act 2003
Pt 8 ........................................................................................................ 82

## EU

Directive 2002/49 – Assessment and Management
of Enviromental Noise of 25 June 2002 ................................................ 153

## Treaties

European Convention on Human Rights
Art 1
Protol 1 ............................................................................................... 72

## Other

General Scheme of Mediation Bill 2012 (Draft) ........................................ 241
Mediation and Consolidation Bill 2010 (Draft)
s 4(1) ................................................................................................. 235n
s 4(2) ................................................................................................. 235n
s 7 ..................................................................................................... 239n
Mediation Bill 2012 ................................................................................ 242

# Boundary Disputes

This chapter deals with disputes in relation to the legal ownership of lands at the boundary between adjoining landowners as distinct from the right to carry out works to a party structure by way of a *Works Order*, as is specifically provided for by way of the statutory framework contained in Pt 8, Chapter 3 of the Land and Conveyancing Law Reform Act 2009. Such applications are dealt with in detail in chapter 2. This chapter deals specifically with attempting to show the means by which one may attempt to establish the actual legal ownership of lands at the boundary between adjoining landowners.

## Slander of Title – A Cautionary Note

In any dispute in relation to lands in the possession of another individual, due care and consideration should always be exercised not to defame the good title of the property owner's lands, or what is more correctly termed as *slander of title*.[1] The Defamation Act 2009 does not only seek to protect the rights of individuals to their good name and character but also affords protection to the property interests of the individual. The publishing of a defamatory statement simply consists of the oral or written communication[2] of the defamatory statement to one or more individuals.[3]

Section 42 of the Defamation Act 2009 allows a plaintiff who is able to prove that a statement about his or her lands was untrue, was published maliciously,[4] and the publication of the statement was calculated to cause

---

[1] Whilst s 6 of the Defamation Act 2009 places the tort of libel and the tort of slander under the new heading of the tort of defamation, s 42, in dealing with malicious falsehood, still refers to *slander of title*.

[2] See the definition of "statement" in s 2.

[3] s 6(2).

[4] s 42(1)(a)-(c).

and was likely to cause financial loss in respect of the property,[5] to state a case before the Circuit Court or the High Court[6] for compensation.

Care must be exercised in the midst of the boundary dispute, or indeed in any context, not to make false and malicious statements in an effort to de-value the adjoining landowner's property value. If, for example, an impending contract for the sale of lands was about to be completed and the intending purchaser was to withdraw from entering into the contract based on an untruthful and malicious statement from an aggrieved neighbour, then the financial repercussions may be most serious for the person who published the statement.

## Boundary Disputes — Avoid at All Costs

Lord Hoffmann, in the English case of *Alan Wibberley Building Ltd v Insley,* perhaps put it best in stating that:

> "Boundary disputes are a particularly painful form of litigation. Feelings run high and disproportionate amounts of money are spent. Claims to small and valueless pieces of land are pressed with the zeal of Fortinbras's army. It is therefore important that the law on boundaries should be as clear as possible."[7]

Fortinbras's army is a reference to Shakespeare's *Hamlet* who considers it pointless for Fortinbras's army to go off and fight a battle over a piece of land too small to build a graveyard to bury the dead that will fight over it.

Boundary disputes between adjoining landowners are perhaps the most contentious area of any kind of legal dispute. It is commonplace that boundary disputes can be fought with a passion which seems disproportionate to what is at stake in practical terms.[8] In the end the Judge must choose between what may be two compelling lines of argument and choose one version of events as being the most likely version on the balance of probabilities. The only certainty in a boundary dispute is that there will only be one winner leaving the court. Very often

---

[5] s 42(2)(a) and (b) note that, alternatively, a claim may be stated for an award of special damages.

[6] See s 41 for the court of appropriate jurisdiction.

[7] [1999] 2 All ER 897 at 898.

[8] *Ali v Lane* [2006] EWCA Civ 1532 as per Carnwath LJ at para. 3, Waller and Maurice Kay LJJ in agreement.

personal relations between neighbours who must continue to live in some proximity will lie in tatters.

## Alternative Dispute Resolution—An Alternative to Court

No individual should allow a boundary dispute to go to court without first having considered the possibility of resolving the matter with their neighbour through an alternative dispute resolution (ADR) process. Chapter 16 deals with ADR in detail and shows the advantages of the process in terms of time, costs, stress and anxiety that invariably accompany a boundary dispute. As boundary disputes can be fought with a disproportionate amount of passion and zeal, legal advisers often regard themselves as under a duty to ensure that their clients are aware of the potentially catastrophic consequences of litigation of this kind and of the possibilities of alternative dispute procedures.[9]

## Matters for Consideration with a Solicitor Prior to Commencing the Boundary Dispute

Any neighbour intending to do battle over a piece of land with an adjoining landowner should seek the assistance of his or her solicitor at the earliest opportunity. One's solicitor will assist in focusing one's attention on the harsh realities of the boundary dispute under the following headings:

### Is the Value of the Land Worth the Dispute?

One will obviously strain the relationship between oneself and one's neighbours and it goes without saying that if one loses the claim in the courts, the costs will usually "follow the event", meaning that not only will one have to pay one's own legal team and expert witnesses but also the legal costs of the winning party.

### Does the Disputed Land Affect the Value of the Property?

Another important consideration is to quantify the value that the property will bring to one's overall parcel of land. There is not much point in putting oneself and one's family through a boundary dispute with all of the worry, stress and general wretchedness that goes with an acrimonious legal battle for what might ultimately be a token victory in consideration of the real worth of the land in economic terms.

---

[9] See Appendix 18 which contains an ADR/Mediation referral form for Mediation Chambers Ireland.

### Would One Buy a Property Affected by a Boundary Dispute?

One has to consider the costs involved in allowing a boundary dispute develop into full blown litigation in the courts as this will impact upon what is termed as the *good marketable title* of the lands. Any party intending to sell the lands that are, were, or more than likely will be, the subject of a boundary dispute will have to declare such disputes to any intending purchaser of the lands. This will invariably act as a major disincentive to any intending purchaser who will want a clean title free from issues of boundary disputes.

### How Does One Propose to Finance Litigation?

As explained above, the rule in litigation is that costs follow the event, meaning that, save for instances of special consideration, the courts will award the costs of a case to the winning side, leaving the losing side to pick up the bill for not only their own legal representation but also that of their opponent. This is a harsh reality of litigation through the courts and it is for this reason that any intending complainant(s) should in the first instance consider ADR as a strong alternative.

## Boundary Disputes and the Court

When a dispute arises as to the ownership of two adjoining pieces of land, and if the two owners are unable to solve matters themselves and fail to come to some agreement in terms of the ownership, then the task falls to a Judge of the Circuit Court or the High Court[10] to decide the matter. Typically boundary disputes will arise where one side seeks a declaratory order of the court in relation to the ownership of lands or, alternatively, where one aggrieved party seeks injunctive relief[11] from the court directing that one party cease to occupy or trespass on the lands of the adjoining landowner.

In this regard both parties will adduce whatever evidence they have in their arsenal in order to affirm their claim. Oral evidence may be adduced

---

[10] Depending on the rateable value of the land. Under s 2(1)(d) of the Courts Act 1981, amending column 3 of the Third Schedule of the Courts (Supplemental Provisions) Act 1961, the Circuit Court has jurisdiction for real property that has a rateable valuation of land that does not exceed €252.95. Note that s 45(2)(b) of the Civil Liability and Courts Act 2004, whilst not yet in law, proposes to enlarge the jurisdiction of the Circuit Court in this regard to land with a market value that does not exceed €3,000.000.

[11] An order issued by a court ordering someone to do something or prohibiting some act after a court hearing.

by one party to show that it has always been custom and practice that one landowner had used the lands up to a certain point of demarcation. Expert evidence may be called from a chartered surveyor who will examine the maps attaching to the deeds to the lands, inspect the lands and give an expert opinion as to ownership.

The difficulty that the Judge has, however, is that such evidence must be weighed and every argument will be met with a counter-argument; each witness may be countered by a witness with an opposing recollection or view and each expert witness such as a surveyor or engineer will have his or her evidence called into question by the other side's surveyor or engineer. It must be remembered that whilst an expert witness is there at that particular party's request and for his or her professional opinion, this expert, nonetheless, owes an overriding duty to the court to assist it in reaching its determination.

## Timeframes for Disputes Involving Land, Squatters' Rights and Adverse Possession

Adverse possession is dealt with in detail in Chapter 4, but in general terms, adverse possession of land, or *squatters' rights* as it is more commonly known, arises where a person or *squatter* is in sole and exclusive occupation of land without the acknowledgment of the legal owner. If such squatting has persisted uninterrupted for a period of 12 years, then one's claim to the squatted lands may be what is termed *statute barred*, meaning that one will be potentially barred from bringing any case before the court to re-gain possession of one's lands. This 12-year rule is laid down under s 13(2) of the Statute of Limitations 1957.[12]

The law rewards individuals for making full use of the land and punishes absentee or careless owners for not paying due care and consideration to their lands. The squatter must have used the property as his or her own for a requisite period of 12 years, thereby *curing* defects in the title to the property claimed, meaning that the squatter will be within his or her entitlement to apply to have him- or herself registered as the owner of the lands.[13]

---

[12] The 12-year limitation period is extended to 30 years' possession in order to bar a State Authority from asserting its prior legal entitlement to the lands in question. See Chapter 4 for more detail in relation to the relevant timeframes.

[13] Or more precisely, the owner by way of what is termed *possessory title*.

The squatter's name will not be on a deed to the lands until such time as he or she has satisfied the requisite test for a claim in adverse possession upon which he or she may then apply to be registered as the owner of the lands in the Land Registry.[14]

From the outset, therefore, it will need to be determined with the assistance of a solicitor if it will be possible to mount an action to re-gain possession or to defend an action against a claim of trespass based on the applicable timeframes.

## Types of Ownership and Shared Ownership of Party Structures and Walls

Under the common law there are varying types of ownership of party structures,[15] and even if the party structure belongs to one individual the adjoining landowner may have a right or *easement*[16] over the party wall in his or her favour. This essentially means that one may have the legal ownership or *title* to a piece of land but this ownership is burdened by the fact that another individual has a right to take an advantage from the land.

Take, for example, the fact that a neighbour's rear kitchen gable wall has derived structural support from a rear wall located on the adjoining lands for over 30 years; that neighbour will have an acquired right of support over the land, or more precisely, the structure located on the land, i.e. the rear wall.[17] Therefore, *absolute* ownership of land at the boundary may be tempered or affected by long-standing rights.

### Type 1 – Outright Ownership

Where the boundary is owned outright by one landowner,[18] that is to say where the boundary of separation belongs to one landowner as distinct from the adjoining landowner, the wall between the two parcels of land is located entirely on lands in the ownership of one of the adjoining landowners.

---

[14] s 49 of the Registration of Title Act 1964.
[15] See JCW Wylie, *Irish Land Law* (1st ed, Professional Books Ltd, London, 1975), pp 374–376.
[16] Chapter 3 deals with this concept of rights or *easements* over the property of another in detail.
[17] See diagram below.
[18] *Hanly v Shannon* (1834) Hay. & Jon. 645.

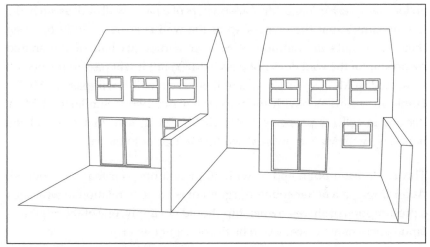

Diagram 1 – Outright Ownership

## Type 2 – Presumed Ownership as Tenants in Common

The common law works under the presumption that party walls on the boundary between two properties are deemed to be shared and are termed to be owned by the two adjoining landowners as *tenants in common*. "Tenants in common" is a legal term describing a type of ownership where owners share a specified proportion of ownership rights in property and upon the death of a tenant in common, i.e. one of the owners, that share is passed on to the estate of the deceased person.

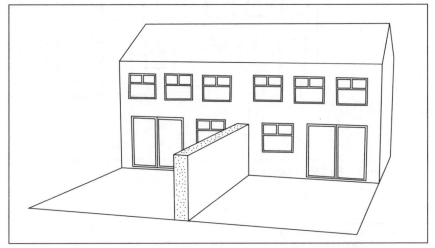

Diagram 2 – Presumed Ownership as Tenants in Common

So for example, Mr X and Mr Y are owners of a party wall and, as such, the law presumes that the ownership of the wall is shared jointly between them as tenants in common. When Mr X dies his half of the shared ownership of the wall does not pass to Mr Y, but it will pass to the person so named in Mr X's will, or where there is no will it will pass to Mr X's family in accordance with the Succession Act 1965.[19] Similarly, if Mr Y decides to sell his property to Mr Z, Mr Z will take that share of the boundary with Mr X as was owned by Mr Y prior to the sale.

This is a presumption and as with all presumptions it may be rebutted. Accordingly, if a better counter-argument is made in relation to why such a presumption of shared ownership should not apply, one of the adjoining landowners may be deemed to be the outright owner.

## Type 3 – Divided Ownership

Alternatively, the party structure may be divided longitudinally down its centre with each of the adjoining landowners owning his or her own share,[20] that is to say, a line is drawn down the centre of the boundary and each respective landowner owns his or her 50 per cent share from the central medial line back.

Diagram 3 – Divided Ownership

---

[19] See s 66 of the Succession Act 1965.
[20] *Matts v Hawkins* (1813) 5 Taunt. 20.

It is open to each of the adjoining landowners to do as he or she so wishes with his or her half of the wall but to remove his or her half of the wall, resulting in the collapse of the adjoining landowner's half, would leave the party that removed his or her section causing the collapse open to a claim for damages and be subject to a mandatory enforcing injunction to reconstruct the wall.

## Type 4 - Divided Ownership with Mutual Rights of Support

Finally, the boundary or party wall may be divided longitudinally down its centre with each adjoining landowner owning his or her own 50 per cent share as per type 3 above. In this instance, however, the ownership of the 50 per cent share is subject to the burden of an easement in favour of the adjoining landowner and vice versa. There is, therefore, a cross-easement, typically of support.

Diagram 4 – Divided Ownership with Mutual Right of Support

One adjoining landowner may not remove his or her 50 per cent share of the wall without ensuring that his or her neighbour's right to support remains. If the wall was to collapse as a result of such removal, the offending adjoining landowner will be open to a claim in damages for the unlawful extinguishment of the easement/right of support and be subject to a mandatory enforcing injunction to reconstruct the wall.

### Type 5 - The Hedge and Ditch Presumption[21]

This presumption applies only to agricultural land. The presumption holds that where two properties are divided by a hedge and a ditch, the property boundary is presumed to be on the opposite edge of the ditch from the hedge. This is based on the principle that the owner would have stood on the boundary facing towards his or her own land, dug the ditch on his or her own land, piled the soil from the digging of the ditch on his or her home side to form a bank, and planted a hedge on the bank.

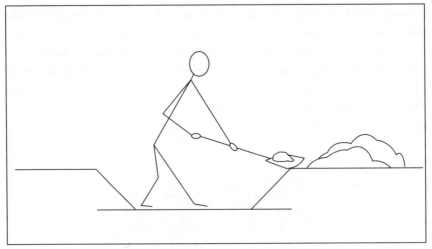

Diagram 5 – The Hedge and Ditch Presumption

### Type 6 – Ownership of the River Bed

In Ireland, and under the common law generally, there exists a presumption that the owner of the lands adjoining the non-tidal river own the land up to the centre of the watercourse,[22] unless it is known to be owned by someone else. The right to fish and take fish from the river which flows over the bed and soil is owned similarly.[23] This means that you have the right to cast the fishing line to the median line of the river only.

---

[21] *Vawles v Miller* (1810) 3 Taunt 137.

[22] *Daly v Quigley* [1960] Ir. Jur. 1.(O'Hagan J).

[23] A *corporeal hereditament* as distinct from an *incorporeal hereditament* where an individual has a right to access a river bank and fish the river therefrom. This type of right is known as a *profit-à-prendre* which are dealt with in detail in chapter 3.

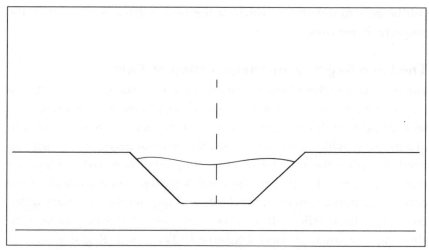

Diagram 6 – Ownership of the River Bed

## Investigation of Title Begins with the Title Documents

In trying to determine the ownership of land between adjoining lands, the starting point is always with the *title documents*. The documents of title are the deed(s) which describe(s) the land, or as it is known in law, the *parcel*,[24] over which a party claims ownership. A solicitor will assist a client in locating and examining title deeds.

There are two separate systems for recording transactions to property or *title*, the term used to describe the ownership of a property in Ireland:

1. The registration of title system (*Land Registry*) which provides a State-guaranteed title to property[25]; and
2. The registration of deeds system (*Registry of Deeds*) which records the priority of the registered deeds and conveyances in relation to lands that are not captured by the *Land Registry* system.[26]

Both systems are mutually exclusive but both are under the control and management of the Property Registration Authority (PRA).[27] A solicitor

---

[24] Parcel of land in essence means the piece of land.

[25] Compulsory first registration in the Land Registry now exists since the 1 June 2011 by virtue of SI No 516 of 2010.

[26] One's solicitor will refer to lands registered in the Land Registry as *registered lands* whilst lands registered in the Registry of Deeds will be referred to as *unregistered lands*.

[27] The PRA is an independent statutory body set up under the Registration of Deeds and Title Act 2006.

will be able to determine which of the two systems is relevant to the property in question.

## The Land Registry and Registration of Title[28]

The Irish land register[29] is a public record and, as such, any person may inspect the folios and *filed plans* or maps,[30] on payment of the prescribed fees. Using the folio one can find out who has the title to or ownership of a property without having to read the original deeds, as the original deeds showing the transfer of ownership from one party to another will have been submitted to the Land Registry who extract all of the necessary information from the deeds and register the necessary detail on a folio. Each folio will also have an associated *filed plan* or map showing the area of land concerned. The Land Registry utilises Ordnance Survey Ireland's topographic mapping to cross-reference and associate its boundary information. This forms the basis of all Land Registry digital map data.[31]

---

[28] The PRA's website—http://www.landregistry.ie—is an excellent resource for any person wishing to further familiarise him- or herself with the process of land registration in Ireland. The Land Registry publishes a number of public guides about land registration which can be viewed or downloaded from its website or obtained free of charge from any Land Registry office. The website also has a "Frequently Asked Questions" section which offers a public guide to registration issues (20 March 2012).

[29] Ireland has a very extensive and well developed system of land registration. Since the foundation of the Land Registry in 1892, there has been a gradual, ongoing and continuous programme of movement away from the older and limited system of recording Deeds (in the Registry of Deeds), to the more modern, flexible and comprehensive "title registration" system provided through the Land Registry. Ninety-three per cent of the total land mass of the State and almost eighty-eight per cent of the legal titles in Ireland are now registered in the Land Registry.

[30] s 84 of the Registration of Title Act 1964 states that the central office shall keep the latest available Ordnance Survey maps for the State and goes on to state that such maps shall be open to public inspection at such times, in such manner, and upon such terms as shall be prescribed.

[31] Both folios and maps are maintained in electronic form. Land Registry maps (digital vector data) are based on Irish Transverse Mercator (ITM) co-ordinate reference system topographic maps that are supplied to the Registry in digital vector form by Ordnance Survey Ireland (OSI). Published scales are 1/5,000 rural, 1/2,500 urban/rural and 1/1,000 urban. The Land Registry represents the extent of all registered land by reference to OSI topographic map data. Where a boundary of the land is not defined by a physical feature on the OSI map, the Land Registry digitises it from either the electronic or paper map(s) lodged by applicants for registration purposes. See Joint Statement OSI-PRA(LR) — 31 January 2011 Joint Statement by Ordnance Survey Ireland and the Property Registration Authority of Ireland http://www.landregistry.ie/eng/News/Joint_Statement_OSI-PRA_LR_-_31_Jan_2011.html. (20 March 2012).

## Land Registry Mapping and Filed Plans

Ordnance Survey Ireland (OSI) is the national mapping agency of Ireland. It is the State agency responsible for the official, definitive surveying and topographic mapping of the Republic of Ireland. This mapping is said to be *topographic*, in that it only represents the physical features on the ground at the time of survey and OSI maps never indicate legal property boundaries, nor do they show ownership of physical features. Although some property boundaries may be coincident with surveyed map features, no assumptions should be made in these instances and consequently it is not possible to identify the position of a legal property boundary from an OSI map.[32]

OSI maps use the same line symbol for a wall, fence, hedge, bank, ditch and stream. Where many features are represented in close proximity it may not be possible to represent them all at the scale of the mapping and it may not be obvious from the map which feature the line represents. For example, where a fence, hedge or wall runs approximately parallel to another feature and so close that they cannot both be plotted correctly at the scale of survey, then only one feature is shown.[33]

Even if a correct interpretation of the map can be made, the line on the map may not be the legal boundary. It is the position of the actual feature on the ground, not the position of the line on the map that is important in attempting to trace the position of the boundary.[34] Accurate analysis of the OSI map can usually only be achieved by taking the map onto the site and comparing it with the features on the ground. This can help decide what has been shown, what has been omitted for the sake of clarity and may also indicate that the map scale does not allow multiple features in close proximity to be shown.

## Land Registry Maps, the Ordnance Survey and the Boundary Dispute

At this stage, given that Land Registry filed plans or maps are based on OSI maps, it will come as little wonder that the boundary system adopted by the Land Registry under the Registration of Title Act 1964 is known

---

[32] *ibid.*
[33] *ibid.*
[34] *ibid.*

as a *non-conclusive boundary system*.[35] Disputing neighbours should only be contacting OSI and the Land Registry for the purposes of taking up copy maps, as both organisations will be unable to answer questions regarding legal property boundaries or to interpret the mapping in a title plan.

The non-conclusive provision dispenses with the need for the land registry to determine the exact location of title boundaries when defining the extent of registered properties, and equally, the ownership of the physical features which mark the limits of a property is left undetermined. As neither the OSI nor the Land Registry will comment on boundary disputes between adjoining landowners it is up to the concerned individual to retain his or her own expert to draw up a report which may be then used to vouch one's claim over certain lands at the boundary. Both the Society of Chartered Surveyors[36] and the Irish Institution of Surveyors[37] maintain a list of land surveyors who offer this service.

## Registry of Deeds System

If one's lands are not registered in the Land Registry then the deeds will normally be registered with the Registry of Deeds. The Registry of Deeds was established in 1707[38] and the primary function of the Registry of Deeds is to provide a system of recording the existence of deeds and conveyances and other documents affecting unregistered property, i.e. unregistered land being land that is not registered under the Land Registry system as detailed above. The effect of registration in the Registry of Deeds is generally to govern priorities between documents dealing with the same piece of land.[39] At registration the registered deed obtains priority over subsequent deeds.

---

[35] s 85 of the Registration of Title Act 1964 states that registered land shall be described by the names of the denominations on the Ordnance Survey maps in which the lands are included, or by reference to such maps, in such manner as the Registrar thinks best calculated to secure accuracy, but, except as provided by this Act, the description of the land in the register or on such maps shall not be conclusive as to the boundaries or extent of the land.

[36] http://www.scs.ie.

[37] http://www.irish-surveyors.ie.

[38] The Registry of Deeds currently operates under the provisions of Pt. 3 of the Registration of Deeds and Title Act 2006 and the Registration of Deeds Rules 2008 (SI No 52 of 2008) which came into effect on 1 May 2008.

[39] http://www.landregistry.ie (20 March 2012).

When a deed is lodged in the Registry of Deeds it must be accompanied by the relevant Registry of Deeds' Application Form.[40] This Registry of Deeds' Application Form replaced the *Memorial* which was a summary of the relevant details of the original deed. The Registry of Deeds' Application Form, and the older Memorials, contain the date of the deed, details of the parties to the deed and a description of the property affected by the deed. Each application is given a serial number in order of the date and time of lodgment and the priority given to registered documents is based on the serial number allocated.[41] The Registry of Deeds does not record ownership of property. It records the existence of deeds relating to transactions with regard to a particular parcel of land.

When the application is completed, the original deed with its scheduled map is not filed in the Registry but is returned to the lodging party, normally the landowner's solicitor. As such, where a party is in dispute with a neighbour over whose title to land is registered in the Registry of Deeds, that person will have no way of taking up a copy of his or her adversary's title deeds and maps as they are not retained by the Registry of Deeds.[42]

Obviously in investigating one's own title, if registered in the Registry of Deeds, then it will be possible for a solicitor to carry out the relevant investigations. However, as the Registry of Deeds does not guarantee the effectiveness of a deed nor does it interpret a deed, an expert opinion by way of a suitably qualified surveyor may be required to consider the detail in the map attaching to the deed by way of reference to the topography or *lie* of the lands at the boundary.

## The Court's View on Determining Boundaries with Reference to Old Deeds and Maps

The court examined and set out these guiding principles in relation to the determining of boundaries in some detail in the case of *McCoy v McGill*.[43] In this case the plaintiffs claimed that the two adjoining properties were

---

[40] As prescribed by the Registration of Deeds Rules 2008 (SI No 52 of 2008).
[41] http://www.landregistry.ie (20 March 2012).
[42] If court proceedings are initiated it may, but not always, be possible for one's solicitor to procure copies of one's neighbour's title deeds through a pre-trial legal process known as *Discovery*.
[43] [2008] IEHC 301.

divided by a natural cliff face, and claimed that the defendants commenced building work in the course of which they removed a substantial quantity of rock from the natural cliff face bounding the two properties.

This, they claimed, was a trespass and constituted a nuisance. Furthermore, the plaintiffs alleged that the work of rock-breaking had a weakening effect on the remaining cliff face and upon the structure of the plaintiffs' house itself. The plaintiffs' claim for trespass was based upon their claim to own the land upon which the rock-breaking and removal took place (the disputed area). In the alternative they claimed to have obtained a possessory title[44] to the disputed area, thereby claiming outright ownership.

The defendants claimed they owned the disputed area. They denied the boundary was the cliff face and argued that the natural cliff face, from the front to the rear of their property, was within their property. They therefore denied any trespass and further denied any damage to the structural integrity of the plaintiffs' house or the natural cliff face. They claimed that the plaintiffs were in fact trying to claim a part of the defendants' property, first by claiming the disputed area under their title document and subsequently by claiming by way of adverse possession.

The issue in the case resolved itself to the question of how to interpret a deed[45] of 1910. It was agreed by the plaintiffs at the hearing that this deed was the key to the case. The key issue was whether that deed granted[46] a right to the lands seven feet from the then boundary of the defendants' property at 5, Ardbrugh Villas to the eastern edge of a pier drawn thereon as a square and described therein as a pier.

The plaintiffs claimed the existing pier was not the pier referred to on the 1910 map. They claimed there must have been another pier since demolished and either the one existing in April 2007 was a twin of that pier or else was constructed after the pier they alleged existed in 1910. The defendants claimed the pier existing in April 2007 was one and the same as that shown on the map and described in the deed of 1910.

---

[44] See chapter 4 on Squatters' Rights.
[45] In this case a deed of assignment.
[46] Or assigned.

In the course of the trial of the action, the court set out the following principles:

**In Relation to Determining Boundaries:**
(a) The primary source for defining a boundary line is the deeds in the chain of title;
(b) The plan attached (if there is one), is usually for the purposes of identification only. It cannot normally be relied upon as delineating precise boundaries; and
(c) If necessary the deeds will have to be supplemented by such inferences as may be drawn from topographical features which existed or probably did when the conveyance was executed.

**In Relation to Rules of Construction of a Deed:**
(a) The court must give effect to the intention of the parties as expressed in the deed; and
(b) To determine this, the court must determine what is meant by the words actually used rather than what the court might conjecture as to what they actually meant. The court should only do so where absolutely necessary to avoid defeating the object which the parties clearly had intended.

**In Relation to the Role of a Map:**
(a) A map or plan may be the determining matter where the parcels provide that the map is to determine the nature and extent of the land in question;
(b) A map may be an essential part of the grant where it is worded such as to make it so and where there can be no certainty without it; and
(c) Any conflict between dimensions set out in figures on a plan by which the property is conveyed or transferred and those calculated by scaling off the plan, may be resolved by reference to topographical features which existed when the conveyances or transfer was executed.

In surmising the case the court found that it was highly probable that the pier that was inspected in April 2007 was one and the same as the pier delineated as a square on the map attached to the 1910 deed. This pier was made of materials and in a manner that showed it was pre-First World War, i.e. 1914 at the latest. In any event, it seemed highly improbable that the pier clearly referred to in the 1910 deed would have been demolished and replaced by another which formed a part of the wall on Ardbrugh Road. Furthermore, the fact that the hoarding which was erected in place of the wall to the road frontage of Redan House and ended at the pier strongly suggested a belief, or at least a suspicion on the part of the plaintiffs and their predecessors in title,[47] that the western boundary of their interest ended at the existing pier.

The decision in *McCoy v McGill*[48] clearly demonstrates that in boundary disputes the court will look very carefully at the dispute in a structured and ordered manner as laid out above in relation to the interpretation of deeds and maps. Perhaps more importantly, the case also clearly demonstrates the need and reliance of the courts on the actual topographical features on the lands and the interpretation of the maps with reference to such topographical features.

In lay terms, the deed tells a story, the map is the accompanying picture, but only when viewed in the context of the actual topography and physical features, both natural and man-made, can a true picture be adduced on the balance of probabilities. Perhaps the court in the English case of *Cook v JD Wetherspoon PLC*[49] put it best in stating that:

> "…[w]here there is a conflict between (1) dimensions in figures on a plan by which the property conveyed or transferred is described, (2) dimensions arrived at by scaling off the plan, the conflict is to be resolved by reference to such inferences as may be drawn from topographical features which existed when the conveyance or transfer was executed."

## Conclusion

Boundary disputes between neighbours are wretched affairs: they cause misery and stress; they lead to costs which are often grossly disproportionate to the value being fought over; not to mention the fact they put a blight on the properties, because no sane person would want to buy a

---

[47] Those in ownership prior to the then current owners.
[48] [2008] IEHC 301.
[49] [2006] EWCA Civ 330 as per Sir Martin Nourse at para 15.

property affected by a boundary squabble, except perhaps at a significantly discounted price.[50]

Little wonder therefore that the Land Registry, Registry of Deeds and the OSI remain silent on the issues of boundaries and even more reason for adjoining landowners to strongly consider an alternative dispute resolution such as mediation as opposed to a long and costly protracted legal battle.

---

[50] *Childs v Vernon* [2007] EWCA Civ 305.

# CHAPTER TWO

# Carrying Out Works
# on a Shared Boundary

## Carrying Out Works on a Shared Boundary

Whilst chapter 1 dealt with disputes in relation to the actual ownership of lands at the boundary between two adjoining landowners, this chapter will deal specifically with the instance of where one of two adjoining landowners refuses consent in relation to any works being carried out to a shared boundary. Works may consist of maintaining hedges, trees, fences, walls, drains and building extensions to the home.

In an ideal world there will be no dispute in relation to the boundary with both neighbours accepting jointly shared ownership and being happy to work together for its maintenance and sharing associated costs. However as the previous chapter demonstrates, ownership of the boundary may often lead to litigation in the courts costing far more than the disputed ground is worth. There are of course instances where a neighbour cannot simply sit idly by as inaction in relation to the maintenance of the shared boundary may spell disaster. Take, for example, the shared ownership of a diseased tree at the boundary that one party feels may be a threat to his or her home if it falls in a storm. In such an instance it is not acceptable for one party to refuse consent for the felling of the dangerous tree in an orderly fashion even if the tree is entirely located on the lands of that non-consenting neighbour.

## Legal Issues in Carrying out Works at the Boundary Without a Neighbour's Consent[1]

*Ownership of the wall*: As discussed in chapter 1, the presumption is that each landowner owns his or her respective longitudinal section of the shared boundary and if the party structure was held under such shared ownership as a *tenancy in common*,[2] this indicated that neither tenant in

---

[1] Chapter 15 deals in detail with the various civil remedies open to parties in seeking to protect their proprietary rights.
[2] For a full explanation of the legal concept of tenancy in common, see chapter 1, pp 7–8.

common may pull it down[3] nor prevent the other from enjoying rights over it.[4] There is a presumption under the law that a boundary is a shared boundary and that, as such, both parties may own their own longitudinal half; however, it is not permissible for one party to knock his or her longitudinal half without the consent of the shared owner. This is because the adjoining landowner will have an implicit right of support for his or her half of the wall against his or her neighbour's half; so while a person may own one's half, this ownership is restricted in terms of implicit *easements*[5] or rights that the neighbour will have over that part of the wall.

## Legal Issues in Relation to Building at the Boundary

*Trespass/Injunctions*: In the absence of consent of the adjoining landowner the party intending to do the works will be trespassing onto the lands of his or her neighbour. This will leave any such party open to a claim for damages in the courts. At the same time the aggrieved neighbour may seek an order of the court that forces the neighbour carrying out the works to desist from trespassing onto lands which are not in his or her ownership.

*Nuisance/Negligence*: Again, if no consent is forthcoming and the works proceed the party carrying out the works may leave him or herself open to a claim not only for trespass but also for nuisance for dust, noise and loss of privacy caused during the construction phase. If the party carrying out the works has the misfortune of hitting an underground pipe causing property damage and flooding to the neighbour's land, there again he or she may be found to have been negligent in the manner the works were undertaken.

*Cost*: Obviously the re-construction or the making safe of the boundary will be to both parties' benefit and, as such, it is only fair and equitable that both parties pay their fair share. So even if a neighbour has no objection to the works taking place, he or she may not be willing to shoulder his or her half of the costs for demolition, and re-construction causes yet another dilemma.

---

[3] *Jones v Read* (1876) IR 10 CL 315.
[4] *Stedman v Smith* (1858) 8 El & Bl 1.
[5] See chapter 3 for a definition and discussion of easements generally.

## Planning Permission is Not a Declaration of Ownership of the Boundary

Very often disputes between neighbours will arise where one party has been granted a planning permission or a certificate of exempted development[6] to build an extension to his or her home and, in the course of same, place the gable of the extension on the shared boundary wall. The planning authority does not examine issues of legal title to determine if a neighbour has title to the lands upon which he or she wishes to build his or her extension. Instead they deem same to be a civil issue to be resolved between neighbours. The planning application form simply requires the applicant to state that he or she owns the property over which permission is sought and the planning authority accepts same at face value.

The planning authority cannot be criticised for such an approach as even Ordnance Survey Ireland and the Property Registration Authority remain mute on the issue of the exact ownership of property at the boundary.[7] Therefore, the planning permission or declaration of exempted development is not a legal entitlement to build a development at the shared boundary without the consent of the adjoining landowner. The last thing any neighbour wants is to be faced with a situation where he or she is served with a court injunction demanding that he or she cease his or her development until the matter of ownership can be fully tried before the courts.

## Talk to One's Neighbour

In some instances it will simply not be possible to engage with a neighbour who may be of a difficult and quarrelsome character to such an extent that there will be little point in initiating the conversation. In most circumstances, a neighbour will be at least open to a discussion in relation to one party proposing to carry out works on the boundary. The reaction may be positive in relation to sharing the costs of demolishing an old crumbling boundary wall but may be more difficult in relation to the proposed construction of an extension off the back of one of the homes which will mean a certain amount of construction at and on the boundary. In the latter case, the neighbour intending to build must go and see his or her

---

[6] See chapter 6, p 95 on s 5 certificates of exempted development.
[7] See chapter 1, p 13 in relation to non-conclusiveness of boundary mapping.

neighbour with the plans for the extension, explaining those measures that have been incorporated into the design to alleviate the natural fears of the neighbour.

For example, one should be able to show from the plans that the pitch of the roof of the extension is at an appropriate height so as not to cause the neighbour a loss of light. Similarly, in terms of maintaining the neighbour's right to privacy, one may be able to indicate that certain windows overlooking the neighbouring property will use frosted glass. In some instances, a neighbour may be willing to consent to the development with some changes to be made to the elevation and design for example. Others may be opposed to the development but may remain courteous in their opposition.

It is of course possible for both parties to reduce the terms of an agreement in relation to the works into a written agreement that states the nature of the construction, details the times at which construction may take place and identifies those persons who may enter onto the adjoining lands to effect the works. In return, the neighbour carrying out the works may offer the consenting neighbour an indemnity in relation to damage and loss howsoever arising out of the construction. Indeed the list of conditions and terms are too various to list here, but needless to say the manner and nature of the party structure between the properties will dictate the terms and conditions forming part of the agreement.

A template agreement for such an arrangement is enclosed in Appendix 1. However, it is strongly recommended that any party wishing to avail of same should seek the advices of a solicitor prior to executing same.

## Obtain the Sanction of the District Court by Way of a *Works Order*

Following on from an unsuccessful meeting between neighbours it is advisable to write a brief *memo* in relation to the conversation as one may need to rely on same as part of an application in the District Court for a works order. At this stage the intending developer neighbour will need to consider an alternate route to resolve matters by way of an application to the District Court pursuant to s 45 of the Land and Conveyancing Law

Reform Act 2009 (the 2009 Act).[8] This piece of legislation provides a statutory mechanism for individuals who wish to carry out works to a party structure, in an instance where consent is being withheld from the adjoining landowner, to obtain a court sanction for such works. The s 45 application, if successful, allows the court to set out the works permitted, thereby offering protection to the neighbour[9] carrying out the works from actions in trespass, nuisance and property damage, not to mention an accusation of criminal damage in the criminal courts, once strict adherence to the terms of the works order is maintained.

## Works Orders—Procedure, Terms and Conditions

Section 45 of the 2009 Act, therefore allows individuals who wish to conduct works to a party structure, in a situation where there is no consent forthcoming from the adjoining landowner, to apply to the District Court for a *works order* allowing for the works to take place. The application, however, must be made on notice[10] to the adjoining landowner who will have a right to have his or her own legal representation in court to outline his or her grounds of objection to the proposed scheme of works.

## Party Structures Defined

Section 43 of the 2009 Act comprises a wide definition of party structures which may comprise any arch, ceiling, ditch, fence, floor, hedge, partition, shrub, tree, wall or other structure which horizontally, vertically or in any other way:

(a)  divides adjoining and separately owned buildings; or

(b)  is situated at or on or so close to the boundary line between adjoining and separately owned buildings or between such buildings and unbuilt-on lands that it is impossible or not reasonably practical to carry out works to the structure without access to the adjoining building or unbuilt-on land,

---

[8] The required Commencement Order was issued on 4 September 2009 (SI No 356 of 2009) and fixes 1 December 2009 as the day on which the 2009 Act came into operation (with the sole exception of s 132 pertaining to rent review clauses in business leases). A copy of the District Court (Land and Conveyancing Law Reform Act 2009) Rules 2010 (SI No 162 of 2010) is found in Appendix 2.

[9] And his or her *agents and servants*, meaning the builders retained for the works.

[10] SI No 162 of 2010.

and includes any such structure which is:

(i) situated entirely in or on one of the adjoining buildings or unbuilt-on lands; or

(ii) straddles the boundary line between adjoining buildings or between such buildings and unbuilt-on lands and is either co-owned by their respective owners or subject to some division of ownership between them.

One of the main developments in this area is the provision of a definition of a party structure which allows an adjoining landowner to make an application to the District Court for a works order notwithstanding the fact that the application may pertain to a party wall located entirely on the adjoining property owner's lands.

Indeed, proof of ownership of the lands in question is not relevant to the application as it is only necessary to show that the land the subject of the application forms part of the party structure in order for the application for the works order to be brought before the court. This definition of a party structure also includes *un-built* on lands at the boundary which opens the door for applications for works orders for developments which envisaged, or perhaps already have the benefit of, planning permissions or a declaration of exempted development from the planning authority.[11]

## Types of Works Permitted to Party Structures

The 2009 Act affords a very wide definition of the term *works*, meaning that there remains an inherent discretion vested in the Judge to make an order in respect of any other works deemed necessary in relation to maintenance and repair of the party structure. Such a judicial discretion to grant works orders even where there may be substantial *damage or inconvenience to the adjoining owner* must also be viewed in conjunction with the financial compensation provisions as contained in s 44(2) and (3). In particular, s 44(2)(b)(ii) gives the Judge discretion to fix a level of compensation to be paid to the adjoining landowner who finds him- or herself having to endure ongoing disturbance by reason of the neighbour's scheme of development.

---

[11] See chapter 6, p 96.

The works must be to a party structure, as defined, and for one of the stated purposes under s 44(1). These are:

(a) to carry out works to a party structure to comply with any statute, notice or order;

(b) to carry out exempted developments or developments for which planning permission has been granted or compliance with any condition attached to such permission;

(c) to carry out any work for the preservation of the party structure or of any building or unbuilt-on land of which it forms part; or

(d) to carry out any other works.

Section 44 details the kinds of works that may form part of the works order allowing for the maintenance or repair of the existing boundary, construction works on foot of a planning permission or an exempted development, and gardening works in respect of hedges, trees and shrubs. If one particular neighbour feels that he or she wishes wish to carry out works to the party structure that are not specifically referred to in s 44, then he or she will need to rely on s 44(1)(d) which allows for applications for what are termed *any other works*. *Any other works* may be granted under the terms of a works order once they:

(i) will not cause substantial damage or inconvenience to the adjoining owner; or

(ii) if they may cause such damage or inconvenience it is nevertheless reasonable to carry them out.[12]

The statute is obviously designed to give the District Court Judge a wide degree of discretion in terms of whether to grant permission for the particular works in question. Any *substantial damage or inconvenience to the adjoining owner* caused may be addressed by the Judge in making the works order conditional upon strict adherence to certain terms and conditions.

## Terms and Conditions of Works Orders

Section 46 details the various terms and conditions that may be attached to the works order. For example, the building owner may be required to

---

[12] s 11(1)(d)(i) and (ii).

indemnify or give security to the adjoining owner for damage, costs and expenses caused by or arising from the works or likely so to be caused or to arise.[13]

Thereafter the 2009 Act gives a wide discretion to the Judge in the formulation of the works *on such terms and conditions as the court thinks fit*.[14] The powers to attach specifically tailored conditions to the works order empowers the court to deal with the myriad of applications that may be made in relation to varying types of party structures based on its generous definition.

By way of example, *such terms and conditions as the court thinks fit* may include:

- Restrictions on the times of the day and weeks at which the works may be carried out;
- An obligation to have an independent architect[15] or surveyor appointed to assess and survey the lands prior to the works proceeding and thereby assuring strict adherence to the actual boundaries between the properties;
- The provision of proof of an adequate policy of insurance in relation to any workmen that may be injured on the lands of the adjoining landowner during construction;
- An obligation to designate routes by which the building owner and his or her agents and servants may access and exit the adjoining lands for the purpose of construction; and/or
- An obligation to furnish a schedule of works that provides a satisfactory timeframe for the completion of works.

## Works Orders and Issues of Trespass

A works order may authorise the building owner, and that owner's builders,[16] to enter onto an adjoining owner's building or unbuilt-on land for any purpose connected with the works.[17] In this way the adjoining landowner cannot bring an action against the building owner or his or her

---

[13] s 46(2)(b).
[14] s 46(1).
[15] Independent but usually paid for by the building owner.
[16] The builders being agents, employees or servants of the building owner.
[17] s 46(2)(a).

workmen for trespass as the trespass has now been authorised by the express authority of the court, making any claim for seeking damages for trespass unsustainable.

A word of caution needs to be added, however, in that the works order may sanction an access onto the specific parts of the adjoining landowner's lands and any deviation from the court sanctioned area benefiting from the immunity from trespass may become actionable by way of an injunction to stop the unauthorised trespass and a claim for damages.

## Works Orders and the Right to Structural Support and Other Easements/Rights of Necessity

Perhaps the most important of easements in the context of adjoining landowners is that of the right of support. Under this right it is not possible for a neighbour to demolish a wall at the boundary thereby causing the collapse of one's garden shed that derived its support from that same wall. Structural support in such instances may be said to be derived from what is termed as *necessity* and, as such, this and other easements[18] acquired by necessity are not affected by s 34 of the 2009 Act, which abolishes the acquisition of an easement by prescription at common law and under the doctrine of lost modern grant. Easements of necessity therefore do not have to be registered to be recognised in the law.

If a works order is to granted in relation to works that will potentially interfere with such an easement, the court may refuse the application outright if the works are to permanently interfere with the right. However, a more balanced approach may be for the court to grant the works order with a stipulation that the works may proceed but that certain alleviating measures be taken to protect the integrity of the adjoining landowner's structural support during the carrying out of the works and thereafter.

## Works Orders and the Right to Light and Other Rights

The one proviso in relation to the granting of a works order is that it may not authorise any permanent interference with, or loss of, any easement of light or other easement or other right relating to a party structure.[19] The restriction on a works order not to permanently interfere with easements

---

[18] For a definition and examples of easements see chapter 3.
[19] s 44(3).

is somewhat confusing in that the 2009 Act abolishes[20] the traditional methods of acquiring such rights,[21] instead allowing for two methods of acquiring rights, first by way of a registration of same by mutual consent, or alternatively by way of a court determination of the matter if the existence of the easement is in dispute, and registration of the court order if it declares its existence.[22]

Very few neighbours, as a precautionary measure, will seek to register an easement such as that of light and fewer more would be advised by their solicitor to go to court and effectively sue their neighbour to confirm its existence. However, there would seem to be no alternative for any party seeking to object to a neighbour's application for a works order by reason of loss of light, loss of right of way or any other such easement that is not derived from necessity.

Arguably the easement of light does not fit comfortably into this category of easement of necessity[23] as even if interference with the easement of light occurs, the actual loss of light may not be so serious as to constitute a loss under the law. For example, *Colls v Home and Colonial Stores Ltd*[24] goes some way to describing the degree of light that one may acquire by way of easement. The House of Lords held that Colls, the plaintiff, was entitled to *sufficient light* to light his premises *according to the ordinary notions of mankind*; as he would have in excess of this amount, even after the erection of the new building, he had not suffered an actionable interference with his easement of light.[25]

Accordingly, s 44(3), in specifically prohibiting the extent of the works order permanently interfering with the right to light, is somewhat at variance with the decided case law in this area which does allow for a certain loss of light once that remaining amount of light is deemed to be sufficient. It would appear that this section of the 2009 Act has placed the

---

[20] s 34.
[21] See chapter 3, p 63.
[22] s 35 of the 2009 Act, as amended by s 37 of the Civil Law (Miscellaneous Provisions) Act 2011.
[23] See chapter 3, pp 56–57, where easements of light are explained as deriving from s 3 of the Prescription Act 1832.
[24] [1904] AC 179.
[25] See chapter 3, pp 56–57.

court in a difficult position in this regard, with the common law and statute adopting what appear to be opposing positions.

## Stopping Works Orders Applications Pending Registration of an Easement

Any neighbour fearing the loss of an easement arising out of the building owner's proposed works which are the subject of a works order application will need to seek the advices of his or her solicitor in relation to defending the application for the works order on the basis of interference with an easement that is in the course of being established. This will require a solicitor to effectively seek a *stay*, which is an application to the court stopping the building owner proceeding with the application for the works order until such time as the easement may be established in law. Such applications will need to be brought in the Circuit Court or the High Court as the District Court does not have the necessary jurisdiction or legal authority to hear applications in relation to these disputes.[26] This type of application may also involve one's solicitor seeking an injunction from the court preventing the building owner from carrying out the works and trespassing on the adjoining landowner's land for that purpose until the court determines the easement dispute.

## Financial Obligations of a Building Owner if a Works Order is Granted

Section 44 of the 2009 Act sets out the obligations of the building owner when carrying out works. The building owner must make good all damage caused to the adjoining owner as a consequence of the works, or reimburse the adjoining owner the reasonable costs and expenses of such making good.[27] However, the building owner may claim from the adjoining owner as a contribution to, or deduct from any reimbursement of, the cost and expenses of making good any damage caused an amount that is representative of the proportionate use or enjoyment of the party structure which the adjoining owner makes or, it is reasonable to assume, is likely to make.[28] Damage is not defined but would seem to be directed towards physical damage and may also include loss of enjoyment of lands during construction.

---

[26] See chapter 3, pp 64–67 in respect of timeframes and limitation periods for the recognition of easements.

[27] s 44(2).

[28] s 44(3).

The 2009 Act also provides for reasonable compensation for any inconvenience caused by works as defined.[29] Again, a facility is provided allowing the building owner to deduct from the compensation payable an amount that is representative of the proportionate use or enjoyment of the party structure which the adjoining owner makes or, it is reasonable to assume, is likely to make. So if, for example, one neighbour is granted a works order to demolish and reconstruct a crumbling and dangerous party wall, it is arguable that no compensation of any kind will be payable for inconvenience as the fate of having a dangerous wall at risk of imminent collapse is of equal benefit to both sides of the party wall and would surely outweigh any compensation payable.

The adjoining landowner may also recoup the reasonable costs of obtaining professional advice with regard to the likely consequences of the works.[30] There is no offset of the costs involved in this form of compensation for the building owner. Presumably *professional advice with regard to the likely consequences of the works* infers that the adjoining landowner has the right to compensation for the retention of an architect or engineer in order to make an informed decision as to whether to accede to the building owner's request for permission to pursue the particular works.

For example, an architect may be retained to look at issues of design of the proposed extension. A surveyor may be called upon to examine issues of encroachment of the works beyond the party structure onto the actual lands of the adjoining landowner. A tree surgeon may need to be consulted in relation to how best to lop tree branches to allow the development proceed.

## Where a Demand for Compensation is Ignored

Section 44(4) allows for the landowner, if a building owner fails within a reasonable time to:

- make good the damage caused to the adjoining owner; and/or
- pay the adjoining owner's reasonable costs of obtaining professional advice; and/or
- pay reasonable compensation for any inconvenience caused, and
- to recover such costs, expenses or compensation as a simple contract debt in a court of competent jurisdiction.

---

[29] s 44(2)(b)(ii).
[30] s 44(2)(b(i).

A solicitor will advise in relation to the court of competent jurisdiction whether it be the District Court, Circuit Court or High Court depending on the value of the claim.

Interestingly, the 2009 Act bestows the District Court with the power to grant limited injunctive-type reliefs, which would not normally be within its jurisdiction, in relation to obliging building owners to make good all damage caused to the adjoining owner as a consequence of the works on application of the adjoining landowner. The District Court *may make such order as it thinks fit* in this regard.[31] On the reverse side, if an adjoining owner fails to meet a claim for contribution for proportionate use and enjoyment of the party structure which the adjoining owner makes or is likely to make from the works carried out by the building owner, that building owner may also recover such contribution as a simple contract debt in a court of competent jurisdiction.[32]

## Discharge or Modification of Works Orders

Any person may apply to the court for a discharge or modification of a works order provided that person is affected by the order and the court may discharge or modify the order *on such terms and conditions as it thinks fit*.[33] This provision would be of benefit to the building owner if he or she requires additional access, other than that permitted in the original works order, to the adjoining lands and consent is not forthcoming. It allows for the original works order to be extended without an entire re-opening of the case before the courts.

Similarly, the landowner may wish to seek a modification of the works order to include a limitation on the actual numbers of workers allowed onto his or her lands if he or she is faced with an unreasonable number of workers being present on his or her lands at any one time.

## Dublin Corporation Act 1890

As the name would suggest, the Dublin Corporation Act 1890 (the 1890 Act) is a Dublin-centric piece of legislation[34] that remains on the statute

---

[31] s 44(4)(a).

[32] s 44(4)(b).

[33] s 47.

[34] See JCW Wylie, *Irish Land Law* (Professional Books Ltd, London, 1975), 1st Edition, pp 374–376. The 1890 Act originally applied to the municipal boundaries of Dublin, and was then extended to all areas of the city in 1933.

book notwithstanding the coming into law of s 45 of the 2009 Act and, as such, must be dealt with as an option, at least for Dublin dwellers, in relation to the carrying out of works at the boundary.

Under the 1890 Act, provision is made for the repair of what that Act refers to as *party structures*. The term is not defined but obviously includes party walls and probably boundary walls.[35] It also contains provisions giving a landowner the right to enter upon the property of an adjoining owner to carry out repairs and other works. Under the 1890 Act a person who wishes to execute any work to a party structure is called the *building owner* and the owner of the adjoining premises is called the *adjoining owner*.

Under the 1890 Act, the building owner is given the following rights:

(1) the right to make good or repair any party structure which is defective or in a state of disrepair;
(2) the right to pull down and rebuild any party structure which is so defective as to make it necessary or desirable to pull it down;
(3) the right to pull down any party structure which is of insufficient strength for any building intended to be built and to rebuild the same of sufficient strength for this purpose; and
(4) the right to cut away or take down any part of any wall or building which overhangs his or her ground in order to erect an upright wall.

Before exercising any of the rights, the building owner must give at least three months' notice to the adjoining owner of his or her intention to commence the work and, if within 14 days after service of the notice of intention to carry out the work the adjoining owner refuses to give consent, he or she is then interpreted as having provided a *de facto* refusal to the carrying out of the works and a difference or dispute is deemed to have arisen between them.

At this juncture, the matter is referred to the arbitration of a mutually agreed arbitrator or to the arbitration of three arbitrators, one being appointed by each party and the third being appointed by the two

---

[35] The difference being that boundary walls are said to pertain to one particular owner's lands whilst a party wall is believed to be shared equally between the two adjoining land-owners: see chapter 1, pp 6–8.

arbitrators. When the arbitrators make their award the building owner is then entitled, with workmen, to enter on the premises of the adjoining owner for the purpose of carrying out the work approved by the award of the arbitrators and anyone who obstructs the workmen in those circumstances is guilty of a criminal offence.

The Dublin-centric approach to boundary works has been overhauled by the coming into effect of s 45 of the 2009 Act, which allows all adjoining landowners to make an application to their local District Court for a works order to carry out works on a party structure. In any event, those living in the city of Dublin would be best advised to progress any court applications for works to party structures under s 45 of the 2009 Act based on the grounds of antiquity of the 1890 Act: the practice and procedure in bringing a claim under the latter having long since fallen into abeyance.

## Why One will Need the Assistance of a Solicitor

An application for a works order is a District Court application by way of notice, as contained in the District Court (Land and Conveyancing Law Reform Act 2009) Rules 2010 (SI No 162 of 2010) (see appendix 2 herein). As may be ascertainable from the above, the law in this area draws upon an understanding of various statutory provisions and their interaction with the common law, particularly in relation to the area of easements, and it is therefore not advisable for an individual to bring such an application to court him- or herself without legal representation.

## Conclusion

The Land and Conveyancing Law Reform Act 2009 and, in particular, s 45 thereof finally sees the introduction onto the Irish statute book of a comprehensive mechanism for adjoining land owners in dispute in relation to the carrying out of works at the boundary to refer such matters to the District Court for determination. Whilst such an application will bring finality to the legal issues to be tried, the affects on neighbourly relations are rarely improved through recourse to the courts. It is for this reason that in the first instance disputing neighbours are well advised to consider an alternative dispute resolution[36] remedy such as mediation in an effort to resolve any unhappy differences without recourse to the courts.

---

[36] See chapter 16.

## Appendix 1

**INDEMNITY BY BUILDING OWNER TO ADJOINING LANDOWNER FOR THE PURPOSE OF CARRYING OUT WORKS TO THE BOUNDARY**[37]

**Building Owner(s)**[38]:

**Adjoining Landowner(s)**[39]:

**WHEREAS** the building owner(s) wish(es) to carry out works to a party structure, namely[40]:

**AND IN CONSIDERATION** of the Adjoining Landowner(s) granting permission to the Building Owner(s), agents, employees or servants,[41] to enter onto their lands for any purpose connected with the carrying out of the above mentioned works on the terms and conditions specified in *'Schedule A'* attached hereto,

The Building Owner(s) **hereby INDEMNIF(Y)IES** the adjoining owner(s) for any damage, costs, and expenses caused by or arising from the carrying out of the said works howsoever arising. The Building Owner(s) **further INDEMNIF(Y)IES** the adjoining owner against personal injury or damage to property caused to his/her agents, employees or servants in the course of carrying out the said works howsoever arising whilst on the adjoining lands. For the sake of clarity personal injury and property damage includes such personal injury and damage to property arising on foot of the Occupier's Liability Act 1995.

---

[37] Not to be completed without first obtaining legal advice.
[38] The person carrying out the works.
[39] The lands of the neighbour not carrying out the works.
[40] Insert a brief description of the works.
[41] Agents, employees or servants meaning the building owner's actual builder, the builder's employees, contractors and other people connected with the construction works.

Building Owner(s)

Signed:

Address:


Witnessed:

Address:

Adjoining Land Owner(s)

Signed:

Address:


Witnessed:

Address:

## SCHEDULE A[42]

-Time and Days upon which works may take place:

-Areas of adjoining property upon which workmen are permitted to occupy during construction:

-Independent Surveyor, to be paid for at the expense of the Building Owner to monitor the maintenance of current boundaries:

-Schedule of Works:

-Etc.

---

[42] List hereunder the terms and conditions upon which the agreed works are to proceed. Building Owners and Adjoining Landowners will be able to draw a specific list dependant upon the particular party structure in question.

## Appendix 2

### District Court Rules for Works Orders

District Court Rules

Order: 93A

District Court (Land and Conveyancing Law Reform Act 2009) Rules 2010 (SI No 162 of 2010)

1. These rules may be cited as the District Court (Land and Conveyancing Law Reform Act 2009) Rules 2010.
2. These rules shall come into operation on the 17th day of May 2010 and shall be construed together with the District Court Rules 1997 to 2010.
3. The District Court Rules 1997 (SI No 93 of 1997) are amended by the insertion immediately following Order 93 of the following Order:

"Order 93A
Applications under the Land and Conveyancing Law Reform Act 2009

"1. In this Order,

the "Act" means the Land and Conveyancing Law Reform Act 2009 (No. 27 of 2009);
"adjoining", "adjoining owner", "building owner", "party structure" and "works" each has the meaning provided for each [*sic*] in section 43 of the Act.

2. (1) An application to the Court for an order under section 44(4)(a)(i) of the Act by an adjoining owner for an order requiring damage to be made good shall be preceded by the issue and service by the applicant of a copy of a notice of application in the Form 93A.1, Schedule C on the building owner concerned.

(2) An application to the Court for an order under section 45(1) of the Act by a building owner for a works order shall be preceded by the issue and service by the applicant of a copy of a notice of application in the Form 93A.2, Schedule C on the adjoining owner concerned.

(3) An application to the Court under section 47 of the Act by a person affected by a works order for an order discharging or modifying a works order shall be preceded by the issue and service by the applicant of a copy of a notice of application in the

Form 93A.3, Schedule C on the building owner and every adjoining owner concerned.

(4) The copy of the notice of application referred to in this Order shall be served not later than four days before the date fixed for hearing the application, and the original notice of application shall be lodged with the Clerk not later than two days before the date fixed for the hearing of the application. An order made on such application shall be in the Form 93A.4, 93A.5 or 93A.6, Schedule C as appropriate, and the applicant shall cause a copy of the said order to be served upon the building owner and every adjoining owner concerned, and on any other person whom the Court directs should be served with a copy of the order.

(5) Every application mentioned in this rule may be brought, heard and determined at any sitting of the court for the court area wherein the party structure to which the application relates is situated.

3. Proceedings in the Court under section 44(4)(a)(ii) or under section 44(4)(b) may be commenced by civil summons in accordance with Order 39.

4. An application to the Court for an order under section 98(2) of the Act authorising a mortgagee to take possession of property may be brought, heard and determined at any sitting of the court for the court area wherein the mortgaged property to which the application relates is situated. Such an application shall be preceded by the issue and service by the applicant on the mortgagor concerned of a copy of a notice of application in the Form 93A.7, Schedule C, which notice shall state whether any court is already seised of an application or proceedings relating to the mortgaged property. Without prejudice to the power of the Court to make an order for substituted service or to substitute notice for service, the Court may deem it sufficient service, if the mortgagor is untraceable, if a copy of the notice is affixed to, or posted at, the entrance of the property concerned. An order made on such application shall be in the Form 93A.8, and the applicant shall cause a copy of the said order to be served as directed by the Court."

4. The Forms numbered 93A.1 to 93A.8 inclusive in inclusive in Schedule 1 shall be added to the Forms in Schedule C of the District Court Rules 1997 (SI No 93 of 1997).

Schedule CO. 93A, r. 2(1)

**Schedule 1 No. 93A.1**

LAND AND CONVEYANCING LAW REFORM ACT 2009, Section 44(4)(a)(i)

NOTICE OF APPLICATION FOR ORDER THAT DAMAGE BE MADE GOOD

District Court Area of District No.

_____ Applicant

_____ Respondent

TAKE NOTICE that the above-named applicant, being an adjoining owner of a building or land adjoining premises or land at in the court area and district aforesaid in or on which the respondent building owner is carrying out works to a party structure, namely, will apply to the District Court sitting at on the _____ day of _____ 20 _____ at _____ a.m./p.m. under section 44(4)(a)(i) of the above-mentioned Act for an order against you, , the respondent, of_(in the court area and district aforesaid) requiring all damage caused to the applicant as adjoining owner in consequence of the said works to be made good.

The grounds for this application are that—

[Here set out the grounds of the application, including particulars of the works carried out and the damage caused to the applicant as a consequence of the works.]

Dated this _____ day of _____ 20_____

Signed _____

Applicant/solicitor for the Applicant

To District Court Clerk

District Court Office

At _____

To the Respondent

At _____

## Schedule CO. 93A, r. 2(2)

No. 93A.2

LAND AND CONVEYANCING LAW REFORM ACT 2009, Section 45

NOTICE OF APPLICATION FOR WORKS ORDER

District Court Area of District No.

_____ Applicant

_____ Respondent

TAKE NOTICE that the above-named applicant, being the building owner of a building or land adjoining premises or land atinthe court area and district aforesaid in or on which the applicant wishes to exercise rights under section 44 of the above-mentioned Act to carry out works to a party structure, namely, _____, will apply to the District Court sitting at _____ on the _____ day of _____ 20_____ at _____ a.m./p.m. under section 45 of the said Act for a works order authorising the carrying out of specified works, namely:

[Here set out the works sought to be authorised.]

The grounds for this application are that—

[Here set out the grounds of the application, including any dispute with the respondent adjoining owner concerning the rights of the applicant to carry out the works.]

Dated this _____ day of _____ 20_____

Signed _____

Applicant/solicitor for the Applicant

To District Court Clerk

District Court Office

At _____

To the Respondent

At _____

**Schedule CO. 93A, r. 2(3)**

No. 93A.3

LAND AND CONVEYANCING LAW REFORM ACT 2009, Section 47

NOTICE OF APPLICATION FOR AN ORDER *DISCHARGING/*MODIFYING A WORKS ORDER

District Court Area of District No.

_____ Applicant

_____ Building owner

_____ Adjoining owner

TAKE NOTICE that the above-named applicant, of (in the court area and district aforesaid) will apply to the District Court sitting at _____ on the _____ day of _____ 20 _____ at _____ a.m./p.m. for an order under section 47 of the above-mentioned Act *discharging/*modifying a works order made by the District Court at _____ on the _____ day of _____ 20_____ authorising the carrying out of specified works in a building or on land at _____ in the court area and district aforesaid.

The applicant is affected by the works order because

The grounds for this application *(and the modifications sought to the works order) are that—

[Here set out the grounds of the application, including any modifications sought to the terms of the works order.]

Dated this _____ day of _____ 20_____

Signed _____

Applicant/solicitor for the Applicant

To District Court Clerk

District Court Office

At _____

To the Building owner _____

At _____

To the Adjoining owner _____

At _____

*delete where inapplicable

**Schedule CO. 93A, r. 2(4)**

No. 93A.4

LAND AND CONVEYANCING LAW REFORM ACT 2009, Section 44(4)(a)(i)

ORDER THAT DAMAGE BE MADE GOOD

District Court Area of District No.

_____ Applicant

_____ Respondent

WHEREAS UPON APPLICATION made to the Court today by the above-named applicant, being an adjoining owner of a building or land adjoining premises or land atin the court area and district aforesaid in or on which the respondent building owner of _____ is carrying out works to a party structure, namely, _____, under section 44(4)(a)(i) of the above-mentioned Act, for an order requiring all damage caused to the applicant as adjoining owner in consequence of the said works to be made good.

THE COURT

BEING SATISFIED THAT notice of the application was duly served

BEING SATISFIED THAT the respondent building owner has failed within a reasonable time to make good damage under section 44(2)(a) of the said Act

HEREBY ORDERS pursuant to section 44(4)(a)(i) of the said Act that

Dated this _____ day of _____ 20_____

Signed _____

Judge of the District Court

## Schedule CO. 93A, r. 2(4)

No. 93A.5

LAND AND CONVEYANCING LAW REFORM ACT 2009, Section 45

WORKS ORDER

District Court Area of District No.

_____ Applicant

_____ Respondent

WHEREAS UPON APPLICATION made to the Court today by the above-named applicant, being the building owner of a building or land adjoining premises or land atin the court area and district aforesaid in or on which the applicant wishes to exercise rights under section 44 of the above-mentioned Act to carry out works to a party structure, namely, _____, for a works order under section 45 of the said Act authorising the carrying out of specified works.


THE COURT

BEING SATISFIED THAT notice of the application was duly served

BEING SATISFIED THAT the applicant is in dispute with the respondent adjoining owner with respect to the exercise of rights under section 44 of the said Act

HAVING REGARD to section 44 of the said Act and taking into account all other circumstances the court considers relevant

HEREBY ORDERS that the carrying out of the following specified works by or on behalf of the applicant be authorised, namely


*AND THIS ORDER AUTHORISES the said applicant building owner, and*its/*his/*her agents, employees or servants, to enter on a *building/*unbuilt-on land of an adjoining owner, _____, *for the purpose of _____ /*for any purpose connected with the works,

*AND THIS ORDER REQUIRES the said applicant building owner, _____ to *indemnify/* to give security in the amount of €_____ by way of _____ to the adjoining owner _____ for damage, costs and expenses caused by or arising from the works or likely so to be caused or to arise.

*THE TERMS AND CONDITIONS (which the Court thinks fit in the circumstances of the case) subject to which said authorisation is given in accordance with section 46(1) of the said Act are:

[here set out any terms and conditions]

Dated this _____ day of _____ 20_____

Signed _____

Judge of the District Court

*delete where inapplicable

**Schedule CO. 93A, r. 2(4)**

No. 93A.6

LAND AND CONVEYANCING LAW REFORM ACT 2009, Section 47

ORDER *DISCHARGING/*MODIFYING A WORKS ORDER

District Court Area of District No.

_____ Applicant

_____ Building owner

_____ Adjoining owner

WHEREAS UPON APPLICATION made to the Court today by the above-named applicant, of _____ (in the court area and district aforesaid) for an order under section 47 of the above-mentioned Act*discharging/*modifying a works order made by the District Court at _____ under section 45 of the said Act on the _____ day of _____ 20____ authorising the carrying out of specified works in a building or on land at _____ in the court area and district aforesaid

THE COURT

BEING SATISFIED THAT notice of the application was duly served

BEING SATISFIED THAT the applicant is affected by the said works order

*HAVING HEARD *the evidence adduced and *the submissions on behalf of *the applicant, *the building owner, _____, *and the adjoining owner, _____

*HEREBY DISCHARGES the said works order

*HEREBY MODIFIES the said works order as follows

*and on the following terms and conditions

Dated this _____ day of _____ 20____

Signed _____

Judge of the District Court

*delete where inapplicable

**Schedule CO. 93A, r. 4**

No. 93A.7

LAND AND CONVEYANCING LAW REFORM ACT 2009, Section 98(1)

NOTICE OF APPLICATION FOR ORDER AUTHORISING MORTGAGEE TO TAKE POSSESSION OF ABANDONED PROPERTY

District Court Area of District No.

_____ Applicant

_____ Respondent

TAKE NOTICE that the above-named applicant, being a mortgagee of mortgaged property of which the above-named respondent is the mortgagor at (hereinafter, the "mortgaged property") in the court area and district aforesaid will apply to the District Court sitting at _____ on the _____ day of _____ 20___ at _____ a.m./p.m. under section 98(1) of the above-mentioned Act for an order against you, _____, the said respondent, of _____ (in the court area and district aforesaid) authorising the said applicant to take possession of the mortgaged property on the grounds that the applicant mortgagee has reasonable grounds for believing that—

(a) the respondent mortgagor has abandoned the mortgaged property, and

(b) urgent steps are necessary to prevent deterioration of, or damage to, the mortgaged property or entry on it by trespassers or other unauthorised persons.

*No court is already seised of any application or proceedings relating to the mortgaged property.

*An application *proceedings relating to the mortgaged property *is/*are pending before the Court, under title and record number

Dated this _____ day of _____ 20_____

Signed _____

Applicant/solicitor for the Applicant

To District Court Clerk

District Court Office

At _____

To the Respondent

At _____

*delete where inapplicable

**Schedule CO. 93A, r. 4**

No. 93A.8

LAND AND CONVEYANCING LAW REFORM ACT 2009, Section 98(2)

ORDER AUTHORISING MORTGAGEE TO TAKE POSSESSION OF ABANDONED PROPERTY

District Court Area of District No.

_____ Applicant

_____ Respondent

WHEREAS UPON APPLICATION made to the Court today by the above-named applicant, being a mortgagee of mortgaged property of which the above-named respondent is the mortgagor at (hereinafter, the "mortgaged property") in the court area and district aforesaid, under section 98(1) of the above-mentioned Act for an order authorising the applicant to take possession of the mortgaged property

THE COURT

*BEING SATISFIED THAT notice of the application was duly served

*DEEMING SUFFICIENT service or notice given of the application to the respondent

*HAVING HEARD said applicant *and said respondent

HEREBY ORDERS that the said applicant mortgagee be and is hereby authorised to take possession of the mortgaged property at in the court area and district aforesaid

*THE TERMS AND CONDITIONS (which the Court thinks fit) subject to which said authorisation is given in accordance with section 98(2) of the said Act are:

[here set out any terms and conditions]

*AND THIS ORDER SPECIFIES that the said applicant mortgagee may retain possession of the said mortgaged property for the period from the day of 20__ to the day of 20___,

*AND THIS ORDER SPECIFIES that the said applicant mortgagee may carry out the following works for the purpose of—

*protecting the mortgaged property

*preparing the mortgaged property for sale in exercise of the mortgagee's power under section 100 of the above-mentioned Act

*AND IT IS ORDERED that costs and expenses incurred by the said mortgagee [in connection with this application/and any works authorised by this order] in the amount of €be and they are hereby added to the mortgage debt.

Dated this _____ day of _____ 20_____

Signed _____

Judge of the District Court

*delete where inapplicable

EXPLANATORY NOTE

(This does not form part of the Instrument and does not purport to be a legal interpretation.)

These rules amend the District Court Rules by the insertion of a new Order 93A to facilitate the operation of the Land and Conveyancing Law Reform Act 2009.

# CHAPTER THREE

# Easements and Profits à Prendre

This chapter deals with the types of *profit à prendre* and easements[1] that have long been recognised in Irish law and, in the absence of Irish decisions, on the basis of English law as and between private individuals.[2] To say that the area is complicated and nuanced is perhaps an understatement and, as such, what follows below is aimed to assist the reader to grasp the basic concepts of easements so as they may have an informed discussion with their solicitor in order to protect their rights in this regard into the future. The bottom line, however, is that one will undoubtedly need professional legal assistance and advice in this area.

## Easements[3]

In its most simple form, an easement is a right of a landowner to do something on a part of his or her neighbour's property and/or to prevent his or her neighbour from doing something on that part of the property. Some of the most widely known easements are those that we take for granted, such as the right to light, right of support or a right of way one may enjoy over the land of another. Importantly, an easement is said to *run with the land*, that is to say, it cannot be sold separately from the land but must be passed on with the land whenever the land is transferred to a new owner.[4]

---

[1] For a comprehensive examination of the subject of easements and *profits à prendre*, see Law Reform Commission, LRC 66-2002, *Report on the Acquisition of Easements and Profits à Prendre by Prescription* (Law Reform Commission, Dublin, 2002).

[2] As opposed to public rights such as the right of the general public to pass over the public highway for example.

[3] The starting point for anybody wishing to delve more deeply into the general area of easements and *profits à prendre* is Peter Bland's (SC) excellent book and invaluable resource for practitioners, *Easements* (2nd ed, Round Hall, Dublin, 2009).

[4] An easement is deemed to pass automatically on a conveyance under s 6 of the Conveyancing Act 1881, this section is now repealed in Pt 4, Sch 2 of the Land and Conveyancing Law Reform Act 2009.

## Profits à Prendre

A *profit à prendre*[5] is another form of right allowing an individual to take something from a neighbour's property such as fish or timber, or may even provide for, by way of example, an entitlement to graze on the lands of the adjoining landowner. Every *profit à prendre* contains an implied easement or right for the owner of the profit to enter the other party's land for the purpose of collecting the resources permitted by the profit.[6]

## How Easements and Profits à Prendre are Created and Recognised in Irish Law

### Dominant and Servient Tenement

The easement can only exist if it is annexed to a piece of land. It cannot exist independently of the land which is benefited by it. It must also be connected to the land and must improve its amenity, utility or convenience. An easement essentially involves the existence of two pieces of land, namely, the dominant and servient tenements. The dominant tenement is the land benefited by the easement and the servient tenement is the land over which the easement exists. The dominant and servient tenements will be owned by two different landowners.

### Some Common Easements and Profits à Prendre that are Recognised in the Law

An easement not created by an express written agreement between two parties[7] can only be claimed if the particular easement is one that is recognised in the law generally. The courts have down through time failed to recognise certain easements as existing but have readily recognised others capable of being conveyed from one person to another down through the generations. There is an exception to this rule and that is where the easement is created by express grant, meaning that two individuals draw up a legally binding agreement under a deed which allows one party to sell a right to the use of his or her lands to some degree. An example may be where one individual grants a right to an adjoining landowner to place a septic tank on his or her lands.

---

[5] In middle French for *right of taking*.
[6] In the remainder of this chapter, *easement* may be read to include *profits à prendre* except where specifically indicated to the contrary.
[7] Known as *an express grant*.

How easements are created other than by express grant is dealt with in detail below, and indeed the remainder of this chapter deals with the creation of easements, other than by express grant, but by long usage over time.

**The Right of Way**

The right of way is well recognised in Irish land law, or perhaps more precisely has been long recognised as a source of dispute for adjoining landowners. A right of way in its simplest form is the right of one person, known as the owner of the *dominant tenement*, to pass back and forth over the lands of an adjoining landowner, known as the *servient tenement*. That is not to say that the person with the right of passage over the lands of a neighbour may do so without any restriction whatsoever.

Perhaps Barr J, in the case of *Eircell Ltd v Bernstoff*,[8] put it best when stating that "traditional boreens are the veins of rural Ireland and the definition of the nature and extent of the right of way any one of them provides may well be a difficult task".

For example, a grant of a right of way may allow for access to agricultural lands on foot but may not be extended for use of that same pathway for the transport of materials by cart, so the nature and extent of the right of way will very much depend on the historical usage of the right of way.[9] That said, the dominant owner, i.e. the person exercising the right over the lands of another, may do what is necessary to maintain the right of way for the intended use. For example, in the case of *Carroll v Sheridan*,[10] the court allowed for the dominant user to double the width of the right of way, allowed the clearing of bushes and briars and even allowed the surfacing of the right of way. It follows that the dominant user is also under an obligation not to damage the lands over which he or she passes. In the case of *Rudd v Rea*[11] it was held that the dominant owner may have had an entitlement to use heavy machinery to access the servient lands but it was not permissible for the use of such heavy equipment to damage the lands rendering them useless for the servient owner.

[8] Unreported, High Court, Barr J, February (See P Bland, *Easements* (2nd ed, Round Hall, Dublin, 2009), p 42.
[9] *Maguire v Browne* [1921] 1 IR 148 at 170 per O' Connor LJ.
[10] *Carroll v Sheridan* [1984] ILRM 451.
[11] *Rudd v Rea* [1921] 1 IR 223.

## The Right to Structural Support from an Adjoining Building (Above and Below the Ground)

The right to structural support from an adjoining building has long been recognised in the law. It is obviously common place in the urban townscape for buildings to be physically joined to each other by a party wall, thereby providing mutual support to each other. Even where one of the adjoining buildings is demolished the remaining building has a right of support from the demolished building, and the owner of the adjoining land must provide support to the remaining property's structure. As seen below, however, there is no obligation to protect the remaining structure from the elements of wind and rain.

The same right of support applies if earth is removed too close to a neighbouring building and so the adjoining landowner who takes away the support will leave him- or herself open to a claim for damages in nuisance and negligence as a result and may be obliged by way of a court-ordered injunction to restore support to the subsiding adjoining lands. The right of support also extends to the earthen ground (as distinct from a building) that is in danger of collapse as a result of excavation on neighbouring land.

## The Right to Light

Section 3 of the Prescription Act 1832[12] recognised easements of light, providing for a user period of 20 years without interruption and applied to light benefiting a dwelling house, workshop or other building. Section 4 of the Prescription Act 1832 provides that the period must be without interruption. Any interruptions must be substantial and the user must have actually ceased for a period of one year. The year is not deemed to commence until the claimant is aware of the interruption and the identity of the person interrupting. As such, s 3 of the Prescription Act 1832 did not specifically bestow the potential to acquire the right to light over open ground such as a garden, for example, and it is decided law that no such right to light may be acquired over a garden.[13]

---

[12] The Prescription Act 1832 was extended to Ireland under the Prescription (Ireland) Act 1858 from 1 January 1859. Both these Acts are repealed in Pt 4, Sch 2 of the Land and Conveyancing Law Reform Act 2009.

[13] *Potts v Smith* (1868) LR 6 Eq 311.

Once the right to light is established it will survive even the demolition and reconstruction of a replacement building that has in its design a similar number of windows of similar dimensions to the original building.[14] That said, a landowner is advised not to leave the site vacant for too long a period as the right to light may be deemed to be *extinguished* after a certain number of years.[15]

Once the right is established, the user of the light cannot simply object to a neighbouring development on the grounds that the amount of horizontal light being received by the windows of his or her property will be diminished.

The important case in this area is the English case of *Colls v Home and Colonial Stores Ltd*.[16] Home and Colonial Stores Ltd owned land in London and proposed to erect a tall building on the site. Colls owned a property immediately opposite the proposed site and objected to the erection of the new building due to the effect this would have on light to a clerk's office on the ground floor of his building. He applied for an injunction to restrain the new development, arguing that he was entitled to an easement under s 3 of the Prescription Act 1832 in respect of all the light then currently enjoyed by his building.

The House of Lords held that Colls was entitled to *sufficient light* to light his premises *according to the ordinary notions of mankind*; as he would have in excess of this amount, even after the erection of the new building, he had not suffered an actionable interference with his easement of light.

The extent of the entitlement to light was described by Lord Lindley in the following terms:

> "Generally speaking an owner of ancient lights is entitled to sufficient light according to the ordinary notions of mankind for the comfortable use and enjoyment of his house as a dwelling-house, if it is a dwelling-house, or for the beneficial use and occupation of the house if it is a warehouse, a shop, or other place of business."

---

[14] *Scott v Pape* (1886) 31 Ch D 554 at 570 per Cotton LJ.

[15] See p 68 for more detail as to how easements may be deemed to have been *extinguished*.

[16] [1904] AC 179 p 199 Lord Davey referring to James LJ *Kelk v Pearson* LR 6 Ch. 809.

If, for example, one feels that a development in the lands adjoining a property is causing a loss of light, and that the resulting nuisance of such a loss of light is restricting the reasonable enjoyment of the property, a case may be brought seeking the removal of that structure interfering with the loss of the right to light. The caveat is, however, that the *ordinary notions of mankind* in relation to the concept of comfortable use and enjoyment of one's home seems a somewhat nebulous concept in its own right, making it difficult for legal practitioners to advise their clients in this regard.

### The Right to Water (or Riparian Rights)

These usually take the form of a right to draw water from a natural watercourse such as a river or a spring on a neighbour's land. Under the riparian principle, all landowners whose property is adjoining a body of water, such landowners being known as *riparian* owners, have the right to make reasonable use of it.

A farmer, for example, may allow his or her cattle drink from the river adjoining the farmland. However, that same farmer may not take so much water from the river to irrigate his or her lands to the extent that this will have a detrimental impact upon the rights of other *riparian* owners further up or down stream.[17] Similarly, there is a prohibition on any one *riparian* owner diverting the natural flow of the watercourse.[18]

In relation to watercourses below the ground, known as percolating waters, the rule is that the *riparian* user cannot claim rights over such waters save where the channel or flow of such subterranean watercourses is clearly defined.[19]

Fishing rights on the river are a traded commodity and can be sold to include or exclude ownership of the related bed and soil of the river,[20] so if the land rights and the sporting rights were sold separately one might have the rights to fish but no rights of access onto the banks, or alternatively

---

[17] See P Bland, *Easements* (2nd ed, Round Hall, Dublin, 2009), pp 131–133.
[18] *Masserine v Murphy* [1931] NI 192.
[19] *Chasemore v Richards* (1895) 7 HLC 349.
[20] Memorandum by The River Exe & Tributaries Association (EA 74), House of Commons Select Committee on Environment, Transport and Regional Affairs, October 1999, http://www.parliament.the-stationery-office.co.uk/pa/cm199899/cmselect/cmenvtra/829/829m60.htm (10 May 2012).

one might have ownership of the land but no rights to fish there. Best advice is never to purchase or lease fishing rights to a section of river unless your solicitor is in a position to vouch that the vendor or lessor actually owns them, and has necessary rights of access.

## The Right of Drainage

This common law right refers to the right of what may be termed *natural* drainage. The Irish courts have recognised the right, however, of the landowner of the lower elevation parcel not to accept the percolation of water from the higher lands and allows for the adjacent landowner to use a barrier to stem the flow of water on his or her lands.[21] That said, the owner of the lower lands cannot be so overzealous in stemming the flow onto his or her lands by use of an impervious barrier and must act with due care and skill not to cause damage, such as flooding, to the lands of the higher property. If such damage accrues the owner of the land at the lower elevation may be held liable in an action for nuisance[22] and may be obliged by way of a court order to remove the impervious barrier causing the damage.

## The Right of Eavesdrop and Water from Overhanging Roofs

The right of surface water from overhanging roof tiles/guttering/eaves being discharged onto a neighbouring property would not be considered to be natural drainage. Therefore, the owner of the lower land may dam the water at the property line to protect his or her property by *abating* the nuisance. *Abatement* is the legal term used to describe the justified action in stopping a nuisance that causes property damage. If the nuisance has caused property damage to the lower lands then the neighbouring owner of the higher lands may be liable to pay damages for the nuisance and property damage. Again, the right to *abate* the nuisance of the water from the adjoining property must be exercised with due care and skill that a reasonable individual would exercise in the circumstances so as to not cause property damage to original offending party.

That said, it will be a defence against a neighbour claiming damages for the neighbour to prove that he or she has an established, right of eavesdrop onto the neighbouring lands.[23] Accordingly, if it has been established

---

[21] *Home Brewery v William Davies & Co* [1987] 1 All ER 637.

[22] See chapter 15 for a more detailed examination of civil remedies generally.

[23] *Thomas v Thomas* (1835) 2 CM & R 34.

practice going back over 20 years or more,[24] the landowner discharging his or her waters onto his or her neighbour's roof tiles from his or her own may have secured a right to continue to do so.[25] That said, the property owner with the higher roof and an established right of eavesdrop cannot stop his or her adjoining landowner from conducting alterations to his or her house so as to raise the level of his or her own roof to that of the higher roof.[26]

## Right of Estovers and Turbary or Turf

Estovers refers to wood that a tenant is allowed to take, for life or a period of years, from the land he or she holds, normally under a lease from a landlord, for the repair of his or her house, the implements of husbandry, hedges and fences, and for firewood. It is included here as a mere example of a particular variant of a type of easement as most commentators seem to indicate that the right of estovers has been rarely invoked in Ireland due to various afforestation Acts[27] which have led to a curtailment of the right. The right of estovers was more of an English phenomenon in that, in Ireland, tenants were more reliant on the right of turbary. The right of turbary is the right to dig, extract and take away turf from another's land, normally that of the landlord from whom the lands were rented, for the specific use of fuelling one's home, meaning that the individual with the right of turbary cannot extract and sell the turf for commercial gain.[28]

## Pasturage and Commonage

Pasturage is the right of an individual to use the lands of another to graze his or her cattle and other livestock. Importantly there is no right for the person benefiting from the right to graze his or her animals on the lands in question to instead cut the herbage and take same away for storage to feed his or her animals or indeed to sell on for commercial gain at a later stage.

Very often the rights of pasturage will be shared with other rights-holders in relation to the same area of land, such as is the case, for example, at the Curragh in County Kildare or at The Great Heath of Maryborough in County Laois. The common right of pasturage must also be used in

---

[24] Or now 12 years by virtue of s 33 of the 2009 Act, see p 64.
[25] How easements are obtained in the first place is dealt with at p 54.
[26] *Greatrex v Hayward* (1853) 8 Exch. 291 at 293–294.
[27] JCW Wylie, *Irish Land Law* (3rd ed, Butterworths, Dublin, 1997 p 263).
[28] *Howley v Jebb* (1859) 8 ICLR 435.

moderation so as not to deprive fellow rights-holders of their due portion of the herbage on the commonage. Any individual rights-holder who is seen to be overzealous in the grazing of his or her animals on the commonage leaves him or herself open to the aggrieved parties bringing an application for an injunction and a claim for damages for *overstint*,[29] a *stint* being the amount of grazing rights allotted.

### Car Parking on a Neighbouring Property

Whilst the courts in England and Wales have a series of decided cases recognising and enforcing the easement of car parking,[30] the matter would appear to remain somewhat inconclusive in the Irish context. In any event, and in the first instance, a certain number of criteria must be met before the right will be recognised.

First, the right to park a car on the lands of an adjoining landowner presupposes that such parking is *appurtenant* to a dominant tenement, meaning that the right to park is situated in an area on a piece of ground in the ownership of the adjoining landowner.

Secondly, the right to park does not infringe the *ouster* principle. This means that the person enforcing his or her right to park cannot, in enforcing his or her right, preclude the ordinary uses of property by the actual owner of the lands over which the right is being claimed. So if a neighbour's lands have enough space for the parking of only one car, the adjoining owner cannot enforce a right to park in that space thereby ousting the neighbour's right to park on his or her own lands. In the same vein, the adjoining landowner's own right to use his or her land for any other use associated with his or her actual ownership of the lands may not be wholly denied.[31]

---

[29] *O' Sullivan v O' Connor* (1980) 114 ILTR 63.

[30] "I feel no hesitation in holding that a right for a landowner to park a car anywhere in a defined area nearby is capable of existing as an easement": *Newman v Jones*, unreported, 22 March 1982 *per* Megarry VC quoted in *Handel v St Stephen's Close* [1994] 1 EGLR 70 at 71 per Aldous J.

[31] There can be no prescriptive right in the nature of a servitude or easement so large as to preclude the ordinary uses of property by the owner of the lands affected: see *Dyce v Hay* (1852) 1 Macq. 305.

The closest the Irish courts have come to a decision on this area is in the case of *AGS (ROI) Pension Nominees Ltd v Madison Estates Ltd*,[32] where Keane CJ refused to recognise the existence of an easement claimed through long usage of a particular piece of land due to the fact that the right claimed had not been exercised for a long enough period of time to have allowed for its recognition as an easement. The courts in Ireland have considered the question and have not expressly ruled out the possibility of recognising the easement if the required user period has been satisfied. As will be seen below, it must be shown that the lands have been used by the person enforcing the right to park for a continuous period of years without interruption.[33]

To surmise, in relation to the easement of parking on the lands belonging to an adjoining landowner, perhaps the best way to put it would be that there is no reason why a right to park is not capable of recognition as an easement once certain principles of law have been satisfied, but as yet the courts in Ireland have yet to pronounce themselves in the affirmative on the subject of the independent easement of parking.

### A Right to Turn a Car on a Neighbouring Property

As with the above example of the right to park a car on neighbouring lands, the Irish courts have yet to pronounce themselves on whether the entering onto the lands of a neighbouring property for the purposes of turning a vehicle is capable of being an easement recognised by the law. In the absence of reported decisions in the Irish context, one instead may look to the English courts for an indication as to how the Irish courts may decide such an issue in the Irish context. It is important to remember, however, that the Irish Judiciary are under no obligation to follow the English case law precedent on this subject or indeed any other subject.

However, the English case of *Propertypoint Ltd v Kirri*[34] confirmed that a right to turn or manoeuvre vehicles on adjoining lands is capable of existing as an easement. Mrs Kirri claimed a right, by virtue of long use, to enter onto land owned by Propertypoint for the purpose of turning vehicles which were to be parked in her garage. The plaintiff, Propertypoint

---

[32] *AGS (ROI) Pension Nominees Ltd v Madison Estates Ltd*, unreported, Supreme Court, 23 October 2003, [2003] 11 ICLMD 107, noted in [2004] 9 CPLJ 20.

[33] For an acquisition of the right by prescription see p 65–66 below.

[34] *Propertypoint Ltd v Kirri* [2009] EWHC 2958 (Ch).

Ltd, had argued that the right to turn or manoeuvre vehicles was not of the type or intensity required to establish an easement. The court disagreed seeing no reason why a right of way should not, in theory, be established for the defined purpose of turning vehicles using the garage.

## Some Easements and Profits à Prendre that are not Recognised in the Law

### Right to a View

There is no recognised right to a view[35] in the law, for example, which effectively means that a neighbour cannot be brought to court if he or she constructs a building in accordance with planning permission and it blocks the view of the surrounding countryside. Similarly, the local planning authority will not entertain a ground of objection to a planning application[36] in relation to a loss of a right to a view as no such right exists in Ireland.

Unfortunately, for those people who see the view from their property as a major selling point of the property, there is no right to that view and, as such, it cannot be protected in law. There is nothing to be done about this. Hence, if a neighbour is going to build a development requiring planning permission that will block a view, the local planning office will not entertain an objection on this ground, the logic being if there was such a right then no neighbouring landowners would be able to develop their land and towns and cities would not exist.

### Right of a Structure to Protection from Wind and Rain from an Adjoining Structure

Similarly there is no right to claim that building or lands in general have a right to protection from the weather.[37] If a neighbour, therefore, demolishes a building leaving an adjoining building exposed to the elements, an action may not be brought against that neighbour for the loss of an easement that never existed in the first instance.

## Repeal of the Law on Prescription

Part 8, Chapter 1 of the Land and Conveyancing Law Reform Act 2009 (the 2009 Act) came into force on 1 December 2009 and s 34 of the 2009 Act

---

[35] *Browne v Flower* [1911] 1 Ch 219 p 227 as per Parker J.
[36] Grounds of objection in relation to planning permissions are dealt with in detail in chapter 7.
[37] *Phibbs v Pears* [1965] 1 QB 76.

abolishes the acquisition of an easement or *profit à prendre* by prescription at common law and under the doctrine of lost modern grant. Section 33 of the 2009 Act sets a new *relevant user period* timeframe for the accrual of an easement or *profit à prendre* from 20 years to just 12 years.[38] Prescription at common law and under the doctrine of lost modern grant is dealt with in detail below but generally allows for the recognition of an easement or a *profit à prendre* where the right claimed has been acquired through repeated use which is open and without the landowner's permission, usually for a period of at least 20 years.

Under s 35 of the 2009 Act, as amended by s 37 of the Civil Law (Miscellaneous Provisions) Act 2011, the person claiming an easement or *profit à prendre* is now required to either:

A:  apply to the court for an order confirming the legal entitlement to the easement, and if granted, the court order conferring the easement or *profit à prendre* must be registered with the appropriate arm of the Property Registration Authority, as is a requirement under s 35(4) of the 2009 Act; or

B:  where there is no disagreement between the parties concerning entitlement to an easement or *profit à prendre*, make an application in accordance with s 49A of the Registration of Title Act 1964[39] (the 1964 Act) which permits the Property Registration Authority to register uncontested easements and *profits à prendre*. The Property Registration Authority already operates a broadly similar scheme under the 1964 Act in respect of titles based on adverse possession.[40]

---

[38] *Relevant user period* means a period of user as of right without interruption by the person claiming to be the dominant owner or owner of a *profit à prendre* in gross: (a) where the servient owner is not a State authority, for a minimum period of 12 years; or (b) where the servient owner is a State authority, for (i) a minimum period of 30 years, or (ii) where the servient land is foreshore, a minimum period of 60 years. The reduction to 12 years mirrors the time frame criteria for claims in adverse possession as detailed in chapter 4.

[39] As inserted by s 41 of the Civil Law (Miscellaneous Provisions) Act 2011.

[40] s 49A—(1) Where any person claims to be entitled to an easement or *profit à prendre* and the relevant requirements set out in sections 33 to 38 of the Land and Conveyancing Law Reform Act 2009 have been met, that person may apply to the Authority and the Authority, if satisfied that there is such an entitlement to the easement or *profit à prendre* concerned, may cause it, as appropriate, to be—

(a) registered as a burden under section 69(1)(*jj*),

(b) entered in the register pursuant to section 82 or, in the case of a *profit à prendre* in gross, in the register of ownership maintained under section 8(*b*)(i).

# The Old 20-Year Rule

Prior to Pt 8, Chapter 1 of the 2009 Act coming into force, there were three methods of acquiring easements[41] by prescription: prescription at common law; under the doctrine of lost modern grant; and under the Prescription Act 1832.

## Prescription at Common Law

To succeed in a claim to have an easement recognised at common law the claimant must establish use of a right from before the time of legal memory which was fixed by the courts as being 1189. However, due to the obvious impracticalities of proving usage from the year 1189, the courts gradually waived this onerous requirement in favour of a lesser period of 20 years whereupon it is presumed that the right claimed existed since 1189.[42] Perhaps not surprisingly, an application in the courts to enforce an easement through prescription at common law was seldom heard of, and as such, most claims to assert the acquisition of easements through prescription were by means of applications under the doctrines of lost modern grant and under the Prescription Act 1832.

## Lost Modern Grant

Under this doctrine, where a person can prove the usage of the right for a continuous period of 20 years it is presumed that at some stage in the past a formal grant of the right was made by deed that dated back to a time before the 20 years and was simply mislaid and never found again. The courts recognise that the system of establishing rights is purely imaginary, amounting to a *legal fiction*,[43] but the courts required some device by which

---

(2) Subsection (1) applies only in relation to claims in respect of which—
    (a) the land benefited by the easement or *profit à prendre*, to which other land is subject, is registered land, or
    (b) the claim is made as part of an application for first registration of that land".
Section 69(1) of the 1964 Act was amended by the insertion of the following paragraph after paragraph (j):
    "(jj) any easement or *profit à prendre* where the Authority is satisfied, pursuant to section 49A, that there is an entitlement to such an easement or *profit à prendre*".

[41] Other than by express agreement and by necessity: see p 68 below.

[42] *Time immemorial* is a term used to denote a time before legal memory. In 1275, by the first Statute of Westminster, the time of legal memory was limited to the reign of Richard I (Richard the Lionheart), beginning 6, July 1189, the date of the King's accession. Since that date, proof of unbroken possession or use of any right made it unnecessary to establish the original grant under certain circumstances.

[43] *Hanna v Pollock* [1900] 2 IR 664 at 702–703.

to prevent a claim from being defeated by proof that the easement could only have come into existence after 1189.

### The Prescription Act 1832

The Prescription Act 1832 came into effect in Ireland on 1 January 1859.[44] The aim of this Act was to alleviate the difficulties caused by the two alternative methods of prescription as outlined above by providing for a usage period for easements of 20 years,[45] after which period it was presumed that the easement came into being as a result of a grant made since 1189, which grant has now been lost meaning that a claim cannot be defeated by establishing enjoyment of the easement later than 1189.[46]

## Transitional Framework for the Acquisition of Easements and *Profits à Prendre* under the 2009 Act (as Amended)

Section 38(b), as amended by s 38 of the Civil Law (Miscellaneous Provisions) Act 2011, provides 12 years for a transitional period, i.e. for claims already acquired under the law, or for claims that will *ripen* and will be acquired during the transitional period, i.e. by 30 November 2021.

Take the example of a farmer who has for some 16 years prior to the commencement of the 2009 Act, in December 2009, been herding his or her cattle across an adjoining farmer's lands to reach a river located thereon. The transitional framework allows that farmer to continue to accrue time under the old law of prescription at common law and lost modern grant until the 20-year timeframe pursuant to the old law is satisfied.

The applicant farmer will therefore need to ensure that he or she has either:

---

[44] The Prescription Act 1832 was extended to Ireland under the Prescription (Ireland) Act 1858 from the 1 January 1859. Both these Acts are repealed in Pt 4, Sch 2 of the Land and Conveyancing Law Reform Act 2009.

[45] s 2 also provides for a user period of 40 years for easements and 60 years for *profits à prendre*. Once the requisite longer usage duration is proved, the right is deemed *absolute and indefeasible* unless it is enjoyed by some consent or agreement expressly given by deed or writing.

[46] s 3 applies to easements of light, providing for a prescriptive period of 20 years without interruption. The right shall be deemed *absolute and indefeasible*, unless enjoyed by written consent. See Law Reform Commission, LRC 66-2002, *Report on the Acquisition of Easements and Profits à Prendre by Prescription* (Law Reform Commission, Dublin, 2002), para. 1.16.

A:   met the requirements set down by case law regarding acquisition under prescription, or

B:   met the requirements set down by case law regarding acquisition under common law or under the doctrine of lost modern grant.

Thereafter, the same farmer will have until 30 November 2021 to make a s 35 (as amended), application to have either the easement registered by way of the non-contentious route of the s 49A procedure under the 1964 Act or where the pending claim is contentious, to initiate court proceedings by 30 November 2021 for adjudication by the court and subsequent registration upon successful application.

The important date, therefore, in relation to the maintenance of *old law* easements is 30 November 2021, after which time the claimant farmer will be obliged to set the user time period clock back to zero and thereafter wait for the relevant user period of 12 years to accrue[47] before approaching the Property Registration Authority or the courts to obtain legal recognition of the easement claimed.[48]

## Where an Easement has been Established in Court Prior to the 2009 Act

While s 49A of the 1964 Act does not apply to implied grants or easements of necessity, applications for registration of same can be made by lodging a copy of the relevant court order pursuant to s 69(1)(h) of the 1964 Act with the Property Registration Authority. Therefore, if a user/claimant of an easement has already established the right of the easement in the courts, there will not be a necessity to re-establish the right to the easement under the new legislation.

## Where the 2009 Act Does Not Apply

It is important to remember that the scope of Pt 8, Chapter 1 of the 2009 Act, as amended by Pt 12 of the Civil Law (Miscellaneous Provisions) Act 2011, and the amended s 49A of the 1964 Act, applies to rights acquired by prescription only and does not extend to rights acquired by *express grant/ reservation* or to the acquisition of rights implied under the law of easements of necessity.

---

[47] s 38(b), as amended by s 38 of the Civil Law (Miscellaneous Provisions) Act 2011.
[48] By way of a s 35 (as amended) application.

Easements created by *express grant/reservation*, in simple terms, occur when two landowners come together and create a written record or deed, wherein one party grants the other a right over certain lands. The most common example would be the right of a home owner to have piping running through a neighbour's garden for the purpose of joining up to the public mains which may be located some distance away.

An easement of *necessity* carries a right of way of necessity over a track, for example, that is the only means of access between the public highway and that parcel of land. It is deemed to be necessary as the lack of the easement, i.e. the right of way, would render the landlocked parcel of land to be otherwise useless to its owner. This type of easement of necessity is giving a new statutory footing under s 40(2) of the 2009 Act.[49]

An example, in an urban context, would be the implied right to support between adjoining houses arising out of an easement of necessity of support. Obviously there is not much point in purchasing a house to find that the adjoining structure may be demolished leaving the remaining property at the certain risk of subsidence.

## How Easements are Extinguished

Section 39 of the 2009 Act, as amended by s 39 of the Civil Law (Miscellaneous Provisions) Act 2011, puts in place a statutory mechanism that attempts to simplify the manner in which easements and *profits à prendre* may be extinguished. In accordance with this section, rights acquired by prescription and implied grant that have not been utilised for a continuous period of 12 years are extinguished save where they are protected by registration in the Registry of Deeds or Land Registry, as appropriate.

## How to Stop a Neighbour Acquiring a Right of Way Over One's Lands[50]

Obviously, the first thing to do once a neighbour begins to cross over lands is to approach him or her in a mannerly fashion and inform him or

---

[49] The old common law rule in *Wheeldon v Burrows* is abolished by s 40(1) of the 2009 Act and given a new statutory footing under s 40(2) of the 2009 Act.

[50] Chapter 4 on adverse possession, at p 75, deals in detail with the ways in which one may regularise a situation of someone using one's lands without allowing an actual proprietary right such as a right of way to accrue.

her that a right of way may not be exercised over the lands, i.e. the use of the lands as a shortcut should cease.

If one's complaint goes unheeded then it will be necessary to fence off any gaps in the boundary where the neighbour gains access to the lands. It may also be advisable to erect an appropriate sign at the entrance to the lands.

If at this stage the neighbour insists on crossing the lands, a solicitor may be engaged to write to the neighbour informing him or her that he or she is, in trespassing onto one's lands without permission, committing a trespass and that if such trespass continues court proceedings will commence.

If the offending neighbour is or has caused damage to one's lands arising out of such trespass, it may also be necessary to inform An Garda Síochána of the trespass and damage caused pursuant to s 24 of the Housing (Miscellaneous Provisions) Act 2002, which broadens the rules governing criminal trespass in the Criminal Justice (Public Order) Act 1994. Pursuant to s 19C (1), of the 1994 Act it is now a criminal offence for anyone to enter, occupy or bring anything onto privately owned land or land owned by local authorities if that act is likely to:

- Substantially damage the land;
- Substantially damage any amenity on the land or prevent any person from making reasonable use of that amenity;
- Render the land or any amenity on it unsanitary or unsafe; and/or
- Substantially interfere with the land or an amenity on it.

## Conclusion

The 2009 Act will mean that easements by prescription are nearing their end and, henceforth, such easements will only now be recognised as forming part of the legal title to lands upon registration of the easement. For this to occur, adjoining landowners have three options. First, meet and agree to draw up a Deed of Assurance recognising whatever easements exist as and between them and, thereafter, steps may be taken to register same with the Property Registration Authority. Secondly, meet and agree that there is/are easement(s) pertaining to the adjoining land(s) and thereby make an application on mutual consent to the Property Registration Authority pursuant to s 49A of the 1964 Act to have same registered.

Thirdly, where there is non-agreement as to the existence of the easement(s), court proceedings will need to be initiated by the claimant, and upon successful application, the court order will then be registered in the Property Registration Authority.

In adopting the 2009 Act, the legislature has seemed to put adjoining landowners in the difficult position of having to have a conversation over what rights each has over the lands of the other, and where no formal agreement is forthcoming, will oblige one party to sue the other in order to obtain the court's affirmation of the right claimed. In a country with a myriad of easements and cross-easements, it is a reasonable assumption that the courts will, on the approach to 30 November 2021, become abundant with neighbours being forced into the situation of having to sue neighbours to establish long-standing rights.

The 2009 Act, therefore, is not the most conducive piece of legislation for the fostering of good neighbourly relations and in hindsight many might rue the day that the old system of acquisition of easements by prescription and long lost grant, all based in part on legal fiction, was brought to an end.

# CHAPTER FOUR

# Adverse Possession and Squatters' Rights

A dverse possession of land, or *squatters' rights* as it is more commonly known, arises where a person or *squatter* is in sole and exclusive occupation of land without the acknowledgment of the legal owner(s) and that occupation is inconsistent with the title of the true owner.

The historical purpose of adverse possession was to allow the common law to step in and cure a defective title that an individual may have in relation to lands. The squatter must have used the property as his or her own for a requisite period of 12 years, thereby *curing* potential or actual defects in the title to the property. Otherwise, long-lost heirs of any former owner could come forward with a legal claim to the property. The law, therefore, rewards individuals for making full use of the land and punishes absentee or careless owners for not paying due care and consideration to their lands.

## Timeframes

This 12-year rule is laid down under s 13(2) of the Statute of Limitations 1957. The 12-year limitation period is extended to 30 years' possession in order to bar a State Authority from asserting its prior legal entitlement to the lands in question. The necessary period is reduced to six years where the property is the estate of a deceased person by virtue of s 126 of the Succession Act 1965.[1]

After this 12-year period[2] the legal owner of the lands, that is to say the person with his or her name on the title deeds and/or registered as the

---

[1] The period is 60 years where the claim relates to the foreshore, or 40 years from the date on which land ceased to be the foreshore but remained in the ownership of the State: s 13(1)(a)–(c).

[2] For the remainder of this chapter save where indicated to the contrary it will be presumed that the 12 limitation period applies i.e. the claim to adverse possession is against a private landowner not being the State.

*current* owner with the Property Registration Authority, is not able to bring a claim before the courts to oust the squatter from the lands in question as they will be deemed to be *statute barred*, or out of time to bring such a successful application in the courts.

## Requirements for Adverse Possession

Whether adverse possession can be deemed to exist depends on an examination of the facts and circumstances of each case. The onus of proof lies on the plaintiff to establish adverse possession with the requisite intent. In September 2007, a High Court case, *Dunne v Iarnród Éireann*,[3] set out the test for determining whether a squatter had acquired the property by adverse possession in Ireland. In summary, the court will consider the following two questions when a claim for adverse possession arises:

- is there a continuous period of 12 years during which the squatter was in exclusive possession of the lands in question to an extent sufficient to establish an intention to possess[4] the land itself?; and
- is any contended period of possession broken by an act of possession by the landowner? If so, time will only start to run when the act of the landowner terminates.

The court qualified the second part of the test by holding that the sufficiency of the act of possession required for the landowner to break possession is a very low threshold. This would be satisfied by certain acts of possession on the part of the landowner. In this particular case, the owner, CIE, had carried out works to a station on part of the lands and had also sent out a contractor at one stage to re-establish fences between the lands and a neighbour's lands. The court found that these were sufficient acts of ownership to defeat the claim of the occupier.

## The European Dimension

The very essence of the doctrine of adverse possession was recently tested before the European Court of Human Rights (ECHR) with reference to Article 1, Protocol 1 of the European Convention on Human

---

[3] [2007] IEHC 314.
[4] *Animus possidendi.*

Rights which entitles every person to peaceful enjoyment of its lands. A UK case, *JA Pye (Oxford) Ltd v United Kingdom*,[5] had challenged the doctrine. Following lengthy litigation in the UK courts, the case was ultimately referred to the Grand Chamber of the ECHR, where it was held that the law on adverse possession, at least as it applies in England and Wales, was deemed to be compliant with the European Convention on Human Rights as it was seen to strike a fair balance between with the legitimate public interest in having a limitation period allowing for the extinguishment of title after a particular period had passed and the interests of the individuals concerned. The view being that it was not unreasonable to place a duty on owners of land to take steps to maintain possession of their own lands.

In view of the decision in the *Pye* case, therefore, it may be argued with some authority that the doctrine of adverse possession has now been re-affirmed and is beyond doubt. In Irish law, however, as per the decision in *Dunne v Iarnród Éireann*, the party trying to win title has an uphill battle given how little it takes for the limitation period to be stopped and the clock to be set back to zero.

## Fraudulent Claims

Where there is a fraudulent attempt to possess lands through adverse possession, s 7 of the Statute of Limitations 1957 steps in to remedy the situation by declaring that the requisite time period, that is to say 12 years in the case of lands in private ownership, shall not begin to run until the plaintiff has discovered the fraud or could, with reasonable diligence, have discovered it.

## Disability

In relation to individuals with a disability, for example a mental infirmity, or in the case of a minor, the clock does not begin to run until six years after such a person ceases to be under such a disability or dies, whichever happens first, notwithstanding that the period of limitation has expired.[6] Obviously the law will not allow the adverse possession clock to run as against any landowner who may not be in a position to exercise dominion over his or her lands or lacks the necessary mental

---

[5] *JA Pye (Oxford) Ltd v United Kingdom* [2005] ECHR 921.
[6] s 49 Statute of Limitations 1957.

capacity to initiate proceedings to claim back his or her lands from a squatter.

## An Example of Adverse Possession in a Neighbourhood Context

The house next door has just been sold and the new owners indicate that they have reviewed the map attaching to their deed of sale. It appears from the map that the garden should actually run a further two metres inside the adjoining landowner's property. The new neighbours furnish a copy of their deed and map to the adjoining landowner.

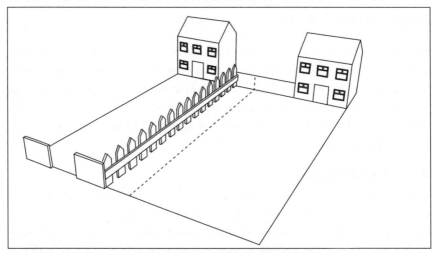

Diagram 7 – Adverse Possession in an Urban Context

The adjoining landowner, who bought the property 14 years ago, is informed by the solicitor acting on his or her behalf that the boundary has indeed been encroached by two metres. Fortunately, the landowner has been holding the property adverse to the new neighbours' legal title, and as the necessary period of 12 years has lapsed since they or their predecessors in title[7] have exercised dominion over the lands in question, the new neighbours no longer have a legal basis upon which to assert ownership of the lands. In essence, the new neighbours cannot mount a successful legal challenge to re-claim the lands as they are *statute barred*, i.e. they are barred from bringing a court action as they are out of time pursuant to s 13(2) of the Statute of Limitations 1957.

---

[7] Meaning all previous owners of the house and garden in question.

## How to Stop Squatters Acquiring One's Title

Given the decision in *Dunne v Iarnród Éireann*, the individual with the title to the lands need not do very much in order to stop the adverse possession clock running for the benefit of the squatter. However, that said, it would be a foolhardy landowner who is not proactive in the assertion of the legal title to his or her property.

In relation to non-residential lands, such as agricultural lands, it is prudent for the landowner to monitor his or her lands, or if he or she is an absentee landowner, to have somebody survey the lands. In every day terms this will mean having somebody survey the lands during any prolonged absences. If there appears to be farm animals grazing, fences newly erected, or indeed any sign of a display of control over the lands, the landowner should immediately seek legal advice to put an end to such trespass and the landowner should also mount a claim for property damage if this is appropriate. The issuance of legal proceedings will immediately stop the adverse possession clock from running.

Thereafter, if a landowner allows individuals onto lands with permission, the landowner will need to have his or her solicitor draw up a lease or licence which will stop the adverse possession clock running and effectively convert the squatter into a lessee or a licensee and, as such, the question of adverse possession falls away.

The landowner, however, must be careful to be seen to act quickly and decisively in contacting his or her legal representative in relation to lessees and licensees who cease paying rents at the end of the term of the lease or licence period. If the lessee/licensee fails to hand possession back to the landowner at the appropriate time, the solicitor for the landowner should serve the appropriate notice in writing on the squatter to vacate the property.

In such an instance, it is only when court proceedings are commenced that the adverse possession clock stops the time accruing in favour of the squatter.

## How to Affirm Ownership of Squatted Lands

Where lands are held adversely to the legal owner, upon instruction, a solicitor may proceed to make an application pursuant to s 49 of the

Registration of Title Act 1964. It will be necessary to prove that the lands have been held for the requisite period of 12 years during which the squatter was in exclusive possession of the lands to an extent sufficient to establish an intention to possess.

As part of this procedure, the squatter will be required to file a form of affidavit[8] which must be comprehensive and detailed in showing when the applicant entered into possession, the use he or she made of the property and his or her acts of possession, i.e. how control was exerted over the property. In addition, it should trace the title to the property from the registered owner stating the names and addresses of all persons whom the applicant claims to have barred.

A map should be lodged where the application is in respect of part of a folio only, unless the property can be identified by reference to a plan number.

Furthermore, notices must be served on affected parties such as the legal owner or the owners of neighbouring/adjoining lands by the Property Registration Authority and objections may follow on foot of the issuance of these notifications. Any objection will cause delays and as such it is not possible to estimate how long any s 49 application will take to process and needless to say a successful objection will prevent registration.

A solicitor will also advise of tax compliance requirements pursuant to s 62 of the Capital Acquisitions Tax Consolidation Act 2003, as no person shall be registered as owner of property based on a claim in adverse possession unless the necessary tax certificate is produced. This is a statutory requirement and the Property Registration Authority has no discretion in this matter.

## The Right to Appeal

Where the Property Registration Authority is not satisfied that the applicant has acquired title, an order refusing registration will issue. This usually occurs when there is an objection and conflicting claims are made by the parties. It is not the function of the Property Registration Authority to make a determination where conflicting claims arise. An order of refusal

---

[8] Land Registry Form 5.

may be appealed to the courts under s 19(1) of the Registration of Title Act 1964. A refusal may also arise in the event of an error in the application or proofs presented.

## Repeal of the Restriction to Claim Adverse Possession on Leasehold Titles

Legal practitioners will be aware that the old rule barring claims for adverse possession against leasehold interests has been repealed by virtue of s 50 of the Registration of Deeds and Title Act 2006, and since the coming into law of this section on 26 May 2006, applications for adverse possession may be made to the Property Registration Authority in accordance with the procedure in s 49 of the Registration of Title Act 1964 as outlined above.

Prior to repeal, it was decided law, as per the ruling in *Perry v Woodfarm Home Ltd*,[9] that it was untenable for a squatter to claim adverse possession to leasehold property. The result of the decision was to affirm that the squatter obtains not the leasehold estate itself but the right to hold possession of the lands during the residue of the term of the lease. Accordingly, this remained as an encumbrance upon the freehold and prevented the freeholder from repossessing the lands during the continuance of the lease.[10]

## Conclusion

Adverse possession or squatters' rights is the laws own mechanism in assuring that land is never seen to lay idle for any significant length of time. There is therefore an economic and social logic to the doctrine in placing an onus on the land owner to assert ownership on an ongoing basis. As mentioned above, the threshold in relation to the positive acts displaying continued use and ownership of the lands are set at a low level making successful applications for possession of lands based on the doctrine, whilst not unheard of, certainly an increasing rarity in the Irish courts.

---

[9] [1975] IR 104.

[10] See Law Reform Commission, Report on Title by Adverse Possession of Land, LRC 67-2002, December 2002, p 8. It should be noted that there remain an unsatisfactory situation of the landlord/free holder may still regain possession of the property for non compliance with the original lease covenants as the person in adverse possession will not be privy to same.

# CHAPTER FIVE

# Trees, Hedges and Roots

## Ownership of the Tree on the Boundary

It will be recalled from chapter 1 that boundary disputes are wretched, drawn out affairs where, at the end of the day, the time, effort and stress involved may far outweigh the value of the piece of land or tree in question. Furthermore, there is no statutory authority in Ireland, whether it be the Property Registration Authority or Ordnance Survey Ireland, who will provide one with a map showing a conclusive line of demarcation between one's garden and that of the adjoining landowner. It is for this reason that one must revert to the common law, or law based on past decisions of the courts, in order to determine the rights of ownership of trees and hedges at and on the boundary.

The English case of *Lemmon v Webb*,[1] is clear authority regarding the rules of ownership in relation to boundary trees, where both the Court of Appeal and the House of Lords[2] agreed with the contention that a tree on a boundary is held in joint ownership as *tenants in common*[3] by each of the adjoining landowners and his or her successors. Each owner of the tree, therefore, in accordance with tenancies in common, would have an equal right to deal with the whole of the tree as both parties would own the whole of the entirety of the tree equally. That said, this is certainly not a licence for one party to unilaterally act in a manner that would lead to the removal of the tree, as such unilateral action would constitute trespass and leave the door open to a wronged party for an award of damages.[4]

A difficult question arises in trying to establish the exact rights of owners of trees in common. In the above case the owner plaintiff was entitled to cut the roots on his own side. Whether he could cut down half the tree

---

[1] [1894] 3 Ch 1.
[2] [1895] AC 1.
[3] See chapter 1, p 7.
[4] *Heatherington v Gault* (1905) 7 F. 708.

longitudinally, the judge did not know. At any rate the plaintiff had no right to cut down the whole tree without the consent of the defendant.

## Overhanging Branches and Encroaching Roots

Under the common law, a person may cut back any branch or root from a neighbour's tree that overhangs or encroaches onto his or her property. The courts have long recognised that branches and roots of trees do not respect legal boundaries and have made clear and unequivocal statements of the law in this regard. The courts deem the transgression of roots and branches as constituting a nuisance and, as such, under the common law one has the right to *abate* or stop such nuisance. In the instances of overhanging trees and branches, a nuisance is defined generally as the unlawful interference with the enjoyment of the property of another.

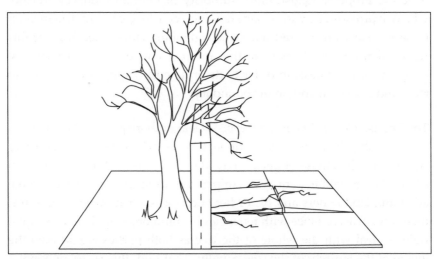

Diagram 8 – Right to Abate Encroaching Roots and Branches

The case of *Lemmon v Webb*[5] involved the cutting of overhanging branches back to a property line. The appellant sold an area of land to the respondent who then cut off the branches from the neighbouring trees which overhung his land. The branches were cut back to the property boundary without first notifying the tree owner (the appellant). The appellant sought damages and an injunction against the respondent to restrain him from the cutting of further branches without his permission.

---

[5] [1894] 3 Ch 1.

During the appeal, Lord Macnaghten said:

> "... if he can get rid of the interference or encroachment without committing a trespass, or entering upon the land of his neighbour, he may do so whenever he pleases, and that no notice or previous communication is required by law."[6]

The opinion of the Court of Appeal was upheld by the House of Lords and this 1894 case from the United Kingdom is still cited as good legal authority in Ireland today.

The following is a checklist to be considered before a neighbour begins to lop trees or extract encroaching roots:

- If the tree is mature, it will be necessary to check with the local planning authority that the tree is not subject to a *Tree Preservation Order*[7];
- It is not permitted to trespass onto the land on which the trees are growing;
- It is not permitted to cut back branches or roots beyond the boundary in anticipation of them overhanging;
- Any branches, fruit or roots that are removed must be returned to the tree owner unless agreed otherwise;
- Care must be taken not to damage property in the ownership of the adjoining landowner;
- Do not carry out work that would render the tree unsafe or dangerous or irreparably damage the tree;
- As a matter of courtesy, notification should be given to the tree owner.

If the tree owner agrees to works that are in addition to common law rights, or if permission is granted to enter the owner's land to undertake the work, it would be advisable to obtain written consent. A standard form of agreement for the carrying out of works at the boundary, including the tending of roots and branches, is contained in Appendix 2.

## Where Consent is Withheld and Section 45 Works Orders

Chapter 2 details the practice and procedure to be followed in making a *works order* application under s 45 of the Land and Conveyancing

---

[6] *Lemmon v Webb* [1891-94] All ER Rep 749 at 751.
[7] See pp 89–90.

Law Reform Act 2009 (the 2009 Act) works order application in the District Court. It will be recalled that works orders allow individuals who wish to conduct works to a party structure, in a situation where there is no consent forthcoming from the adjoining landowner, to apply to the District Court for a works order allowing for the works to take place without fear of accusation of trespass or criminal damage. Section 43 of the 2009 Act comprises a wide definition of party structures which includes any hedge, shrub or tree which horizontally, vertically or in any other way divides adjoining and separately owned buildings and, as such, the works order application finally remedies this often troublesome area.

## Works Orders, Coniferous Trees, the Right to Light and the Right to a View

Fast growing coniferoustrees, such as Leyland Cypress hedges planted between adjoining properties, may cause a nuisance by diminishing the amount of sunlight reaching the neighbouring property or by obstructing the neighbour's view or even access to the property. Whilst the common law provides the remedy in relation to overhanging branches, there is no inherent right to lop the tree branches that are not occupying one's airspace, i.e. those branches and trunks occupying the space perpendicular to the edge of the trimmed tree/hedge-line upwards.

In England and Wales, Pt 8 of the Anti-Social Behaviour Act 2003 tackles this problem by requiring everyone with a high hedge to consider the effect that such a hedge will have on neighbours. An application may be lodged with the local district council and the council will then decide whether the hedge is adversely affecting the reasonable enjoyment of one's property. The council can issue a formal notice setting out what must be done to remedy the problem, including the requirement to reduce the height of the hedge-line.

There is as yet no such specific law in relation to high hedges or tree lines in Ireland, but notwithstanding the lack of specific legislation in this area, it is open to an aggrieved neighbour to bring an application for a s 45 works order to conduct works on the boundary that involves the lopping of the neighbour's trees. Even though the trees may be located on the neighbour's lands, they will still form part of the party structure definition and, as such, an application of this nature will be feasible on this ground.

In terms of the likelihood of success of this application, the District Court has a wide discretion in terms of making an order pursuant to s 44(1)(d) of the 2009 Act which allows for applications for works to the party structure that are termed *any other works*. *Any other works* may be granted under the terms of a works order once they:

(i) will not cause substantial damage or inconvenience to the adjoining owner; or

(ii) if they may cause such damage or inconvenience it is nevertheless reasonable to carry them out.[8]

The statute is obviously designed to give the District Court Judge a wide degree of discretion in terms of whether to grant permission for the particular works in question. Any *substantial damage or inconvenience to the adjoining owner* caused may be addressed by the court in making the works order conditional upon strict adherence to certain terms and conditions. Each such application will be judged on its own merits in the context of the particular case. It is, of course, a potential difficulty that Irish law does not recognise a right to a view and does not recognise a right to light over rear gardens.[9]

## Fruit and Leaves from the Tree Next Door

A tree or shrub belongs to the land on which it grows even if its branches or roots go over or under adjoining land. This includes the branches and the fruit of any tree or shrub. This even applies to what is termed as windfall apples, pears and plums, etc. However, the law does not require the owner to come and sweep up the leaves or pick up the fruit. Nor is there any obligation on the person onto whose land the fruit has fallen to keep it safe for the tree owner. However, there is English authority which states that the adjoining owner is allowed to enter onto the lands to recover the fruit.[10]

In the case of *Mills v Brooker*,[11] the defendant picked some apples from the branches of his neighbour's tree that overhung his garden and sold

---

[8] s 11(1)(d)(i) and (ii).
[9] Chapter 3, p 56.
[10] *Mitten v Faudyre* (1625) Poph. 161; *Patrick v Colerick* (1838) 3 M. & W. 483 at 485 as per F.V. Lee.
[11] [1919] 1 KB 555.

them. It was held that the neighbour had a right to cut overhanging branches but he had no rights of ownership on the cut branches or apples growing on them. The court awarded judgment to the tree owner. The defendant was entitled to remove the branches but could not use the removed branches for his own use. The defendant appealed but this was dismissed. During the appeal it was also cited that fruit remains the property of the tree owner whether carried by overhanging branches or whether blown off by the wind. The appeal court stated that:

> "… the owner of a fruit tree the branch of which grows over the boundary of his land, is the owner of the fruit on the overhanging branch while it is still growing on the tree. The adjoining owner is entitled to sever the branch but that does not divest the owner's right of property. The adjoining owner is not entitled to sell the fruit".

As the fruit from the tree overhanging one's property belongs to one's neighbour,[12] it follows that the leaves from the tree also belong to one's neighbour. Nowhere does the law place an obligation on the tree owner to come and pick the fallen fruit or falling leaves, so in a technical sense the leaves from next door's tree should be collected and returned next door along with any lopped overhanging branches and fallen fruit.

## Dangerous Trees and the Risk to Property and Personal Safety

In a situation where it is feared that a neighbour's tree may fall and cause a hazard to personal safety and/or property, and where consent to fell the tree is not forthcoming, it will be necessary to make an application for a s 45 works order pursuant to s 44(1)(d) of the 2009 Act which allows for applications for *any other works* to party structures. Obviously the court will consider all of the necessary factors and may even adjourn matters to allow the parties to have the trees examined by an expert such as an arboriculturist[13] in order to assess the risks of the tree falling. The adjoining landowner may also recoup the reasonable costs of obtaining professional

---

[12] As does the overhanging lopped branch.

[13] Arboriculturists manage all aspects of felling, preserving, planting and protecting trees with a focus on maintaining a safe relationship between the trees, their immediate environment and the general public.

advice with regard to the likely consequences of the works.[14] Presumably *professional advice with regard to the likely consequences of the works* infers that the adjoining landowner on whose land the tree is situated has the right to compensation for the retention of the professional advice in order to make an informed decision as to whether to accede to the building owner's request for permission to pursue the particular works. The party making the application, if successful, may seek a contribution for proportionate use and enjoyment of the party structure which the adjoining owner makes or is likely to make from the works carried out by the building owner.[15]

## Where a Tree Falls Causing Property Damage and/or Personal Injury

In this situation the ordinary rules of negligence law apply, meaning that the courts ask themselves the question as to what an *ordinary, prudent landowner* would have done or would have been expected to have known in relation to the dangerous tree that falls causing damage to property, or worse again, personal injury to an adjoining landowner or a member of the public. In this way the law seems to indicate that the reasonably-minded tree owner in more populated urban areas, or tree owners beside busy roads, should exercise greater prudence in checking their trees for defects, as the risks of not doing so are far greater than for the tree owner on a country lane.

The decision in *Gillen v Fair*[16] involved an appeal to the High Court from the Circuit Court, in which it was held that the standard of care required was that of the *ordinary, prudent landowner*.[17] The case concerned a fatal accident caused by the fall across a public road in County Mayo of a very large ash tree, 70-feet high, five-feet in diameter and about 130 years old. It was proved that the tree was rotten in some respects. The defects were

---

[14] s 44(2)(b(i).

[15] For a complete detail of the financial provisions on foot of works orders, see chapter 2, pp 26–31.

[16] (1956) 90 ILTR 119.

[17] As per the definition of Lord Normand in *Caminer v Northern & London Investment Trust Ltd*, [1951] AC 88, where he states that "the test of the conduct to be expected from a reasonable and prudent landlord sounds more simple that it really is. For it postulates some degree of knowledge on the part of the landlords which must necessarily fall short of the knowledge possessed by scientific arboriculturists but which must surely be greater than the knowledge possessed by the ordinary urban observer of trees or even of the country-man not practically concerned with their care".

high up the tree. There was a black spot and fungus on it and portions of the bark had come off. It was said that these defects might be apparent to an expert but the court did not think that every farmer in the country should employ an expert to examine every tree growing on his or her lands beside a highway.[18] It was also posited that the standard of care required of a farmer in County Mayo having trees growing on his or her land adjoining a highway might not be as high as that required of an owner of a tree growing beside a highway in a thickly populated, built-up area. The court found the fact that the tree in this case had a defect, which in a storm might cause it to fall, was such a latent defect that it was not discoverable by ordinary inspection or reasonable care. The case failed in nuisance as well as in negligence.

The above decision is still seen as good law and has been upheld in the courts in relatively more recent times. In the case of *Lynch v Hetherton*,[19] Hanlon J laid down the following indications as to the appropriate level of care to discharge the test of the *ordinary, prudent landowner* which may lead to a successful defence of any claims arising in this context:-

1.  that a landowner having on his or her lands a tree or trees adjoining a highway or his or her neighbour's land is bound to take such care as a reasonable and prudent landowner would take to guard against the danger of damage being done by a failing tree, and if he or she fails to exercise this degree of care and damage results from such failure on his or her part, a cause of action will arise against him or her;
2.  that for a plaintiff to succeed in an action for damages arising out of an incident of this kind, he or she must establish as a matter of probability that the landowner was aware, or should have been aware, of the dangerous condition of the tree;
3.  that the onus of proof will be discharged if the plaintiff can show that a proper inspection of the tree at reasonable intervals would have forewarned the owner that it was getting into a dangerous condition and that the danger should be averted by lopping or felling or by other suitable means;

---

[18] *Gillen v Fair* (1956) 90 ILTR 119, 20.
[19] [1991] 2 IR 405.

4. that the standard of care required was that of the *ordinary, prudent landowner*[20];

5. that the defendant had exercised the degree of care that would have been exercised by a reasonable and prudent landowner in satisfying him or herself that the tree which fell should not be regarded as a danger to persons using the highway and, accordingly, he was not liable for the accident.

As per the decision in *Gillen v Fair* discussed above, a word of caution is required for the landowner in urban or built-up areas or along busy road ways to take a greater responsibility to discharge the test of the *ordinary, prudent landowner*. In such instances, it would be looked upon very favourably by the courts if the landowner was able to demonstrate systematic inspection of the trees on the lands. Whilst this may not always amount to retaining experts to conduct the inspection, if the landowner discovers what may appear to be a defect in the tree that may constitute a danger, or is simply unsure, then expert assistance, such as from an arboriculturist, should be retained in order to address the risk.

As Lord Oaksey said in *Carminer v Northern & London Investment Ltd*[21]:

> "Landowners are not all experts in the management of trees, and those who are not perform their duty if they take reasonable steps to employ persons who are experts."

## Liability for Poisonous Trees

Much of the English case law[22] in this area pivots on the death of farm animals from eating overhanging yew branches, and therefore the case law would appear to be sub-divided into two distinct categories: first those animals that die as a result of eating the poisonous foliage of the adjoining landlord where the relationship is that of tenant and landlord; and the second category relates to adjoining lands where the relationship of landlord and tenant is not seen to exist.

---

[20] As per *Carminer v Northern & London Investment Ltd* [1951] AC 88 and *Quinn v Scott* [1965] 1 WLR 1004.

[21] [1951] AC 88 at 104.

[22] See C Mynors, *The Law of Trees, Forests and Hedgerows* (Sweet and Maxwell, London 2002), pp 69–71 for a more in-depth review of the case law in this area.

Where the relationship of landlord and tenant does exist, the case law in this area is quite explicit in demonstrating that any individual who leases lands is not essentially obliged to lease such lands, and as such, if he or she chooses to do so he or she should inspect his or her boundaries to see if any potential risks by way of poisonous shrubs or branches exist for the animals that he or she brings onto the leased lands. The case of *Erskine v Adeane*,[23] for example, demonstrates an instance where the plaintiff's cattle died as a result of feeding on overhanging yew tree branches coming onto the lands that the plaintiff was leasing from the defendant.

The plaintiff's action failed in relation to the overhanging branches due to the fact that the courts decided that as the plaintiff was the lessee of the defendant he had ample opportunity to survey the lands and discover any inherent dangers represented by the yew trees on the boundary. This case is also demonstrative of the fact that the lessor need not be responsible for the blocking of gaps in the boundary in order to deter his or her tenant's animals from straying onto his or her lands where there might be found such poisonous foliage.

The case of *Cowhurst v Amersham Burial Board*,[24] however, is authority for the fact that an adjoining landowner with poisonous foliage on his or her boundary may be held liable for the damage or loss of the adjacent landowner's animals that eat such overhanging foliage. In this case the plaintiff's horse had eaten from the branches of yew trees that were located on the defendant's land but the branches of which were overhanging the plaintiff's property. The horse ate the poisonous foliage and died and the plaintiff sued for his loss. The court held in favour of the plaintiff and the judge's ruling was clear in its assertion that it is not incumbent upon the animal owner to be constantly surveying and cutting back the poisonous foliage encroaching onto his or her lands.[25]

Best practice, therefore, would seem to indicate that the landowner should take care in not planting potentially poisonous foliage on or near a boundary. Any adjoining landowner who feels restricted in releasing his or her animals onto his or her lands due to the fact that he or she is

---

[23] (1873) LR 8 Ch App 756.
[24] (1878) IV Ex D5.
[25] *ibid* at 10.

aware of an inherent risk from such foliage on adjoining lands should seek legal advice from his or her solicitor in relation to injunctive relief if the adjoining landowner is being unreasonable in refusing to cut back or remove such foliage. If a loss has already accrued to an adjoining landowner then a claim for damages under nuisance, negligence and the rule in *Rylands v Fletcher*[26] may be considered. Chapter 15 gives a brief description of civil remedies available to individuals in such instances.

## Tree Preservation Order (TPO)

Notwithstanding that neighbouring trees may be a source of nuisance, it may equally be the case that certain trees add character and improve the aesthetic amenity of the neighbourhood. If this is the case and one is fearful that an adjoining property owner may fell a tree that adds to the aesthetic amenity of its surrounds, an application may be made to the local authority pursuant to s 205 of the Planning and Development Act 2000 which enables any individual to ask the local authority to consider making a TPO. For the local authority to make such a designation, the tree must be of such aesthetic merit that it warrants the protection and as such should become the subject of a TPO.

Whilst the ultimate discretion in the decision to make the order rests with the local authority, the decision of the local authority to make a TPO may be appealed by the tree owner to An Bord Pleanála. A TPO will prevent the cutting down, topping, lopping or willful destruction of a tree without the specific consent of the local authority. Importantly, any individual who fells a tree that is the subject of a TPO, or a tree the subject of the TPO decision-making process, is guilty of an offence and on summary conviction may be liable to a fine of €5000, or to imprisonment for a term not exceeding six months, or to both.[27]

## Tree Felling and the 10-Year Rule

Section 37 of the Forestry Act 1946 (the 1946 Act) makes it unlawful for any person to uproot any tree over 10 years old or to cut down any tree, unless the owner of the land on which the tree stands has, not less than 21 days and not more than two years before the commencement of the uprooting or

---

[26] *Rylands v Fletcher* (1868) LR 3 HL 330.

[27] s 156(1)(b) of the Planning and Development Act 2000 as amended by s 46(a) of the Planning and Development (Amendment) Act 2010.

cutting down (as the case may be) of the tree, given to the sergeant in charge of the Garda Síochána station nearest to the tree a notice in writing of intention to uproot or cut down (as the case may be) the tree.[28]

Thereafter the Minister for Lands, or as the Minister is now known, the Minister for Communications, Energy and Natural Resources, may make and serve an order under s 39 which prohibits the uprooting or cutting down of the tree. Certain exemptions are afforded under this Act to allow the ESB to by-pass this regulatory framework in its statutory role in the provision of energy to the State.[29]

If any person uproots or cuts down or causes or permits to be uprooted or cut down any tree in contravention of s 37(3) of the 1946 Act, such person may be tried on indictment and, on conviction on indictment, shall be liable to a fine not exceeding €2,540[30] together with an amount not exceeding €64[31] for each tree in respect of which the offence is committed or, at the discretion of the court, to imprisonment for a term not exceeding two years, or to both the fine and the imprisonment.[32]

## Can the ESB Enter Private Lands and Fell One's Trees?

By virtue of s 53(1) of the Electricity (Supply) Act 1927 (the Act), the ESB[33] may enter onto the lands of private citizens for the purposes of the installation of power lines both above and below the ground and the Act provides for notification periods in relation to this right of entry to install.[34] Furthermore, s 98(1) of the Act allows the ESB[35] to enter onto an individual's lands for the purpose of felling or lopping trees, shrubs or hedges which obstruct or interfere with any electric wires of the ESB.

---

[28] s 37 should be consulted in full as statutory exemptions are provided for in certain circumstances.

[29] See p 91.

[30] The euro equivalent of £2,000.

[31] The euro equivalent of £50.

[32] s 6(3) of the Forestry Act 1988.

[33] Or any of those entities as permitted by the Commission for Electricity Regulation under s 49 of the Electricity Regulation Act 1999.

[34] s 53(3) of the Act.

[35] Or, as amended by s 45 of the Electricity Regulation Act 1999, an authorised undertaker or a holder of an authorisation under s 16 of the Electricity Regulation Act 1999, or holder of a direct line permission under s 37 of the Electricity Regulation Act 1999, as the case may be.

However, before the removal of the obstructing foliage the ESB is obliged to serve on the affected occupier[36] a seven-day notice in writing of its intention to exercise its statutory rights under s 98(1). Under s 98(2), the occupier of the lands may then, within seven days of receipt of the notice, inform the ESB that he or she is him- or herself going to carry out the works. The ESB is obliged under s 98(3) to refund the expenses associated with such works as undertaken by the occupier of the lands. In default of agreement in relation to the costs of the works carried out by the occupier of the lands affected, the matter may, again in accordance with s 98(3), be referred to an arbitrator, by the Minister for Industry and Commerce, and the arbitrator will fix the costs to be paid to the occupier.

## Can Telecoms Providers Enter Private Lands to Fell Trees?

Under s 58(1) of the Communications Regulations Act 2002 a network operator, or any person authorised by him or her in that behalf, may lop or cut any tree, shrub or hedge which obstructs or interferes with any physical infrastructure of the network operator. However, before lopping or cutting any tree, shrub or hedge under this a network operator shall give to the landowner or occupier of the land on which the tree, shrub or hedge is standing, notice in writing of its intention to do so and, after the expiration of 28 days from the date of such service, the network operator may lop or cut any tree, shrub or hedge where the landowner or occupier has not already done so[37] at any reasonable time.[38] Where a network operator carries out the cutting or lopping he or she must do so in a manner which causes the least damage to property or the environment or amenities.[39] Where an occupier or landowner, upon receipt of the 28 day notice decides to carrying out the necessary works themselves, the expense incurred by him or her in so doing shall be paid to him or her on demand by the network operator and the amount of such expenses shall be recoverable from the network operator, in default of agreement, as a simple contract debt in any court of competent jurisdiction.[40]

---

[36] *Occupier* is not defined under the Act, but presumably the term *occupier* is used to include not only the actual landowner but also any individual holding the lands by way of a lease, licence, conacre agreement, etc.

[37] s 58(2) of the Communications Regulations Act 2002.

[38] s 58(3) of the Communications Regulations Act 2002.

[39] s 58(4) of the Communications Regulations Act 2002.

[40] s 58(5) of the Communications Regulations Act 2002.

A network operator is prohibited from the cutting or lopping of trees in contravention of an order under s 205 of the Planning and Development Act 2000 which, as discussed above, relates to the preservation of trees.[41]

## The Law on Hedges

Section 46 of the Wildlife (Amendment) Act 2000 (the 2000 Act)[42] amends s 40 of the Wildlife Act 1976 (the 1976 Act), recognising hedgerows as important heritage features as well as providing food and shelter for a range of wildlife, including birds, insects and wildflowers. The legislation makes it an offence to *cut, grub, burn or otherwise destroy any vegetation growing in any hedge or ditch*[43] during the nesting season beginning on the first day of March and ending on the 31st day of August.

## Exemptions for Domestic Gardeners and Farmers

Gardeners are exempted from these restrictions as the prohibition in relation to the controlling of hedges during this period does not apply to *any vegetation growing on any land not then cultivated*.[44] Hedges surrounding domestic dwellings and gardens will constitute cultivated lands and, as such, the prohibition on cutting back and trimming such hedges does not apply.

Exemptions also exist for certain categories of activity such as farming where an exemption applies for the destroying, in the ordinary course of agriculture or forestry, of any vegetation growing on or in any hedge or ditch,[45] as well as the cutting or grubbing of isolated bushes or clumps of gorse, furze or whin or the mowing of isolated growths of fern in the ordinary course of agriculture.[46] An exemption also applies for the cutting, grubbing or destroying of vegetation in the course of any works being duly carried out for reasons of public health or safety by a Minister of the Government or a body established or regulated by or under a statute.[47]

---

[41] s 58(6) of the Communications Regulations Act 2002.
[42] Commencement date: 12 March 2001.
[43] s 46(a) of the 2000 Act.
[44] s 46(a) of the 2000 Act.
[45] s 40(2)(a) of the 1976 Act.
[46] s 40(2)(b) of the 1976 Act.
[47] s 46(b) of the 2000 Act.

Any person concerned about the illegal cutting of hedgerows will need to make contact with the Gardaí or the National Parks and Wildlife Service,[48] citing the above legislation and the alleged breach thereof. Obviously the breach may only occur between the first day of March and the 31st day of August in any given year.

Where a person is guilty of cutting a hedge in contravention of the Wildlife Acts 1976 to 2010, such person will be liable on summary conviction in the case of a first offence to a fine not exceeding €1,000.[49]

## Conclusion

As see above, s 45 of the Land and Conveyancing Law Reform Act 2009 now provides for the first time a statutory mechanism for neighbours to now apply to the court for permission to interfere with trees, hedges, shrubs and bushes that form part of the party structure in the absence of the adjoining landowner's consent. This new statutory framework does not replace the common law principles in relation to the right to abate nuisance but where one adjoining landowner is objecting to the exercise of such common law rights the better opinion would be to stay the works and apply for court sanction by way of the s 45 works order application.

---

[48] The National Parks and Wildlife Service of the Department of Environment, Community and Local Government have a designated sites information line. Freephone 1800 40 50 00 from 9am to 5pm.

[49] See s 68 of the 2000 Act as amended by s 7 of the Wildlife (Amendment) Act 2010.

# CHAPTER SIX

# Planning, Exempted Development and Unauthorised Development

## The Laws Governing the Planning Code

The Planning and Development Act 2000 (the 2000 Act) consolidated all previous planning statutes into one self-contained piece of legislation. The 2000 Act remains the basis for the Irish planning code, setting out the detail of regional planning guidelines, development plans and local area plans as well as the basic framework of the development, management and consent system. Among other things, it provides the statutory basis for protecting our natural and architectural heritage, the carrying out of Environmental Impact Statements and the provision of social and affordable housing.

The principal regulations underpinning the Planning and Development Acts 2000-2011 are the Planning and Development Regulations 2001 (the 2001 Regulations). They prescribe the detail of the various processes and procedures that make up the planning code.

## When Planning Permission is Required

The safe rule to follow in this area is that all development requires planning permission save for those proposed developments that are described as exempted development in the 2001 Regulations. The term *development* is defined under s 3 of the 2000 Act and includes the carrying out of works (building, demolition, alteration) on land or buildings and the making of a material change of use of land or building of a significant nature.

## Exempted Development

Exempted development is development for which planning permission is not required. Categories of exempted development are set out in planning law. There are usually certain thresholds relating to, for example, size or height. Where these thresholds are exceeded, the exemptions no longer apply and planning permission will then be required.

Exempted development is given a comprehensive definition under s 4 of the 2000 Act and, in particular, under s 4(2)(2) the Minister for the Environment, Community and Local Government may, by regulations, provide for any class of development to be exempted development for the purposes of the 2000 Act where he or she is of the opinion that by reason of the size, nature or limited effect on its surroundings the carrying out of such development would not offend against principles of proper planning and sustainable development. Such class of development constituting exempted development has been laid out in detail in the 2001 Regulations. Of particular interest to prospective developers is the exempted development criteria as detailed in Art 6, which in turn refers to Sch 2, Pt 1 of the 2001 Regulations.[1]

## Declarations or Certificates of Exempted Development

Section 5 of the 2000 Act allows for any individual to submit a request to his or her local planning office for written confirmation that a particular proposed development is a development that does not require planning permission. It is always recommended that any individual who is planning to construct a significant exempted development, such as a side or rear extension to a dwelling house, should as a matter of course make the application for the s 5 declaration from his or her local planning authority as it may be used as bone fide proof to protect against the complaints from aggrieved neighbours at a later date.

## Section 5 Declarations and Section 45 Works Orders

A s 5 declaration is of some merit if it is intended to build at or on the boundary to adjacent lands. In chapter 2 it was seen that s 45 of the Land and Conveyancing Law Reform Act 2009 (the 2009 Act) allows applications to be brought before the District Court for works orders to obtain the court's sanction to interfere with the shared boundary whilst carrying out a scheme of works. Section 44 of the 2009 Act[2] states that a building owner may carry out works to a party structure for the purpose of carrying out development which is exempted development or development for which planning permission has been obtained or compliance with any condition attached to such permission.

---

[1] See Appendix 3.
[2] See s 44(1)(b).

## Section 5 Declarations, Section 45 Works Orders: the Right to Light and the Right to a View

Section 46 of the 2009 Act allows the District Court Judge to set out the terms and conditions in the works order as he or she thinks fit in the circumstances of the particular case. That said, the District Court does not have the legal capacity to grant a works order that may cause *any permanent interference with, or loss of, any easement or of light.* In this respect the obtaining of a s 5 declaration is not just a prudent course of action but should be regarded as a necessary precursor to any such application for a works order.

The s 5 declaration allows the applicant for the works order to go some considerable distance in convincing the District Court Judge that the granting of the works order does not interfere with the loss of the adjoining landowner's right to light. This may be implied by virtue of the fact that the proposed development is an exempted development, and exempted developments by their very nature are considered of such modest scale that they will not impact upon neighbouring residential amenity, in this instance a loss of light.

It will also be worthwhile for any intending developer to peruse the local development plan as there will be a reference therein to that which constitutes residential amenity which will invariably include a reference to a right to light. Again in this regard it may be stated that such provisions in the local development plan will only apply to developments that require permission and not to exempted developments, the presumption once again being that developments of a minor nature will not give rise to a loss of light. Chapter 2, at p 29–31, deals in more detail in relation to applications for works orders and the right to light.

## Section 5 Declarations of Exempted Development – How to Apply

Each planning authority has its own application form for the s 5 declaration and most are downloadable from the particular authority's website. Very often applicants may employ an architect or draughtsman to submit the application on their behalf as it does require the furnishing of:

- a site location map;
- drawings of the proposed development in question; and
- full details and description of the proposed development including accurate measurements.

Each application must also be submitted with the prescribed fee for such applications.[3] The planning authority is obliged to issue the declaration within four weeks of the receipt of the request. This timeframe may be extended if the planning authority requires further information from the applicant in order to make its determination. If such further information is required the local planning authority must then issue its decision as to whether or not the proposed development is exempt within three weeks of receipt of such further information.

If the applicant is not satisfied with the determination of his or her local planning authority, he or she has a statutory right of appeal to An Bord Pleanála in relation to the decision. This appeal must be made within three weeks of the notification of the decision to refuse the granting of the s 5 Declaration.[4] The planning appeals process is dealt with in detail in chapter 6.

## Common Types of Development that are Exempt

Much caution is needed in this area as it is a criminal offence to have carried out or to be in the process of carrying out an unauthorised development, meaning a development for which planning permission is required but has not been obtained. An individual contemplating carrying out works which he or she considers to be exempted development, in accordance with Art 6 of the 2001 Regulations,[5] should always err on the side of caution and apply to his or her local planning authority for a s 5 declaration of exempted development in the first instance.

Generally, and keeping in mind that a party is advised to obtain a s 5 declaration, the following types of development may be classed as exempted development in certain circumstances:

### Certain House Extensions

Building an extension to the rear of the house which does not increase the original floor area of the house by more than 40 square metres and is not higher than the house may be an exempted development. The extension should not reduce the open space at the back of the house to less than 25 square metres which must be reserved exclusively for the use of the

---

[3] Currently €80.
[4] s 5(4) of the 2000 Act.
[5] See Appendix 4.

occupants of the house. If a house has previously been extended the floor area of the new extension and the floor area of any previous extension, including those for which planning permission was previously obtained, must not exceed 40 square metres. There are also other height restrictions.

### Garage Conversions

Converting a garage attached to the rear or side of the house to domestic use may be exempted so long as it has a floor area of less than 40 square metres. Building a garage at the back or side of a house may also be exempted so long as it does not extend out in front of the building line of the house and does not exceed four metres in height (if it has a tiled/slated pitched roof) or three metres (if it has any other roof type). This building may be exempt from planning permission once the floor area is limited to 25 square metres. Garages or sheds to the side of the house must match the finish of the house and may not be lived in, used for commercial purposes or for keeping pigs, poultry, pigeons, ponies or horses.

### Front Porches

The construction of a front porch, so long as it does not exceed two square metres in area and is more than two metres from a public road or footpath, may be deemed to be exempted. If the porch has a tiled or slated pitched roof, it must not exceed four metres in height or three metres for any other type of roof.

### Walls and Fences

Capped walls made of brick, stone or block, and wooden fences but not security fences, can be erected without planning permission as long as they do not exceed 1.2 metres in height or two metres at the side or rear. Gates may be built provided that they do not exceed two metres in height. Permission is always required if it is intended to widen or create new access to the public road.

### Boiler Houses

A central heating system, chimney, boiler house or oil storage tank (up to 3,500 litres capacity) may be exempt.

### Aerial and Satellite Dishes

A TV aerial on the roof may be exempt so long as it is less than six metres higher than the roof. Similarly, a satellite dish (up to one metre in diameter and no higher than the top of the roof) at the back or side of the house (a dish on the front needs planning permission) may also be exempt.

## Complaining about an Unauthorised Development

If an individual is concerned that an unauthorised development has commenced a complaint should be made to the local planning authority. Each of the local planning authorities has a team of planning enforcement officers who are obliged to react and investigate such complaints in accordance with Pt VIII of the 2000 Act. The first step in this process is for the person fearing that a development may be in the process of construction, or has been constructed without the benefit of a planning permission, to complete and lodge an *Unauthorised Development Complaint Form*. There is no indication in the planning laws as to the format for the submission of such complaints. In light of same the Unauthorised Development Complaint Form, found in Appendix 4, will guide anyone through the complaints submission procedure.

## Unauthorised Development Complaints and Anonymity

Part VIII of the 2000 Act does not make any reference to how the details of any individual making a complaint in relation to an unauthorised development are to be held and whether any member of the public has a right to attend at and inspect the unauthorised development file. That said, it has been for a long time now the custom and practice of planning authorities not to reveal the personal details of any person who has made a complaint of unauthorised development. This is obviously to the advantage of the planning enforcement section of the planning authority as it encourages members of the public to complain those individuals who may be in breach of the planning code. This approach is also beneficial to the maintenance of positive relations with adjoining and surrounding landowners who will be unaware as to the identity of the person who made the original complaint. The unauthorised development complaint form in Appendix 4 specifically requests the planning enforcement office to treat any complaints in the strictest confidence.

## Warning Letters

Upon receipt of the unauthorised development complaint form or indeed any representation in writing, and where it appears to the planning authority that the representation is not vexatious, frivolous or without substance or foundation, or the development complained of is not of a trivial or minor nature, the planning authority has no further discretion but to issue a warning letter, which must be issued *as soon as may be*,[6] but not later than six weeks after receipt of the representation from a third party,[7] to the owner, the occupier or any other person carrying out the development. The legislation does not oblige the planning authority to make a copy of the warning letter available to the complainant but it may give a copy, at that time or thereafter, to any other person who in its opinion may be concerned with the matters to which the letter relates. Again, it is custom and practice for the complainant to be forwarded a copy of the warning letter.

The warning letter must inform the alleged unauthorised developer that it is an offence to undertake any work needing permission without that permission and that he or she may be required to rectify any unauthorised works, and will have to pay whatever costs are involved. If the six-week period has elapsed and the warning letter has not issued, the complainant should immediately write to the planning authority asking for an update in relation to the complaint, and in the absence of a response the matter may need to be referred on to the Office of the Ombudsman for review. The Ombudsman has responsibility for examining complaints concerning the administrative actions of government departments, including planning authorities. The complaints procedure, along with a more detailed examination of the role of the Ombudsman, is found in chapter 15.

## Enforcement Notices

As soon as may be after the issuance of a warning letter, the planning authority must make such investigation as it considers necessary to enable it to make a decision on whether to issue an enforcement notice.[8] Whilst there is no specific timeframe for the planning authority to make its decision, it is its statutory duty to ensure that decisions on whether to issue an enforcement notice are taken as expeditiously as possible. That said, it must be the statutory objective of the planning authority to ensure that the decision on whether to issue an enforcement notice is taken within 12 weeks of the issue of a warning letter.[9] Where the planning authority decides not to issue an enforcement notice, it must notify any person to

---

[6] s 152(3).
[7] s 152(3)(e).
[8] s 153(1).
[9] s 153(2)(b).

whom the warning letter was copied and any other person who made a representation in relation to the warning letter of the decision in writing within two weeks of the making of that decision.[10]

If the planning authority proceeds to issue the enforcement notice, s 154(5) of the 2000 Act stipulates that the notice must refer to the land concerned and shall:

(a) (i) in respect of a development where no permission has been granted, require that development to cease or not to commence, as appropriate, or

    (ii) in respect of a development for which permission has been granted under Part III, require that the development will proceed in conformity with the permission, or with any condition to which the permission is subject,

(b) require such steps as may be specified in the notice to be taken within a specified period, including, where appropriate, the removal, demolition or alteration of any structure and the discontinuance of any use and, in so far as is practicable, the restoration of the land to its condition prior to the commencement of the development,

(c) warn the person or persons served with the enforcement notice that, if within the period specified under paragraph (b) or within such extended period (not being more than 6 months) as the planning authority may allow, the steps specified in the notice to be taken are not taken, the planning authority may enter on the land and take such steps, including the removal, demolition or alteration of any structure, and may recover any expenses reasonably incurred by it in that behalf,

(d) require the person or persons served with the notice to refund to the planning authority the costs and expenses reasonably incurred by the authority in relation to the investigation, detection and issue of the enforcement notice concerned and any warning letter under s 152, including costs incurred in respect of the remuneration and other expenses of employees, consultants and advisers, and the planning authority may recover these costs and expenses incurred by it in that behalf, and

(e) warn the person or persons served with the enforcement notice that if within the period specified by the notice or such extended period, not being more than 6 months, as the planning authority may allow, the steps specified in the notice to be taken are not taken, the person or persons may be guilty of an offence.[11]

---

[10] s 154(2).

[11] s 154(9) states that any person who knowingly assists or permits the failure by another to comply with an Enforcement Notice also commits an offence.

If, within the period specified under s 154(5)(b) of the 2000 Act or within such extended period, not being more than six months, as the planning authority may allow, the steps specified in the notice to be taken are not taken, the planning authority may enter on the land and take such steps, including the demolition of any structure and the restoration of land, and may recover any expenses reasonably incurred.[12]

## Penalties for Offences

On conviction in the District Court, fines of up to €5,000 and/or a term of imprisonment of six months may be imposed[13] together with fines of up to €1,500 for each day upon which the offences continues or to a term of imprisonment of six months or to both.[14] On conviction in the higher courts, the maximum fine is €12,700,000 (€12,700 per day for continuing offences) and up to two years' imprisonment, or both. The planning authority may also may an application to recoup all its costs involved in bring a prosecution.[15]

## Cases of Urgency

Where, in the opinion of the planning authority, due to the nature of an unauthorised development and to any other material considerations, it is necessary to take urgent action with regard to the unauthorised development, the planning authority do not have to issue a warning letter but may issue an enforcement notice directly.[16] Obviously, such power should be exercised only in relation to the more extreme breaches of the planning code as this option negates the alleged unauthorised developer's right of response to the allegations as made by the planning authority upon receipt of the warning letter.[17]

## Planning Injunction

Section 160 of the 2000 Act provides for a procedure whereby an application may be made to either the Circuit Court or the High Court[18]

---

[12] s 154(6).

[13] s 156(1)(b) of the 2000 Act as amended by s 46(a) of the Planning and Development (Amendment) Act 2010.

[14] s 156(2)(b) of the 2000 Act as amended by s 46(b) of the Planning and Development (Amendment) Act 2010.

[15] s 156.

[16] s 155.

[17] s 152(4)(b).

[18] The Circuit Court will now have jurisdiction to hear and determine an application under s 160 where the rateable valuation of the land concerned does not exceed the euro

for orders in respect of an unauthorised development. The wording of s 160(1) of the 2000 Act is very wide and provides for the making of an order requiring *any person* to do or not to do, or to cease to do, as the case may be, anything that the court considers necessary. The applicant in most instances will be the planning authority; however, individuals who do not have an interest in the land the subject of the application for injunctive relief may also bring an application before the court.[19] This opens the door for individuals who may not be happy with the response of the planning authority in relation to how it has responded to an allegation of unauthorised development to bring the matter into the courts themselves and seek a court order directing:

(a)  that the unauthorised development is not carried out or continued;

(b)  in so far as is practicable, that any land is restored to its condition prior to the commencement of any unauthorised development; or

(c)  that any development is carried out in conformity with the permission pertaining to that development or any condition to which the permission is subject.[20]

Furthermore, in making an order and where appropriate, the court may order the carrying out of any works, including the restoration, reconstruction, removal, demolition or alteration of any structure or other feature.[21]

Chapter 15 deals with injunctions generally in the context of civil remedies and provides more detail in relation to the practice and procedure with reference to how such applications are brought before the court. It is worth reiterating at this point, however, that an application for an injunction may be a costly and arduous affair and any party considering such a course of action should only do so after much consultation with his or her legal advisors.

---

equivalent of £200. If a rateable valuation has not been given for the land in question or forms part of other land to which a rateable valuation has been given, the Circuit Court may determine the rateable valuation of the land in order to determine whether it has jurisdiction to deal with the application. If an application is made to the Circuit Court by any person having an interest in the proceedings in circumstances where the rateable valuation of the relevant land exceeds the euro equivalent of £200 the Court is obliged to transfer the proceedings to the High Court.

[19] Injunctions generally are dealt with in detail in chapter 15.

[20] s 160(1)(A) – (C).

[21] s 160(2).

## Where the Warning Letter Issues and the Alleged Wrongdoer Applies for Retention Planning Permission

Once a warning letter or enforcement notice issues to the person who has or is in the process of carrying out the unauthorised development it is not uncommon for such person(s) to then apply for what is known as *retention planning permission*. In the case of development which is unauthorised, the developer may apply for the sanction of the planning authority by way of a planning application that may, notwithstanding the fact that it was built in breach of the planning code in the first instance, be granted permission to retain the otherwise unauthorised development.[22] As per s 162(3) of the 2000 Act, an application for retention planning permission does not, under any circumstances, allow the planning authority to freeze or withdraw any enforcement proceedings by reason of an application for retention of permission.[23]

If, therefore, a complaint has been lodged with the planning authority in relation to an unauthorised development and it is perceived that the planning authority is delaying taking enforcement proceedings by virtue of the fact that a retention permission has been lodged with the planning authority, the complainant should immediately bring the details of s 162(3) of the 2000 Act to the attention of the planning authority. In circumstances where no response or an unsatisfactory response is received from the planning authority, the matter will need to be referred to a solicitor or a complaint may be lodged with the Ombudsman.[24] A letter of complaint in this regard is contained in Appendix 5.

In terms of more substantive matters, any concerned complainant will need to also see his or her solicitor in relation to the possibility of bringing an application for injunctive relief, as s 162(3) of the 2000 Act specifically

---

[22] s (12).

[23] The Irish system of planning development control and planning enforcement in relation to unauthorised developments seems to be self defeating at times. Take for example s 23 of the Planning and Development (Amendment) Act 2010 amending s 34 (12) of the 2000 Act which states that an application for development of land in accordance with the permission regulations may be made for the retention of unauthorised development, whilst s 162(3) of the 2000 Act states categorically no enforcement action shall be stayed or withdrawn by reason of an application for retention permission. In any event s 162(3) remains clear, unambiguous and unamended by the Planning and Development (Amendment) Act 2010.

[24] See chapter 15.

states that an application for retention will not act as a bar on bringing an application for injunctive relief.

## Time Frames in Relation to Enforcement Generally

In relation to unauthorised developments generally, s 157(5) of the 2000 Act states that proceedings for other offences under this Act shall not be initiated later than seven years from the date on which the offence concerned was alleged to have been committed. If a planning authority wishes to bring a person to court, therefore, for an alleged unauthorised development, it will have had to have initiated enforcement proceedings within seven years of the date of the alleged breach of the planning code.[25]

## Conclusion

The fact that the local authority will maintain anonymity of complainants is an incentive to individuals to bring to the attention of their local authority that unautorised development has/is or may about to be taking place.

Furthermore it is not acceptable for the enforcement section of the planning office to adopt a await and see policy in relation to an unauthorised development where the development in question has since become the subject of a retention application. As seen above, s 162(3) of the 2000 Act is more than explicit in this regard. As a last resort any aggrieved complainant who feels that the local authority is not carrying out its enforcement obligations with due expediency will need to make contact with the Ombudsman or, in relation to more serious breaches of the planning code, their solicitor for advice in relation to the s 160 of the 2000 Act planning injunction.

---

[25] In accordance with s 160(6)(a), an application to the Circuit Court or High Court for an order for injunctive relief shall not be made: (i) in respect of a development where no permission has been granted, after the expiration of a period of seven years from the date of the commencement of the development; or (ii) in respect of a development for which permission has been granted under Pt III, after the expiration of a period of seven years beginning on the expiration, as respects the permission authorising the development, of the appropriate period (within the meaning of s 40) or, as the case may be, of the appropriate period as extended under s 42.

# Appendix 3

## Planning and Development Regulations 2001

Article 6

Part 1

| Column 1 | Column 2 |
| --- | --- |
| Description of Development | Conditions and Limitations |
| Development within the curtilage of a house | |
| CLASS 1 | |
| The extension of a house, by the construction or erection of an extension (including a conservatory) to the rear of the house or by the conversion for use as part of the house of any garage, store, shed or other similar structure attached to the rear or to the side of the house. | 1. (a) Where the house has not been extended previously, the floor area of any such extension shall not exceed 40 square metres. |
| | (b) Subject to paragraph (a), where the house is terraced or semi-detached, the floor area of any extension above ground level shall not exceed 12 square metres. |
| | (c) Subject to paragraph (a), where the house is detached, the floor area of any extension above ground level shall not exceed 20 square metres. |
| | 2. (a) Where the house has been extended previously, the floor area of any such extension, taken together with the floor area of any previous extension or extensions constructed or erected after 1 October 1964, including those for which planning permission has been obtained, shall not exceed 40 square metres. |

(Continued)

| Column 1 | Column 2 |
| --- | --- |
| | (b) Subject to paragraph (a), where the house is terraced or semi-detached and has been extended previously, the floor area of any extension above ground level taken together with the floor area of any previous extension or extensions above ground level constructed or erected after 1 October 1964, including those for which planning permission has been obtained, shall not exceed 12 square metres. |
| | (c) Subject to paragraph (a), where the house is detached and has been extended previously, the floor area of any extension above ground level, taken together with the floor area of any previous extension or extensions above ground level constructed or erected after 1 October 1964, including those for which planning permission has been obtained, shall not exceed 20 square metres. |
| | 3. Any above ground floor extension shall be a distance of not less than 2 metres from any party boundary. |
| | 4. (a) Where the rear wall of the house does not include a gable, the height of the walls of any such extension shall not exceed the height of the rear wall of the house. |
| | (b) Where the rear wall of the house includes a gable, the height of the walls of any such extension shall not exceed the height of the side walls of the house. |

(c) The height of the highest part of the roof of any such extension shall not exceed, in the case of a flat roofed extension, the height of the eaves or parapet, as may be appropriate, or, in any other case, shall not exceed the height of the highest part of the roof of the dwelling.

5. The construction or erection of any such extension to the rear of the house shall not reduce the area of private open space, reserved exclusively for the use of the occupants of the house, to the rear of the house to less than 25 square metres.

6. (a) Any window proposed at ground level in any such extension shall not be less than 1 metre from the boundary it faces.

(b) Any window proposed above ground level in any such extension shall not be less than 11 metres from the boundary it faces.

(c) Where the house is detached and the floor area of the extension above ground level exceeds 12 square metres, any window proposed at above ground level shall not be less than 11 metres from the boundary it faces.

7. The roof of any extension shall not be used as a balcony or roof garden.

CLASS 2

The provision, as part of a central heating system of a house, of a chimney, boiler house or oil storage tank.

The capacity of any such oil storage tank shall not exceed 3,500 litres.

(*Continued*)

| Column 1 | Column 2 |
|---|---|
| CLASS 3 | |
| The construction, erection or placing within the curtilage of a house of any tent, awning, shade or other object, greenhouse, garage, store, shed or other similar structure. | 1. No such structure shall be constructed, erected or placed forward of the front wall of a house. |
| | 2. The total area of such structures constructed, erected or placed within the curtilage of a house shall not, taken together with any other such structures previously constructed, erected or placed within the said curtilage, exceed 25 square metres. |
| | 3. The construction, erection or placing within the curtilage of a house of any such structure shall not reduce the amount of private open space reserved exclusively for the use of the occupants of the house to the rear or to the side of the house to less than 25 square metres. |
| | 4. The external finishes of any garage or other structure constructed, erected or placed to the side of a house, and the roof covering where any such structure has a tiled or slated roof, shall conform with those of the house. |
| | 5. The height of any such structure shall not exceed, in the case of a building with a tiled or slated pitched roof, 4 metres or, in any other case, 3 metres. |
| | 6. The structure shall not be used for human habitation or for the keeping of pigs, poultry, pigeons, ponies or horses, or for any other purpose other than a purpose incidental to the enjoyment of the house as such. |

## CLASS 4

(a) The erection of a wireless or television antenna, other than a satellite television signal receiving antenna, on the roof of a house.

The height of the antenna above the roof of the house shall not exceed 6 metres.

(b) The erection on or within the curtilage of a house, of a dish type antenna used for the receiving and transmitting of signals from satellites.

1. Not more than one such antenna shall be erected on, or within the curtilage of a house.

2. The diameter of any such antenna shall not exceed 1 metre.

3. No such antenna shall be erected on, or forward of, the front wall of the house.

4. No such antenna shall be erected on the front roof slope of the house or higher than the highest part of the roof of the house.

## CLASS 5

The construction, erection or alteration, within or bounding the curtilage of a house, of a gate, gateway, railing or wooden fence or a wall of brick, stone, blocks with decorative finish, other concrete blocks or mass concrete.

1. The height of any such structure shall not exceed 2 metres or, in the case of a wall or fence within or bounding any garden or other space in front of a house, 1.2 metres.

2. Every wall other than a dry or natural stone wall bounding any garden or other space shall be capped and the face of any wall of concrete or concrete block (other than blocks with decorative finish) which will be visible from any road, path or public area, including public open space, shall be rendered or plastered.

3. No such structure shall be a metal palisade or other security fence.

*(Continued)*

| Column 1 | Column 2 |
|---|---|
| **CLASS 6** | |
| (a) The construction of any path, drain or pond or the carrying out of any landscaping works within the curtilage of a house. | The level of the ground shall not be altered by more than 1 metre above or below the level of the adjoining ground. |
| (b) Any works within the curtilage of a house for— | |
| (i) the provision to the rear of the house of a hard surface for use for any purpose incidental to the enjoyment of the house as such, or, | |
| (ii) the provision to the front or side of the house of a hard surface for the parking of not more than 2 motor vehicles used for a purpose incidental to the enjoyment of the house as such. | |
| **CLASS 7** | |
| The construction or erection of a porch outside any external door of a house. | 1. Any such structure shall be situated not less than 2 metres from any road. |
| | 2. The floor area of any such structure shall not exceed 2 square metres. |
| | 3. The height of any such structure shall not exceed, in the case of a structure with a tiled or slated pitched roof, 4 metres or, in any other case, 3 metres. |
| **CLASS 8** | |
| The keeping or storing of a caravan, campervan or boat within the curtilage of a house. | 1. Not more than one caravan, campervan or boat shall be so kept or stored. |
| | 2. The caravan, campervan or boat shall not be used for the storage, display, advertisement or sale of goods or for the purposes of any business. |

3. No caravan, campervan or boat shall be so kept or stored for more than 9 months in any year or occupied as a dwelling while so kept or stored.

## Sundry Works

### CLASS 9

The construction, erection, renewal or replacement, other than within or bounding the curtilage of a house, of any gate or gateway.

The height of any such structure shall not exceed 2 metres.

### CLASS 10

The plastering or capping of any wall of concrete blocks or mass concrete.

### CLASS 11

The construction, erection, lowering, repair or replacement, other than within or bounding the curtilage of a house, of —

1. The height of any new structure shall not exceed 1.2 metres or the height of the structure being replaced, whichever is the greater, and in any event shall not exceed 2 metres.

(a) any fence (not being a hoarding or sheet metal fence), or

(b) any wall of brick, stone, blocks with decorative finish, other concrete blocks or mass concrete.

2. Every wall, other than a dry or natural stone wall, constructed or erected bounding a road shall be capped and the face of any wall of concrete or concrete blocks (other than blocks of a decorative finish) which will be visible from any road, path or public area, including a public open space, shall be rendered or plastered.

*(Continued)*

| Column 1 | Column 2 |
|---|---|
| **CLASS 12** | |
| The painting of any external part of any building or other structure. | Such painting may not, except in the case of a hoarding or other temporary structure bounding land on which development consisting of works is being or will be carried out in pursuance of a permission granted under Part III of the Act or as exempted development, be for the purposes of creating a mural. |
| **CLASS 13** | |
| The repair or improvement of any private street, road or way, being works carried out on land within the boundary of the street, road or way, and the construction of any private footpath or paving. | The width of any such private footpath or paving shall not exceed 3 metres. |

## Appendix 4

*Unauthorised Development Complaint Form*
*Pursuant to Part V of the Planning and Development Act 2000*

*Please Treat Complaint in the Strictest Confidence*

*To* _____

*The Planning Authority for the County*

*of* _____

*Name and Address of person making complaint*

*I* _____ *of* _____

_____

*hereby formally lodge a complaint in relation to a development that I believe to be an unauthorised development located at:*

*Address of Unauthorised Development*

_____

_____

_____

_____

*Description of Unauthorised Development*

_____

_____

_____

_____

_____
_____
_____
_____
_____
_____
_____*(attach additional information on a separate sheet(s) if necessary).*

*Map of Location Attached*  Yes  No

*tick as appropriate*

*Photos of Development Attached*  Yes  No

*tick as appropriate*

*Owner's Name and Address*

_____

_____

_____

*Brief Description of Unauthorised Development*

_____
_____
_____
_____
_____
_____
_____
_____
_____

_____

_____

_____

*Date of Commencement of Unauthorised Development (if known)*

_____

*Date of Completion of Unauthorised Development (if known)*

_____

**THE PLANNING AUTHORITY TO COPY AND DATE STAMP AND RETURN ONE COPY TO COMPLAINANT**

## Appendix 5

*The Manager,*
*County Council,*
*County [Insert Name].*

*RE: RETENTION PLANNING APPLICATION REFERENCE [INSERT REFERENCE NO.]*

*APPLICATION FOR RETENTION OF AN UNAUTHORISED DEVELOPMENT AT NO. 1, STRAWBERRY DRIVE, HILL TOWN, COUNTY.*

*Dear Sirs,*

*I refer to the above retention planning application under planning register reference number [Insert Reference No.]. I wish to inform you that this development is already the subject matter of an unauthorised development complaint by me lodged with your planning office on the day of [Insert Date].*

*I wish to inform you that I have the impression that your planning authority is staying the issuing of enforcement proceedings against the applicant pending the outcome of the retention application for permission.*

*I remind you that in accordance with Section 162(3) of the Planning and Development Act 2000 that such a course of action is not permitted by your planning office which has no discretion but to commence and continue with enforcement proceedings notwithstanding that application for retention permission.*

*I ask that enforcement proceedings be brought in accordance with your statutory obligation and to inform me of your intended action in this regard within 10 days of the date hereof, or I will be obliged to bring this matter to the attention of my solicitor for legal redress.*

*Furthermore, I reserve my right to lodge a complaint with the Ombudsman's office in relation to the planning authority's breach of its statutory obligations under the planning code.*

*Yours faithfully,*

_____.

# CHAPTER SEVEN

# Planning Objections and Appeals

## Objecting to a Planning Permission

This section is specifically addressed to those individuals who wish to object to a development in their locality with which they are unhappy. The planning process itself does also accept written submissions from individuals who wish to add their support to a particular development. This chapter is addressed, however, to those individuals who have real concerns in relation to what the planners call *loss of residential amenity*, generally meaning what makes it pleasant to live in a particular area.

In relation to an extension to a neighbouring home, for example, a party will need to go to the local planning office, or increasingly, review the application online through the council's website, and request to see the planning file by quoting the address of the development in the planning office. The first step must be to inspect the application and understand it, thereby allowing an informed decision to be made as to whether one wishes to lodge a formal objection to the planning application.

## Objections, Defamation and a Word of Warning

It is important to remember the planning process is a public process and the planning file, along with any objections submitted, will be available for the public at large to view. Any submissions will be made public and could therefore be placed on the planning authority's website. An objector must use due care and attention not to include any personal information about him- or herself or others and should never use an objection to launch or vent a grievance about a neighbour. The last thing one needs is to be defending an accusation of defamation[1] arising out of an objection placed on a public planning file. Any objection must be rational, impersonal and

---

[1] The tort of defamation consists of the publication, by any means, of a defamatory statement concerning a person to one or more than one person (other than the first-mentioned person), and *defamation* shall be construed accordingly: s 6(2) of the Defamation Act 2009.

directed principally to the planning issues raised by the proposal in the context of the development plan.

## Timeframes and Procedure for Objecting

The Planning and Development Regulations 2001 to 2011[2] set out the procedures to be followed in respect of submissions/objections in relation to planning applications. First, one must know that permission is being sought in order to object. An applicant for planning permission must publish notice of the application in an approved newspaper[3] and the planning application must then be received by the planning authority within two weeks of the newspaper notice. The planning authority will be able to provide a list of such newspapers. Needless to say, all of the major daily national newspapers suffice and, together with local newspapers, will normally be acceptable by the planning authority for this purpose.

A site notice must be put up on or before the date the application is lodged with the planning authority and must be kept in a prominent position, in a legible condition, for at least five weeks after the submission of the planning application.[4] It is not acceptable for an intending developer to place the site notice in an obscure area of the site where it may not reasonably be seen by the public. If ever there is more than one entrance from public roads, on or near all such entrances, or on any other part of the land or structure adjoining a public road, the notice must be placed in such a position so as to be easily visible and legible by persons using the public road.[5]

Any objections to a proposed development must be made in writing within five weeks[6] beginning on the date of receipt of the planning application by the planning authority. If the last day of this five-week period falls on a Saturday, Sunday or public holiday, objections can be accepted on the next working day.

Strict adherence to the five-week deadline is of paramount importance. If an objection is forwarded to the planning authority outside of the five-week period, the objection will be returned with the fee and this obviously means that the opportunity to object will be lost.

---

[2] SI No 600 of 2001 — Planning and Development Regulations 2001, Pt 4, Chapter 1, art 29.
[3] SI No 600 of 2001 — Planning and Development Regulations 2001, Pt 4, Chapter 1, art 81(1).
[4] SI No 600 of 2001 — Planning and Development Regulations 2001, Pt 4, Chapter 1, arts 16–47.
[5] SI No 600 of 2001 — Planning and Development Regulations 2001, Pt 4, Chapter 1, art 81(3).
[6] SI No 600 of 2001 — Planning and Development Regulations 2001, Pt 4, Chapter 1, art 29(1)(a).

All objections must be made in writing and forwarded to the planning section of the local authority, and the objection must include:

- the name of the person or body making the submission/objection;
- the planning reference number of the application concerned;
- the address to which any correspondence relating to the application may be sent; and
- a fee of €20[7] which can be payable by cheque or cash. Again, if no fee is included with the objection it will not be considered and the objection will be returned as invalid.

Upon submission of a valid planning objection the planning authority is obliged to provide a certificate of objection[8] and same should be kept safely as, in the event of the planning authority deciding not to uphold an objection and to issue a decision to grant permission, it will be necessary to produce the objector's certificate in order to proceed to appeal the decision to An Bord Pleanála.

## Group Objections

If it is the case that one is among a number of individuals objecting to the proposed development, then it will make more sense for all individuals concerned to sign the objection and thereafter nominate one person as the point of communication between the planning authority and the group. Such an approach also means that only one planning objection fee will be payable for the entirety of the objectors.

## Preparing An Objection—Understanding the Application and Plans

Prior to lodging the objection one must know and understand that for which planning permission is being sought. In circumstances where an objector is unable to understand the plans and drawings submitted with the planning authority, a member of the technical staff of the planning authority may be asked to assist. Similarly, it may be worthwhile asking to speak with the planner for the area concerned and have him or her explain the plans. Different planning authorities would seem to have different procedures in relation to the role of planners in this respect. It would only seem fair and reasonable that if planners are to make themselves available

---

[7] This fee is subject to change from time to time and contact should be made with the planning authority to confirm the objector's fee prior to lodging.
[8] SI No 600 of 2001 — Planning and Development Regulations 2001, Pt 4, Chapter 1, art 29(2).

to the individual seeking permission by way of a pre-planning meeting then that same courtesy should be extended to a potential objector.[9]

An applicant will not be automatically entitled to request copies of drawings and plans on copyright grounds.

## Check the Planning History of the Property

If the property in question has already been the subject of a past refusal then a lot of the work may already be completed by the reasons given by the planning authority for refusing the application in the first instance. It will be necessary to attend at the planning office and to ask for a list of previous applications on the site, or if the planning authority has an online searchable planning database it may be possible for an applicant to run the search him- or herself and view a copy of the reasons for refusal. It might also be of benefit to search for other applications of a similar nature in the vicinity as a previous refusal for a like development in the vicinity of that which is proposed may act as a persuasive precedent to the planner.

## Planning Applications are Determined Having Regard to the Development Plan

The planning authority will have copies of its Local Development Plan available for viewing at its public counter. In assessing any objections received, the planning authority will consider the *proper planning and development* of its area and the preservation and improvement of amenities, having regard to the provisions of the development plan. *Amenity*, in planning terms, refers to the pleasant or normally satisfactory aspects of a location which contribute to its overall character and the enjoyment of residents or visitors. As previously mentioned, *residential amenity* is a term used to specifically describe what makes it pleasant to live in a particular area.

## How to Word an Objection

To be effective, any objection must focus upon the planning merits of the application only. The planning objection should be as brief as possible, as a rambling, personalised objection based on non-planning issues will make for poor persuasive authority with the planner. The planning authority is simply not interested in personal dislikes, grievances or histories of a long-standing boundary dispute with a neighbour.

---

[9] See chapter 15, pp 228–231 in relation to the role of the Ombudsman in relation to complaints against local authorities.

There is no set format of an objection; however, the example below will be of assistance in relation to the various grounds of objection based on purely planning considerations. Each relevant ground of objection may be briefly expanded upon if required.

## Example: Letter of Objection

*Re: Proposed Development at No. 1, Strawberry Drive, Hill Town, County [insert county].*

*Planning Register Reference Number: [insert ref no]*

*Dear Sirs,*

*I refer to the above planning application currently under adjudication with your office and hereby formally object to the proposed development on the following grounds:*
- *overshadowing*
- *overlooking or loss of privacy*
- *adequate parking and servicing*
- *overbearing nature of proposal*
- *loss of trees*
- *loss of ecological habitats*
- *design and appearance*
- *layout and density of buildings*
- *effect on listed building(s) and Conservation Areas*
- *access/road safety issues*
- *traffic generation*
- *noise and disturbance from the scheme*
- *disturbance from smells*
- *public visual amenity[10]*
- *drainage/flood risk*
- *at variance with precedent of development in the area*

*Based on the objections outlined above, I say that the proposed development does not represent proper planning and sustainable development and is contrary to the aims and objectives of the development plan and call upon the planning authority to refuse same.*

*I enclose herewith objection fee of €[insert fee] and look forward to receipt of acknowledgment in early course.*

*Yours faithfully,*

_____.

---

[10] But not loss of private individual's view.

## Issues the Planning Authority will not Consider

Below is a list of the various concerns that one may have in relation to a neighbouring development but that should not form part of one's planning objection as they are not planning issues; these are private, civil matters between adjoining landowners.

Issues the planning authority will not consider, include:
- loss of value to individual property;
- loss of view;
- boundary disputes including encroachment of foundations;
- boundary disputes including encroachment of gutters;
- the applicant's personal conduct or history;
- the applicant's motives;
- potential profit for the applicant or from the application;
- private rights of way;
- damage to property;
- disruption during any construction phase;
- time taken to do the work;
- capacity of private drains;
- building or structural techniques;
- issues of personality.

That is not to say that the above issues are not relevant; the point is they are not generally relevant to the planning process but should be addressed under the civil law.

## The Granting of Planning Permission is not a Permission for an Unjust Attack on Property Rights

Even if the planning objection or any subsequent appeal to An Bord Pleanála is lost, and the development proceeds, as the civil law provides a range of legal remedies that will be of assistance in the case of the development constituting an unjust attack on an adjoining neighbour's property rights. For example, if a neighbour's development is encroaching and building upon adjoining lands or damaging the connection to sewage and water mains causing nuisance and damage to those adjoining lands, one should consult a solicitor with a view to mounting a challenge to the trespass, nuisance and property damage by way of a court application for injunctive relief and damages.[11]

---

[11] See chapter 5 for more detail on civil remedies.

Where an objection and subsequent appeal fail, and the application for permission is granted, there will still be a statutory remedy available in relation to any attempt by a neighbour to build on the shared boundary under s 45 of the Land and Conveyancing Law Reform Act 2009 as discussed in chapter two.

In the context of boundary ownership disputes, it was discussed in chapter one, and it is worth re-emphasising here, that neither the Property Registration Authority nor Ordnance Survey Ireland pronounce themselves on the issue of ownership of lands at the boundary and it is certainly the case that a grant of permission is in no means an intended declaration of any legal merit in this regard.

## Notification of the Planning Authority's Decision

Once the five-week period for the submission of objections has elapsed, the planner reviews the application, taking account of all information submitted, including objections, and has a further three weeks to make a decision; eight weeks in total from the lodgment date. This timeframe may be extended, however, if the planner needs to revert back to the applicant by way of a request for further information.[12] All objectors are informed as a matter of course in relation to the decision of the planning authority.[13]

An appeal lies to An Bord Pleanála (the Board) in circumstances where an applicant feels that the decision does not take full account of the issues raised in the objection or decision.

## An Bord Pleanála

The Board was established in 1977 under the Local Government (Planning and Development) Act 1976 and is responsible for the determination of appeals under the Planning and Development Acts 2000 to 2011. Appeals of planning decisions made by a planning authority are made to the Board pursuant to s 37 of the Planning and Development Act 2000 (the 2000 Act).

## Appeals to An Bord Pleanála—Timeframe and Procedures for Lodging of Appeals

As mentioned, any individual who has objected to a planning permission is obliged to be notified by the planning authority as to its decision to

---

[12] SI No 600 of 2001 — Planning and Development Regulations 2001, Pt 4, Chapter 1, art 33(1).
[13] SI No 600 of 2001 — Planning and Development Regulations 2001, Pt 4, Chapter 1, art 31.

either grant or refuse permission. If an objector is dissatisfied with the outcome a period of four weeks is allowed for the lodging of an appeal with the Board.[14] In practice, however, it should be assumed that 27 days are allowed to lodge the appeal as the day that the decision issues is counted as one of the 28 days.

These are strict statutory time limits and, as such, the Board is unable to accept late appeals. Care should also be taken in relation to submitting appeals by post as an appeal posted within the permitted period but received outside it will be deemed invalid and returned. If the appeal is to be delivered by hand it must delivered to an employee of the Board at the Board's offices during office hours 9.15 am to 5.30 pm on Monday to Friday, except on public holidays and other days on which the offices are closed.[15] It is recommended that upon lodging the application in person a receipt is obtained from the Board prior to leaving its office as is the standard practice.

Appeals placed in the Board's letterbox are invalid and appeals that are not accompanied by the appropriate fee will not be accepted by the Board.

## Who May Appeal?

Appeals fall into three categories, namely:

- First party appeals against decision of planning authorities to refuse permission. The first party is the person who lodged the original application that was refused by the planning authority;
- First party appeals against conditions proposed to be attached to permissions by planning authorities. As seen above, whilst the planning authority may grant permission it may attach certain

---

[14] An Bord Pleanála, 64 Marlborough Street, Dublin 1.

[15] When the last date for the receipt of an appeal or other material falls on a weekend, public holiday or other day when the Board's offices are closed, the deadline for receipt is the next day on which the offices of the Board are open. The period from 24 December to 1 January inclusive is excluded for the purposes of the calculation of all periods of time in relation to planning appeals. If the last day of the four-week period for making an appeal falls in the period from 24 December to 1 January inclusive, the last day for making one's appeal is extended. For example, if the last day of the four-week period falls on 24 December, the last day for making an appeal is 2 January; and if the last day for the four-week period falls on 29 December, the last day for making an appeal is 7 January. The exclusion of the Christmas and New Year period also applies to any other matter in relation to an appeal where a time period is specified. If the last day of the 18-week statutory objective period within which the Board should decide an appeal falls within the Christmas and New Year period, the period is extended by the appropriate number of days.

terms and conditions to the granting of permission. The first party or the developer can, if he or she so wishes, appeal one or more of these conditions to the Board for its determination; and

- Third party appeals, which are normally against decisions of planning authorities to grant permission. The third party will be the person who objected to the permission in the first instance and will, in the neighbourhood context, very often be the adjoining landowner.

It is for this reason that the certificate of objection received from the planning authority when the original objection to the development was lodged should be kept safely as it will need to be produced to proceed with the subsequent appeal to the Board. It is not unusual for the Board to receive both a third party appeal and a first party appeal in relation to a planning application. However the remainder of this chapter will only deal with third party appeals.

## How the Board Determines Appeals

When an appeal is made to the Board, it is normally required to determine the application *de novo* meaning that it will treat the planning application as not yet having been adjudicated upon by the planning authority in the first instance. The Board will apply the same criteria as the planning authority and will generally be restricted to considering the proper planning and sustainable development of the areas outlined in the development plan.

## How to Write an Appeal

As the Board usually assesses applications that have been appealed to it as if no decision had been made in the first instance, the drafting of an appeal may simply consist of the letter previously submitted to the local planning authority.[16]

## Can One Appeal if One Did not Originally Object to the Development?

Section 37(6)(a) of the 2000 Act allows, notwithstanding that a person may not have objected to the original application, a person who has an interest in land adjoining land in respect of which permission has been granted

---

[16] Obviously being addressed to the Board, with change of address, etc.

28 days[17] to apply to the Board for leave to appeal against a decision of the planning authority. There is also a prescribed fee for this application.[18] The person with an interest in the land would normally be the owner or occupier of the lands next door to the development. Where a person is granted leave to appeal, the planning appeal must be received by the Board within two weeks of him or her having received notification of leave to appeal.[19]

The letter seeking leave to appeal may be as follows:

*The Secretary,*
*An Bord Pleanála,*
*64 Marlborough Street,*
*Dublin 1.*

*Re: Planning application reference [insert ref no]*

*Application for development at No.1, Strawberry Drive, Hill Town, County [insert county].*

*Dear Sir,*

*I refer to the above planning application under planning register reference number [insert ref no] that was granted by County [insert county] planning authority on the 1 January 2013. I confirm that I am the owner occupier of the development at No. 2 Strawberry Drive, Hill Town, County [insert county] and hereby apply, pursuant to s 37(6)(a) of the Planning and Development Act 2000 for leave to appeal the above decision.*

*I enclose your prescribed fee of €[insert fee] in this regard and look forward to hearing from you in early course.*

*Yours faithfully,*

_____.

---

[17] In theory one should work under the assumption that one has 27 days to lodge the appeal as the day that the decision issues is counted as one of the 28 days. See the section on timeframes below.

[18] At the time of publishing: €110. A list of the Board's fees is downloadable at http://www.pleanala.ie, 21 March 2012.

[19] s 37(6)(f).

## Making An Observation Where No Original Objection to the Planning Application Was Made

Where an appeal has already been made, any person may become an *observer*,[20] and may make submissions or observations on the appeal. A copy of the appeal may be obtained at the planning authority's office. Even though a person may not have originally objected to the proposed development, the Board will consider any observations and submissions received. A submission or observation must be made in writing, state the name and address of the person making the submission or observation, state the subject matter of the submission or observation, state in full the reasons, considerations and arguments on which the submission or observation is based and be accompanied by the appropriate fee.

The timeframes for receipt of observations and submissions is the period of four weeks beginning on the day of receipt of the appeal by the Board or, where there is more than one appeal against the decision of the planning authority, on the day on which the Board last receives an appeal.[21] The onus is on any person intending to make an observation or submission to monitor the planning application with both the local planning authority and the Board in order to determine if an appeal has been lodged.

## Timeframe for Adjudicating Appeals

It is the duty of the Board to ensure that appeals are disposed of as expeditiously as may be; it shall be the objective of the Board to ensure that every appeal or referral is determined within a period of 18 weeks beginning on the date of receipt by the Board of the appeal.[22] However, whilst this is an objective of the Board, in some instances decisions on appeals may take longer than 18 weeks.

## Oral Hearings

The Board has absolute discretion to hold an oral hearing with or without a request from a party[23] and will generally only hold one where this will

---

[20] s 130 of the 2000 Act.
[21] s 130(3)(c) of the 2000 Act.
[22] s 126 of the 2000 Act.
[23] s 134(1) of the 2000 Act.

aid its understanding of a particularly complex case or where it considers that significant national or local issues are involved.

It would not be appropriate, therefore, to request an oral hearing where the issues involved in the planning application do not affect the wider community. So whilst one may not be afforded an oral hearing to make oral submissions in relation to developments of a standard nature, applications for large-scale infrastructural projects or developments near sites of particular environmental significance may be afforded an oral hearing.

The Board may also direct the holding of an oral hearing to determine whether an appeal is made with the sole intention of delaying development or of securing the payment of money, gifts, considerations or other inducement by any person.[24]

## Board May Dismiss Appeals or Referrals if Vexatious

As stated in relation to planning objections, an appeal must be rational, impersonal and directed principally to the planning issues raised by the proposal in the context of the development plan for it to be seen as an appeal of merit.

The Board shall have an absolute discretion to dismiss an appeal if it considers it to be vexatious, frivolous or without substance or foundation[25] or if the appeal is made with the sole intention of delaying the development or with the intention of securing the payment of money, gifts, considera-tion or other inducement by any person.[26] If the Board makes such a determination then the person whose appeal is dismissed must be issued with the formal decision made, stating the main reasons and considerations on which the decision is based.[27]

As all appeals to the Board are a matter of public record, after the case has been determined, care must be taken not to find oneself on the wrong side of the defamation laws in relation to any personal statements as to the

---

[24] s 138(3) of the 2000 Act.
[25] s 138(1)(a)(i) of the 2000 Act.
[26] s 138(1)(a)(ii) of the 2000 Act.
[27] s 138(2) of the 2000 Act.

character and nature of any person mentioned in written statements to the Board.[28]

## If the Board Rejects an Appeal are there Grounds for Judicial Review?

Once an appeal has been rejected by the Board, the planning process is at an end and the only recourse thereafter will be by way of a judicial review application to the High Court. However, even then the court will not re-open the planning merits of the case; instead the court will look at the legal basis upon which the decision was arrived; for example, the decision-making power of the Board must be made within the statutory framework,[29] the Board must be reasonable in making its decision and fair procedures must be shown to all parties involved.

The party applying for leave to bring judicial review against a decision of the Board on any appeal or referral must have been a party to the original appeal or a person who made submissions or observations in relation to that appeal or referral.[30] It is not, therefore, open to a person who was not involved in the appeal to bring the judicial review application without first having obtained the permission of the court on the basis of showing good and sufficient reasons for not having made an objection or observation in the first instance.[31]

Any person who believes that there may be possible grounds for judicial review will need to move swiftly in contacting a solicitor, as the timeframes for bringing judicial review proceedings are rigid in that any such applications for leave must be brought within a period of eight weeks commencing on the date of the decision of the Board.[32] The court may extend this timeframe where there are *good and sufficient reasons* for doing so.[33]

Finally, it is also open to any person who has applied for permission or objected to a permission to bring an application for leave to bring judicial

---

[28] See chapter 6, p 119 in this regard.
[29] The 2000 Act and the Planning and Development Regulations 2001 to 2011.
[30] s 50(4)(c)(i)(III).
[31] s 50(4)(c)(ii).
[32] s 50(4)(a)(i).
[33] s. 13(8)(a) Planning and Development (Strategic Infrastructure) Act 2006.

review against the local planning authority,[34] but this course of action is used sparingly as it obviously makes more economic and procedural sense to simply appeal the result of the matter to the Board, and thereafter revert to considering possible grounds for a judicial review.

## Conclusion

To surmise, the lay person when drafting planning objections and appeals must adhere rigidly to issues of planning, It will be of no benefit to the objector/appellant to be diverted into airing personal grievances and the importance of refraining from making defamatory statements cannot be over emphasised as all files of the local authority and the Bord will be open to public inspection.

---

[34] s 50(2)(a)(i).

# CHAPTER EIGHT

# Derelict Sites, Dangerous Structures and Unsanitary Sites

## Derelict Sites Act 1990

If a person is living next door to lands that have been abandoned and left decrepit over a number of years to the extent that the adjoining lands have become unsightly and perhaps even unsafe for children in the neighbourhood, there is redress available for concerned residents under the Derelict Sites Act 1990[1] (the Act). The Act came into law in June of 1990 and provides remedies for individuals by empowering the local authority to take actions to protect the public and the environment against dereliction. Any member of the public concerned by such a site will need to be pro-active in ensuring that his or her local authority is using its full powers in trying to regularise such sites.

## What is a Derelict/Dangerous Site?

The law in this area is more than clear as s 9 of the Act states that:

> "It shall be the duty of every owner and occupier of land, including a statutory body and a State authority, to take all reasonable steps to ensure that the land does not become or does not continue to be a derelict site."

Under s 3 of the Act a derelict site means any land that detracts, or is likely to detract to a material degree from the amenity, character or appearance of land in the neighbourhood of the land in question because of:

- the existence on the land in question of structures which are in a ruinous, derelict or dangerous condition; or
- the neglected, unsightly or objectionable condition of the land or any structures on the land in question; or
- the presence, deposit or collection on the land in question of any litter, rubbish, debris or waste, except where the presence, deposit

---

[1] Repealing the Derelict Sites Act 1961.

or collection of such litter, rubbish, debris or waste results from the exercise of a right conferred by statute or by common law.

Under s 8 of the Act, the local authority is obliged to maintain a register of derelict sites within its administrative boundaries which may be inspected by the general public during office hours. In this regard, any individual concerned about an adjoining property being in or falling into a state of dereliction should, in the first instance, check the register as the local authority may already have commenced taking action to regularise the derelict site.

Before making any entry on the register in relation to any land, the local authority is, in accordance with s 8(2) of the Act, obliged to give to any owner and occupier, where they can be ascertained by reasonable enquiry, notice of its intention to make an entry on the register in relation to their lands. The local authority must also shall consider any representations any owner or occupier may make in writing within such period as may be specified in the notice and may either make the entry or not as it thinks proper having regard to such representations.

It is the duty of a local authority to take all reasonable steps (including the exercise of any appropriate statutory powers) to ensure that any land situated in its functional area does not become or continue to be a derelict site.[2] The local authorities are empowered to take certain measures to uphold this statutory obligation.

The local authority may on its own initiative or by way of direction from the Minister for the Environment, Community and Local Government[3] serve a notice in writing on any person who appears to it to be the owner or occupier of the affected lands, specifying the measures which the local authority or the Minister, as the case may be, consider to be necessary in order to prevent the land from becoming, or continuing to be, a derelict/ dangerous site. Once the local authority is satisfied that the works schedule, as per the notice of remedial works required, has been carried out to the satisfaction of the local authority, the entry of the site on the derelict/dangerous sites register may be removed.

---

[2] s 10 of the Act.
[3] s 12 of the Act.

## Criminal Sanction Where Works are not Carried Out to Remedy Derelict/Dangerous Sites

Under s 28 of the Act, a person who contravenes a condition of the statutory notice to make good a derelict/dangerous site[4] of the local authority may be guilty of an offence and will be liable, on summary conviction, to a fine not exceeding €1,270 and also a fine not exceeding €127 for every day on which the offence continues and not exceeding €1,270 in total.[5] A person convicted might also be sentenced to imprisonment for a term not longer than six months. The court may also decide to impose both a fine and imprisonment.

On conviction on indictment for failing to carry out the measures required by the local authority to prevent a property from being classed as derelict within an allotted time, a person faces a fine not exceeding €31,750 with a further fine not exceeding €2,540 for every day the offence is continued, or imprisonment for a term not exceeding two years. The court may also decide to impose both a fine and imprisonment.

## Powers of Local Authority and Minister to Acquire Derelict Sites

In more extreme situations, s 14 of the Act allows a local authority to acquire by agreement or compulsorily[6] any derelict/dangerous site situated within its functional area. Any person upon whom notices of the proposed compulsory acquisition of a derelict site have been served may, within the time specified in the notices, submit an objection in writing to the local authority to the proposed compulsory acquisition referred. If such an objection is received by the local authority, then the local authority must seek the consent of An Bord Pleanála[7] to compulsorily acquire the site and must outline its comments to An Bord Pleanála in relation to the objection of the landowner whose land is to be compulsorily acquired.

An Bord Pleanála, as it thinks fit, may grant or refuse to grant its consent to the compulsory acquisition of all or part of the derelict site. A local

---

[4] A s 11(4) Statutory Notice.

[5] This figure does not include the original fine of €1,270 for committing the offence in the first place.

[6] The compulsory purchase order is subject the Derelict Sites Regulations 2000 (SI No 455 of 2000).

[7] The functions of the Minister in s 16(3) were transferred to the Board by virtue of s 214 of the 2000 Act.

authority may use any derelict site acquired by it under the Act for any purpose connected with its functions.[8] The local authority may also sell on the acquired derelict site and apply the monies received from any sale for the purpose of its functions in such manner as the local authority, with the consent of An Bord Pleanála, shall think proper.[9] In many instances the local authority will use the derelict site as future social housing.

## Compensation for Acquisition of Derelict Sites

Where, immediately before a vesting order[10] is made, any person who has any estate or interest in or right in respect of the derelict site acquired by the order may apply to the local authority not later than 12 months after the making of the order for compensation in respect of the estate, interest or right, and the local authority must pay to that person by way of compensation an amount equal to the value (if any) of the estate, interest or right.[11] However, if the owner of the derelict site owes any monies to the local authority, this amount will be deducted from the compensation payable. Similarly, if the amount owed is equal to or greater than the derelict site acquired, then no compensation will be payable to such owner.

The compensation to be paid by a local authority in respect of any estate or interest in or right in respect of the derelict site shall, in default of agreement, be determined by arbitration under and in accordance with the Acquisition of Land (Assessment of Compensation) Act 1919.[12] Both parties, the landowner and the acquiring local authority, are bound by the arbitrator's decision.

On lodgment of the original vesting order made under s 17 of the Act with the Property Registration Authority,[13] the local authority is registered as full owner of the derelict site free from equities and all other burdens,[14]

---

[8] s 20 of the Act.

[9] s 31 of the Act.

[10] The vesting order is the legal instrument giving rise to the change of ownership to the local authority pursuant to s 17 of the Act.

[11] s 19(3) of the Act

[12] s 19(2) of the Act.

[13] See Property Registration Authority practice direction on Local Authority Vesting Orders, published on 1 December 2009: http://www.prai.ie/eng/Legal_Professional_Customers/Legal_Practices_Procedures/Practice_Directions/14_Local_Authority_Vesting_Orders/LOCAL_AUTHORITY_VESTING_ORDERS.html#1., 21 March 2012.

[14] s 18(2) of the Act directs that the local authority becomes full owner free from all encumbrances, all estates, rights, titles and interests save for the Land Purchase Annuity or other annual sum payable to the Land Commission or Commissioners of Public Works.

meaning that the local authority will appear as full owner and the interest of the bank or any other person or body with an interest in the land is effectively abolished.

## Ghost Estates

The structural safety of unfinished property developments is of growing concern throughout the country as partly constructed housing developments can become structurally unsound if only partially completed and left exposed to the elements.

The statutory framework, of compulsory acquisition, as per the provisions laid out in the Act and the Local Government (Sanitary Services) Act 1964, are of relevance in dealing with the phenomenon of so called *Ghost Estates*. The issue becomes somewhat troublesome, however, in instances where the derelict site may be heavily mortgaged leaving the site in negative equity. A legal person in Irish law is an entity that has standing to sue or be sued in Irish courts. These entities include natural persons and companies such as the bank with the mortgage being entitled to seek compensation from the local authority, in the event of compulsory acquisition, as it clearly has an *interest* in the land.[15]

The compensation sought would be the unpaid amount of the mortgage loan, which creates obvious difficulties where the value of the mortgage is substantially less than the market value of the property. The situation of a compulsory acquisition by the local authority may again be fraught with difficulty where the bank has reserved a power under the mortgage contract to appoint a receiver to dispose of the asset so as to discharge as much of the debt of the mortgage as is possible.

Then again, if the financial institution so happens to be the National Asset Management Agency, in accordance with its statutory remit *to contribute to the social and economic development of the state,*[16] it may adopt a more holistic approach to the resolution of unfinished housing estates in accordance with its legislative role and the role of the local authority in making safe derelict and unsanitary sites.

---

[15] s 11(1) of the the Local Government (Sanitary Services) Act 1964.
[16] s 2(b)(viii) of the National Asset Management Agency Act 2009.

In any event the local authority would need to have sufficient economic resources to pay for lands at the determined market value. The local authority would also need to come to some arrangement with the financial institution irrespective of the somewhat simplistic approach espoused in s 17 of the Act.

## Taking in Charge

The taking in charge by a local authority of a private housing estate is carried out in accordance with s 180 of the Planning and Development Act 2000[17] (the 2000 Act) and s 11 of the Roads Act 1993. A private housing estate can be defined as one comprising two or more houses[18] which are served by access road(s), open spaces, car-parks, sewers, watermains and drains.

Most modern private housing/apartment developments will have a condition in the planning permission that a properly constituted management company be established for the purpose of maintaining the public lighting, roads, footpaths, parking areas, services and open spaces which shall then be conveyed to the management company. This condition is imposed pursuant to s 34(4)(i) of the 2000 Act which allows the local authority to impose conditions for the maintenance or management of the proposed development (including the establishment of a company or the appointment of a person or body of persons to carry out such maintenance or management) as a condition of the grant of permission.

Obviously, the problem in the modern era is that many of the developers and development companies, who were effectively the management company, are now insolvent and no longer have the financial resources to complete the developments and are obviously not in a position to pass over management of the public areas of the estate.[19] In the past, s 180(2) of the 2000 Act allowed, even where the development had not been completed to the satisfaction of the local authority, the majority of the qualified electors who were the owners or occupiers of the houses to insist on the local authority taking the estate or development in charge.

---

[17] As amended by s 59 of the Planning and Development (Amendment) Act 2010.
[18] s 180(1) of the 2000 Act.
[19] As opposed to the common areas which the local authority would not be responsible to take charge of in any respect.

If the local authority's hand was forced in this regard, it was able to call in the security provisions, being that condition attaching to a grant of permission requiring the giving of adequate security for satisfactory completion of the proposed development by the developer. In the normal course of affairs, a construction bond[20] was provided by the developer. The problem with construction bonds was that they were generally renewable on a yearly basis, meaning that when the insurance company issuing the bond did not receive the premium from the developer to pay for the policy of insurance for the coming year, the policy lapsed and also the bond. This meant that the local authority was then left exposed with no security to call in to finish off the public works aspect of the development when called upon by the residents, as was their statutory entitlement pursuant to s 180 of the 2000 Act.

Unsurprisingly, therefore, s 59 of the Planning and Development (Amendment) Act 2010, which amends s 180 of the 2000 Act, now refers to a request by a *majority of the owners of the houses,* as opposed to *owners and occupants* as was the situation under the 2000 Act, and the previous obligation to take the estate in charge has been replaced with an *absolute discretion* as to whether the local authority takes the estate in charge.

## Annual Levy on Derelict Sites

The Act provides for an annual levy[21] by local authorities on all urban land which had been entered onto the derelict sites register on the 1st January of that year and where its market value has had been determined. This levy acts as an impetus on the landowner to maintain the site and have it removed from the derelict site register and in this way avoid the payment of the levy. The amount of the derelict sites levy is three per cent of the market value of the urban land concerned. The Minister for the Environment, Community and Local Government may prescribe a higher percentage but it may not be greater than 10 per cent of the market value. The market value of the land is determined by the local authority but the owner of the site may appeal the valuation to the Valuation Tribunal.[22]

---

[20] s 34(4)(g).
[21] ss 21–24 of the Act.
[22] As established under s 2 of the Valuation Act 1988.

## Local Government (Sanitary Services) Act 1964

The Act to a large degree mirrors the statutory framework as laid out in the provisions of the Local Government (Sanitary Services) Act 1964 (the 1964 Act). In this regard, the 1964 Act places obligations on property owners and empowers local authorities to require the owners of dangerous places and dangerous structures to make them safe so as not to constitute a public or indeed a private hazard.

As per s 1 of the 1964 Act, a *dangerous place* is defined as an excavation, quarry, pit, well, reservoir, pond, stream, dam, bank, dump, shaft or land that, in the opinion of the sanitary authority in whose sanitary district it is situated is or is likely to be dangerous to any person.

A *dangerous structure* is defined as any building, wall or other structure of any kind, or any part of, or anything attached to, a building, wall or other structure of any kind, that, in the opinion of the sanitary authority in whose sanitary district it is situate is or is likely to be dangerous to any person or property.

Section 3 bestows a comprehensive set of powers on the local authority to fulfill its objective to make safe such hazards. For example, a notice may be served on the landowner requiring the carrying out of works, including the demolition of the structure or any part of it and the clearing and levelling of the site thereof, as will, in the opinion of the authority, prevent the structure from being a dangerous structure, to remove any debris and to erect a wall or barrier between any open area created by the works and any road, street or public place.[23]

Alternatively the local authority may step in, complete the works and recover the costs of such works from the owners of the relevant properties. In more extreme cases, the local authority may, having served the necessary notice(s), demolish the dangerous structure if the hazard posed by the structure demands such a radical course of action.[24]

In certain cases, the local authority can direct the occupier of a dangerous structure to leave and remove all his or her property. This is done in the

---

[23] s 3(1)(a) of the 1964 Act.
[24] s 3(2)(a) of the 1964 Act.

interests of the occupier's safety. If it is necessary, the local authority can obtain a court order, which allows it to use whatever force it considers necessary to remove the person and his or her property from the dangerous structure.

Section 6 of the 1964 Act allows the local authority acquire, by agreement or compulsorily, any land situated in its functional area that is a dangerous place or that has ceased, by reason of the carrying out of works under the 1964 Act by the authority, to be a dangerous place. As with derelict site acquisitions, compulsory purchases have to be advertised in the local newspaper, with details of the land in question, and a notice must be sent to the owner or occupier of the land giving information about how and where he or she can make an objection to the purchase.

Furthermore, in the case of a dangerous place, a notice must be posted either on or near the land, giving details of the local authority's intentions. If an objection is made to the compulsory purchase, the local authority cannot acquire the land without the consent of An Bord Pleanála.

If the acquisition is allowed by An Bord Pleanála, as per the Act, any person with an interest in the lands may make an application for compensation within 12 months of the acquisition of the site. In determining the amount of compensation, regard is had to any expenditure incurred by the authority in mitigating the hazards on the site.[25]

## Criminal Sanction where Works are not Carried Out to Remedy Dangerous Places/Structures

Under s 3(4) of the 1964 Act, a person who contravenes a condition of the statutory notice to make good a dangerous place/structure is guilty of an offence and will be liable, on summary conviction, to a fine not exceeding €1,270.[26]

---

[25] s 9 of the 1964 Act deals with compensation generally in relation to the local authority's acquisition of sites deemed to be dangerous places or structures. In default of agreement, compensation is to be determined by arbitration under and in accordance with the Acquisition of Land (Assessment of Compensation) Act 1919, as amended.

[26] The fine was increased from £100 to £1,000 by s 113 of the Environmental Protection Agency Act 1992.

## Conclusion

Both the Derelict Sites Act 1990 and the Local Government (Sanitary Services) Act 1964 provide a range of powers to local authorities to deal with sites which become unsightly, unsanitary and constitute a danger. With such legislation the local authority has the authority to demand that all necessary remedial works be carried out within a specified timeframe and in certain circumstances may even empower the local authority to set about acquiring such sites for the purpose of demolition if needs be.

Normally the threat of an entry on the derelict/dangerous sites register and the associated levy will be enough to spur a landowner into taking the necessary course of action in returning his or her lands to a proper state so as not to constitute a general nuisance or danger. Any person living beside such sites should contact his or her local authority to verify if the site is listed in the mandatory register of derelict/dangerous sites and, if not, he or she needs to submit a formal written request to the local authority for the site to be placed on the register. This will allow the local authority to then proceed with the various enforcement mechanisms as outlined above and hopefully bring resolution to the matter. Very often the approach to the local authority may be made by a group of local residents adding extra weight to such requests.

A template letter requesting that a local authority inspect a particular site for this purpose is provided at Appendix 6.

# Appendix 6

*[your address 1]*
*[your address 2]*
*[your address 3]*

*County Manager,*
*Local Authority,*
*County [insert county].*

**Re. Derelict Sites Act 1990 and the Local Government (Sanitary Services) Act 1964**

*Dear Sirs,*
*I refer to the above Acts and note that you are the body responsible for the implementation of the provisions of the Derelict Sites Act 1990 and the Local Government (Sanitary Services) Act, 1964.*

*I wish to make you aware of a site located at: [insert full address], that I consider to be in such poor structural state and so badly maintained that it may very well constitute a dangerous/derelict site as per the above statutory provisions.*

*Furthermore, I fear that it is only a matter of time before one of the children who frequent the site will suffer a serious injury such is the ruinous state of the structure. I should also bring it to your attention that the above site has also become a magnet for anti-social behaviour.*

*I would be most grateful therefore if you could revert to me at the above address and inform if this site has already been included on your statutory register of Derelict/Dangerous sites and further inform what steps you have taken to have the landowner of the site restore the site to a satisfactory degree.*

*If the site is not as yet on the register I request that an inspection be made of the site in order to determine if it should now be included on this register.*

*I look forward to hearing from you in early course*

*Yours faithfully,*

————————————.

# CHAPTER NINE

# Noisy Neighbours

"He showed the pills he was taking for his nerves. He showed the prescription sleeping pills. He didn't have to. It was enough to look at his quivery hands, the frazzle in his eyes. The weekend before, he had gathered up his garbage, dragged it downstairs and hurled it into the bar. He said he was contemplating drilling a hole through his floor, inserting a hose attached to his faucet and flooding the place. "I can't stand it! he said. "I need help!""[1]

The above account from a noise inspector from New York city's Department of Environmental Protection exemplifies the devastating effect sustained noise disturbance may have on residents as they try to go about their daily lives. Studies of the physiological and psychological effects of noise indicate that protracted noise can impair one's hearing, dry the mouth, dilate pupils, raise cholesterol, elevate blood pressure and burden the heart. Constant noise can bring on irritability, depression and aggression. It can also interfere with the learning ability of children.[2] Little wonder, therefore, that noise disturbance is perhaps the most prominent issue of disputes between neighbours.

The law in Ireland governing this area is s 108 of the Environmental Protection Agency Act 1992 (the Act) and the Environmental Protection Agency Act (Noise) Regulations 1994.[3] Unfortunately the law does not specifically mention an exact level or standard of noise that constitutes a nuisance for residential dwellers. Even though s 106 of the Act specifically allows for the Minister for the Environment, Community

---

[1] NR Kleinfield, *New York Quiet? Never. Quieter? Maybe. Listen Up* (*New York Times*, date unknown), http://tenant.net/Rights/Noise/noise4.html, (21 March 2012).
[2] *ibid*.
[3] SI No 179 of 1994.

and Local Government to make regulations with reference to specific noise levels for the purpose of the prevention or limitation of any noise causing nuisance or dis-amenity, no such regulations have been published.

Instead, the aggrieved party is left with the s 108 definition being noise amounting to nuisance where it is found to be *so loud, so continuous, so repeated, of such duration or pitch or occurring at such times as to give reasonable cause for annoyance to a person in any premises in the neighbourhood or to a person lawfully using any public place.*

## Noise and Nuisance Diary

Given the above definition and lack of any decibel levels indicating breaches of the legislation, any aggrieved party is well advised to commence filling out a noise and nuisance diary to log all instances of noise nuisance as it must be proven that the noise is *so loud, so continuous, so repeated, of such duration or pitch or occurring at such times* as to give reasonable cause for annoyance. Any person wishing to make a complaint, therefore, must be able to satisfy this test and the best way to do this is to compile the noise and nuisance diary found at Appendix 7. As will be seen below, it will prove an invaluable resource if ever an application must be made by the complainant to the District Court for the purposes of obtaining a noise order from the court. In terms of filling out the diary, any intending complainant needs to readily identify how the noise affects him or her in terms of his or her daily routine.

Whilst it is not always necessary, some individuals may also purchase a handheld decibel reader and will fill entries in the diary sheet that they recorded at the time of the noise disturbance. Whilst the veracity of such devices is not always accepted by the courts, it may act as a persuasive element for the court if they are included as part of the diary.

*Example of Noise/Nuisance Diary Entries*

| Date | Start Time | Finish Time | Type of Noise | How it affects me |
|------|-----------|-------------|---------------|-------------------|
| 14/06/2012 | 1 am | 2.30 am | Music with heavy base. | Unable to sleep, children unable to sleep and crying. All the family tired and stressed the following day. |

| Date | Start Time | Finish Time | Type of Noise | How it affects me |
|------|-----------|-------------|---------------|-------------------|
| 17/06/2012 | 2.30 pm | 5.00 pm | Party with loud music, shouting, loud laughter, revving cars in driveway. | Unable to read the newspaper in my living room, Sunday dinner was ruined by the noise from next door. |

## Decibel Levels

Individuals may use the decibel level chart below as an indication of the amount of noise that they may be enduring by benchmarking decibel level readings against certain everyday noise levels.[4]

| Sound level in decibels dB(A) | Description |
|-------------------------------|-------------|
| 0 | Absolute silence |
| 25 | Very quiet room |
| 35 | Rural night-time setting with no wind |
| 55 | Day-time, busy roadway 0.5 km away |
| 70 | Busy restaurant |
| 85 | Very busy pub, voice has to be raised to be heard |
| 100 | Disco or rock concert |
| 120 | Uncomfortably loud, conversation impossible |
| 140 | Noise causes pain in ears |

[4] Environmental Protection Agency, *Guidance Note For Noise In Relation To Scheduled Activities* (2nd ed, EPA, Johnstown Castle, 2006), p 6, http://www.epa.ie/downloads/advice/noise/name,14605,en.html.

## External Intruder Alarms

A European standard for external intruder alarms replaced all current national standards in September 2003. The new standard incorporates stricter controls regarding minimum and maximum duration for the sounding of alarms. The new limits are 90 seconds minimum and 15 minutes maximum. However, the new controls only apply to alarms fitted from September 2003.[5]

## Roadmap to Resolution

The first thing to do is to inform the offending neighbour of the fact that, at certain times, the noise coming from his or her home is disturbing the daily routine. Ideally at this point the problem will be resolved. Where the problem persists, it will be necessary to record the date on which the neighbour was approached. It may ultimately be necessary to write to the offending neighbour, a template letter is contained in Appendix 8, informing that if the noise continues unabated a noise nuisance application will be brought before the District Court for the purposes of obtaining a noise order to prohibit the continuance of the noise nuisance.

## Where the Property is Rented

In an application for a noise order, where the offending property is a rental property, the complainant needs to also serve a warning letter making the landlord aware of the situation and informing that if a noise order application is to be made, the landlord will be joined to the proceedings along with the tenants.

Such a threat of action will also serve to increase pressure on the landlord to serve a formal notice on his or her tenants to *quit* or leave the property for non-compliance with a term of the rental agreement and/or failure to comply with their statutory obligation not to behave within the dwelling, or in the vicinity of it, in a way that is anti-social.[6] The Private Residential Tenancies Board (PRTB) should assist in providing the name of an unknown landlord[7] and a template letter directed towards the landlord of the property is found in Appendix 9.

---

[5] European Standards Series for Intruder Alarm Systems ref. EN50131.

[6] See s 15(1) of the Residential Tenancies Act 2004 where a landlord of a dwelling owes to each person who could be potentially affected a duty to enforce the obligations of the tenant under the tenancy.

[7] s 77(3) of the Residential Tenancies Act 2004. Technically the PRTB may only release the name of a landlord to allow any intending complainant serve a letter informing the landlord that it was his or her intention to lodge a complaint in respect of the tenement concerned with the PRTB.

## Where the Property is an Apartment/Duplex Unit Forming Part of a Multi-Unit Development

Where the property is an apartment/duplex unit forming part of a multi-unit development such as a block of apartments and it is owner-occupied, a complainant should inform the management company of the nuisance being caused. It will invariably be a condition of the owner's lease[8] that he or she does not interfere with other residents' rights to the *peaceful enjoyment* of their homes. As there is a contract between the management company and the leaseholder/owner[9] causing the disturbance, the management company will be able to pursue the leaseholder/owner of the property the source of the noise for breach of contract. The threat of any such action by the management company would be a persuasive element in trying to alleviate the noise/nuisance.

At this stage, if there is no cessation of the noise/nuisance an application will need to be brought before the District Court pursuant to s 108 of the Act. It is not necessary to be represented by a solicitor for the making of this application but many complainants would engage a solicitor to prepare the necessary application and make the application in court which may require the hearing of oral evidence from the complainant and cross-examination of evidence given by the respondent to the complaint.

An intending complainant wishing to proceed without legal representation will need to fill out the prescribed notice of application form[10] in Appendix 10 and contact the clerk of the local District Court about an appointment for the hearing of the case. Once a date is assigned by the clerk, one will need to serve the notice of application form on the respondent to the complaint either personally or by registered post and thereafter having effected service, fill out a statutory declaration of service[11] which must be returned to the District Court office at least four days prior to the court date. It is also important to remember that the listing of the matter in the District Court must be at least seven days later than the date on which one serves the respondent. The local District Court clerk will be able to

---

[8] In strict legal terms the owner of the unexpired term of the lease.
[9] Or his or her tenants, as the case may be.
[10] s 108 of the Act and the Environmental Protection Agency Act 1992 (Noise) Regulations 1994 (SI No 179 of 1994).
[11] See Appendix 11.

assist in relation to the practice and procedure of preparing the application.

## Adjournments to Allow for an Attempt at Mediation

Parties to the hearing of the matter need to be aware that once the matter is listed for hearing the Judge may hear a brief synopsis of the matter and adjourn the matter for a period of time to allow both parties enter into a process of mediation in an attempt to find a mutually convenient resolution of the matter.[12] The court is well aware that arguments over noise can be long-running and turn hostile, with the result being that neighbourly relations may be damaged beyond repair. Very often if the court believes that a matter is better served by an attempt at an amicable settlement in an Alternative Dispute Resolution process such as mediation, it will allow for a reasonable amount of time to explore this avenue. As mentioned in chapter 16, various community law centres provide a free service in this regard and if parties can resolve the issue amicably themselves it is obviously to everyone's advantage as both parties must continue to live side-by-side once the battle ends.

## Where Mediation Fails or is Deemed Unsuitable

In some instances the court will realise that the matter is not amenable to mediation and will choose to list the matter for full hearing. It will be necessary to bring the noise/nuisance diary to court in order to provide evidence to the court that the noise is not just a once-off incident but that it is *so loud, so continuous, so repeated, of such duration or pitch or occurring at such times as to give reasonable cause for annoyance to a person in any premises in the neighbourhood constituting a nuisance.* It is this threshold that must be reached for the court to make the noise order. The court may also permit the playback of sound recordings of the noise.

After hearing both sides, and if the court is satisfied that the necessary test pursuant to s 108 of the Act has been met, the court may order the person or body responsible to:

— limit the noise;
— reduce the level of noise; or
— stop the noise completely.

---

[12] See p 237 in relation to mediation in the context of disputes between neighbours.

Obviously the more proof available to a party, the stronger the likelihood of a successful outcome to the application. It will be a good defence to a noise order application to prove that the defendant has taken reasonable care to prevent or limit the noise.[13]

## The Problems with Enforcing the Order

Unfortunately it can be the case that a neighbour will continue to cause a noise nuisance subsequent to a successful noise order application. Section 8(1) of the Act states that any person who contravenes any provision of the Act is guilty of an offence[14] and a fine on summary conviction of up to €3,000 or imprisonment for up to 12 months, or both, may be imposed.[15] However, a criminal prosecution will need to be brought by the EPA, or to whomever the Minister for the Environment, Community and Local Government delegates this power, normally the local authority.[16] In this regard any aggrieved neighbour should make contact with his or her local authority in order to progress matters in this regard as it is not open to the private citizen to bring a case before the courts that results in the imposition of criminal sanction on a fellow citizen.

## Noise Orders and An Garda Síochána

If the noise nuisance continues unabated to a degree that it becomes truly intolerable, it will be necessary to call the Gardaí to have them approach the neighbour with a copy of the court order; the Gardaí may approach the nuisance neighbour and may attempt to have him or her desist from causing such nuisance.

Obviously the arrival of the Gardaí should have good persuasive effect but in terms of arrest for non-compliance with a direction of the Gardaí, s 8 of the Criminal Justice (Public Order) Act 1994 states the person must be in a *public place*, meaning that the powers of arrest of the Gardaí may be

---

[13] s 108(2) also states that it is also a defence if the noise is in accordance with a licence issued under the Environment Protection Agency Act 1992 (Noise) Regulations 1994 (SI No 179 of 1994); however, such licences are granted for commercial/industrial enterprises.

[14] s 8(1).

[15] s 9(1)(a) as amended by s 10 of the Protection of the Environment Act 2003.

[16] s 11(1) and (2) states that the Minister may, by regulations, provide that an offence under the Act, specified in the regulations, may be prosecuted summarily by such person (including the Minister) as may be so specified.

somewhat limited given the fact that the nuisance will be coming from a *private dwelling*.

## Complaining a Landlord to the PRTB

Section 15 of the Private Residential Tenancies Act 2004 (the 2004 Act) states that a landlord of a dwelling owes to each person who could be potentially affected a duty to enforce the obligations of the tenant under the tenancy. As there is a statutory obligation on the tenants of a landlord not to behave within the dwelling, or in the vicinity of it, in a way that is anti-social, the landlord must take responsibility for the actions of the people that he or she brings into his or her property. Complaints are made pursuant to Pt VI of the 2004 Act.[17]

The PRTB's dispute resolution function consists of two stages; stage one is either mediation or adjudication and is confidential, and stage two is a public hearing by a Tenancy Tribunal. The Tribunal is composed of three persons drawn from the PRTB's Dispute Resolution Committee.[18] A mediated agreement or the determination of an adjudicator or of a Tribunal will result in a determination order of the PRTB. The Tribunal's determination of a matter may be appealed to the High Court within 21 days on a point of law only. The enforcement of determination orders of the PRTB that are not complied with will be dealt with by the Circuit Court.

## Reform of the Law on Noise Nuisance

The Government Legislation Programme, as issued on 14 September 2011, proposes new legislation to address issues of enforcement and also seeks to bestow increased powers on the local authority, including the introduction of a system of fixed payment notices for noise nuisance offences. The legislation also proposes to allow for local authority authorised officers and Gardaí to enter premises to disable continuously sounding intruder alarms and new on-the-spot fines for noisy house parties and loitering.[19]

---

[17] More information and an application form may be obtained through the PRTB's website at www.prtb.ie.
[18] As described in s 103 of the 2004 Act.
[19] The new legislation was not published at the time of writing.

## Civil Remedies for Noise Nuisance

In the most extreme of situations it may be necessary to instruct a solicitor to issue proceedings for compensatory damages arising out of a neighbour's activities that unreasonably interfere with an aggrieved party's family's right to the peaceful enjoyment of their home.[20] It will be necessary to satisfy the court that the noise is excessive and disturbing to such an extent that one's enjoyment of the property is diminished. A noise nuisance diary, copies of complaints to the Garda Síochána and sound recordings, together with witness testimony, may be used as evidence in support of such a claim.

Such claims will normally need to be stated in the Circuit Court as an award of damages arising out of nuisance caused may also be coupled with an application for mandatory injunctive relief, i.e. the court may prohibit the neighbour from continuing to cause the nuisance complained of. The breaching of an injunction is a most serious offence and may lead to the person found to be in breach being brought before the court, with the assistance of the Gardaí.

## Barking Dogs, Noise and Nuisance

Noise and nuisance caused by barking dogs is dealt with under specific provisions of the Control of Dogs Acts 1986 to 2010, and chapter 12 details the available remedies in such instances.

## Noise from Aircraft, Rail and Road

The Environmental Noise Regulations 2006 (the Regulations)[21] give effect in Ireland to Directive 2002/49 of 25 June 2002 relating to the assessment and management of environmental noise,[22] or more precisely, *noise emitted by means of transport, road traffic, rail traffic, air traffic, and from sites of industrial activity.*[23]

A two-stage approach to the assessment and management of environmental noise is provided for in the Regulations. First, the preparation of strategic noise maps for areas and infrastructure falling within defined criteria,

---

[20] Civil remedies are discussed in more general detail in chapter 15.
[21] SI No 140/2006.
[22] OJ L 189, 18.7.2002, pp 12–25.
[23] Art 3(1) of the Regulations.

such as large agglomerations, major roads, railways and airports. Responsibility for making the strategic noise maps based on the results of the mapping process rests with the relevant local authorities, relevant airport authorities, the National Roads Authority, Iarnród Éireann and the Railway Procurement Agency, as appropriate.[24]

Secondly, the Regulations require the preparation of *noise action plans* which must aim to protect so called *quiet areas*.[25] It is the task of the local authorities to make the noise action plan.[26] Local authorities are obliged to make the information for the public on noise maps and action plans clear, comprehensive and accessible, and must include a summary of the most important points. The public must be consulted on proposals for action plans and must be afforded early and effective opportunities to participate in the preparation and review of action plans. The Regulations clearly state that the results of public participation are to be taken into account in finalising action plans. Strategic noise-maps and action plans must be made available to the public no later than one month after the date on which they are made[27] and local authorities must review noise action plans not later than five years after the date on which they were made or last reviewed.[28]

Normally a community rights association will be formed to act as a conduit for proposals to the appropriate local authority tasked with drafting the noise action plan. If at any stage of this consultative process the public fear that their views and opinions have not been fairly represented in the noise action plan in breach of the Regulations, they will need to make contact with the EPA in its capacity as the national competent authority for implementing the Regulations, with general

---

[24] Art 6 of the Regulations.

[25] Art 5(b) refers to the protection of noise areas whilst Art 1 defines quiet areas as follows: "quiet area in an agglomeration" means an area, delimited by an action planning authority following consultation with the Agency and approval by the Minister, where particular requirements on exposure to environmental noise shall apply; "quiet area in open country" means an area, delimited by an action planning authority following consultation with the Agency and approval by the Minister, that is undisturbed by noise from traffic, industry or recreational activities.

[26] Art 7.

[27] Art 12.

[28] Art (7)(b)(iii).

supervision over noise-mapping bodies and action-planning authorities and reporting duties.

If at this stage members of the public still fear that there are issues in relation to adherence to the Regulations and the correct functioning of the process as a whole, then they will need to make contact with their solicitors for the purposes of exploring the possibility of seeking the leave[29] of the court to bring a judicial review application in order to oblige all the relevant agencies to operate in strict compliance with the Regulations, ensuring the rights of individuals to participate in the process are respected.

## Noise from Commercial Facilities and the Planning and Development Act 2000

Whilst general noise issues or nuisance are regulated by the Act and associated Noise Regulations 1994, the powers of s 34 of the Planning and Development Act 2000 (the 2000 Act) should not be overlooked in terms of its power to abate potential noise and nuisance. Under s 34 of the 2000 Act, the local planning authority, if it decides to make a decision to grant permission for a particular development, may attach conditions for regulating the hours and days during which a business premises may operate[30] and may impose measures to reduce or prevent the emission of any noise which might give reasonable cause for annoyance to persons in any premises in the neighbourhood of the development.[31]

Such conditions, if imposed, would usually be restricted to commercial/ industrial developments if located within proximity to residential areas. Any person so affected will need to consult his or her local planning register to take up a copy of the planning permission and verify if there are any such restrictive conditions attaching to the grant of permission of the development complained of. If it transpires that the restrictive conditions are attached, and the operator of the premises is acting outside the remit of the planning permission with respect to those conditions, a formal unauthorised development complaint should be lodged with the planning office. Chapter 6 deals in detail with the operation of the

---

[29] Or permission.
[30] s 34(4)(q).
[31] s 34(4)(c)(i).

unauthorised development complaints[32] and investigation procedure as well as the s 160 of the 2000 Act planning injunction.

## Noise from Commercial/Industrial Facilities and the EPA

As previously mentioned, whilst general noise issues or nuisance are regulated by the Act and associated Noise Regulations 1994, noise issues in relation to commercial facilities are dealt with via licences issued by the EPA for certain scheduled activities specified in the First Schedule to the Act and the Protection of the Environment Act 2003. Where an application is made to the EPA for a licence[33] it may grant the licence subject to certain conditions which seek to prevent or limit any noise which may give rise to a nuisance or disamenity, constitute a danger to health, or damage property.[34] The EPA can take specified measures to prevent or limit the noise under the licensing agreement. If these orders are not adhered to, the person concerned may face prosecution.

In relation to commercial and industrial premises that have not been issued with such a licence it is then open to the local authority and to the EPA where necessary to issue a s 107[35] notice for the prevention or limitation of noise. The notice will specify the measures which appear to the local authority or the EPA, as the case may be, to be necessary in order to prevent or limit the noise and direct the person on whom the notice is served to take such measures as may be specified in the notice to prevent or limit the noise. The notice will specify a period, which the local authority or the EPA considers reasonable in all the circumstances of the particular case to allow for such measures to be taken.

If a person on whom a notice under this section has been served by a local authority or the EPA does not, within the period specified in the notice, comply with the requirements of the notice, the local authority or the EPA may take *such steps as it considers reasonable and necessary to secure compliance with the notice*[36] and may recover any costs and expenses thereby incurred from the person on whom the notice was served as a simple contract debt in any court of competent jurisdiction.

---

[32] Appendix 4 is a template unauthorised development complaint form.
[33] s 83(1) of the Act.
[34] See s 106 of the Act.
[35] s 107 of the Act.
[36] s 107(5).

It shall be a good defence, in a prosecution for a contravention of this section in the case of noise caused in the course of a trade or business, for the accused to prove that he or she took all reasonable care to prevent or limit the noise to which the charge relates by providing, maintaining, using, operating and supervising facilities, or by employing practices or methods of operation that, having regard to all the circumstances, were suitable for the purposes of such prevention or limitation. As per s 9 of the Act, a person guilty of an offence under the Act shall be liable on summary conviction to a fine not exceeding €3,000 or to imprisonment for a term not exceeding 12 months or, at the discretion of the court, to both such fine and such imprisonment.[37]

Any intending complainant should write a formal letter of complaint to the local authority's environment section and ask that it investigate the noise nuisance complained of with a view to issuing a s 107 notice if the situation so demands it. In certain circumstances, the EPA has the authority to direct the local authority to carry out, cause to be carried out, or arrange for, such action related to the function in question as the EPA considers necessary for the purposes of environmental protection.[38]

## Conclusion

Noise disturbance is a most serious matter especially when the detrimental effects on health are considered in the more extreme cases. The importance of the integrity and the right to peaceful enjoyment of the home of the citizen is recognised and will be protected by the courts but the onus is on the suffering party to assist their solicitor in compiling the necessary nuisance/diary sheets in some detail order to allow for a more satisfactory outcome. After all a judge cannot impinge the right of another citizen to make noise where no evidence of the detrimental affect of the noise complained of is forthcoming.

---

[37] The fine under s 9 was increased from £1,000 to €3,000 by virtue of s 10 of the Protection of the Environment Act 2003.
[38] s 63 of the Act.

## Appendix 7

Noise Diary Sheet – Environmental Protection Agency Act 1992

To help us investigate your noise complaint, we need you to keep a record of the noise problem that is bothering you.

Please keep a note below and over the page, details of the date the noise occurs, the time it starts and finishes, and the way it affects you.

YOUR DETAILS:

Name: _____

Address: _____

_____

Source of Noise Problem: _____

| Date | Start Time | Finish Time | Type of Noise | How it affects me |
|------|-----------|-------------|---------------|-------------------|
|      |           |             |               |                   |
|      |           |             |               |                   |
|      |           |             |               |                   |
|      |           |             |               |                   |
|      |           |             |               |                   |

I certify that the above record is a true statement of the noise/vibration complained of.

Signed: _____

Date: _____

## Appendix 8

*[Insert date].*
*[insert name and address of neighbour].*

*Dear [Insert name],*

*You will recall that on [date] I called to your apartment to talk to you about what I feel is excessive noise coming from your apartment which continues to cause my family and I stress and anxiety. I asked in a reasonable and friendly manner that you take care not to play your music too loud after 10.30 pm.*

### Option 1[39]

*Unfortunately, as the problem has continued to persist since we last spoke, I am now left with no alternative but to pass this matter on to the management company/landlord[40] as I believe that you are in breach of the terms of your lease.*

### Option 2

*Unfortunately, as the problem has continued to persist since we last spoke, I now regrettably feel that I have no option but to apply to the District Court, as is my entitlement under s 108 of the Environmental Protection Agency Act 1992, in order to seek a noise order from the court to prohibit you from causing my family any further stress and anxiety from the excessive noise coming from your apartment/house.*

*I do remain open to meeting with you again if you wish to try and resolve this problem in a mutually convenient fashion but in the meantime I intend to proceed as detailed above.[41]*

*Yours sincerely,*

---

[39] There is nothing to stop a complainant using option 1 and option 2 in the correspondence if the source of the noise is an apartment/duplex.

[40] If the property is owner-occupied and is an apartment/duplex in a multi-unit development, then the occupant of such apartment/duplex will be obliged to adhere to the terms of his or her lease which will invariably require him or her to refrain from causing annoyance and nuisance to other dwellers within the development.

[41] If a resolution is arrived at, all complaints may be withdrawn and the action in the District Court may be withdrawn with the consent of all of the parties involved.

## Appendix 9

*[Insert date]*

*[insert name and address of neighbour].*

**Re: Noise and Nuisance from Rental Property at** _____

*Dear Sir,*

*I refer to the above and note that you are the landlord of the property concerned.*

*Unfortunately, I must inform you that for some time now, there has been an excessive amount of noise and general disturbance coming from the property which is having a serious impact of my enjoyment of my own home at* _____*

*I explained to your tenants on the* _____ *day of* _____ *20*_____ *that the excessive noise and general disturbance was causing my family and I a great deal of stress and anxiety. I asked your tenants in a reasonable and friendly manner that they take care not to play their music so loud in the evenings or constant parties but to no avail.*

*Unfortunately, as the problem has continued to persist since we last spoke, I now regrettably feel that I have no option but to apply to the District Court, as is my entitlement under s 108 of the Environmental Protection Agency Act 1992, in order to seek a noise order from the court to prohibit your tenants from causing my family any further stress and anxiety from the excessive noise coming from your property. As you are responsible for the actions of your tenants pursuant to s 15 of the Residential Tenancies Act 2004, I intend to join you to my application for the noise order.*

*I do remain open to meeting with you if you wish to try and resolve this problem in a mutually convenient fashion, but in the meantime I intend to proceed as detailed above.*[42]

*Yours sincerely,*

_____

---

[42] If a resolution is arrived at, all complaints may be withdrawn and the action in the District Court may be withdrawn with the consent of all of the parties involved.

# Appendix 10

## Schedule

ENVIRONMENTAL PROTECTION AGENCY ACT 1992.

Notice pursuant to s 108(3) of the Environmental Protection Agency Act 1992 of intention to make a complaint to the District Court in relation to noise giving reasonable cause for annoyance.

Complainant    _____

of               _____ [1]

Defendant    _____

of               _____ [2]

WHEREAS the above-named complainant alleges that the above-named defendant is the *person *body [3] making, causing or responsible for the following noise, namely,_____ [4] _____ at _____ [4] in District Court district no_____and District Court area of_____ [4], which noise is so loud/so continuous/so repeated/of such duration or pitch/occurring at such times[5] as to give reasonable cause for annoyance to

   *the complainant,
   *a person in any premises in the neighbourhood,
   *a person lawfully using a public place,[3]

NOTICE IS HEREBY GIVEN to the defendant that the complainant intends to make a complaint pursuant to s 108(1) of the above Act to a sitting of the District Court for the said court area and district to be held at_____ _____on the_____day of\_\_\_\_\_ 20\_\_\_\_\_ at\_\_\_\_\_am/pm,[6] being a date not earlier than seven days from the date of this notice, and to seek an order pursuant to that section in relation to the said noise.

Dated this_____day of_____, 20_____ [7].

Signed_____ [8]

To_____

of_____²

The above-named defendant.

NOTES FOR COMPLETING THIS FORM

1. Insert name and address of person or local authority making complaint.
2. Insert name and address of person or body alleged to have made or have caused or have been responsible for the noise (see s 14 of the Act in regard to the service of notice).
3. *Delete as appropriate.
4. Insert details of the noise complained of — including location in the court area and district, nature, source, date, time, etc.
5. Delete whichever of these terms and conditions may not be appropriate in the case of the noise concerned.
6. Insert details of court sitting concerned.
7. Insert date.
8. To be signed by the complainant, i.e. the local authority or person concerned.

## Appendix 11

SI No 132 of 2009:

FORM 1B

ENDORSEMENT OF SERVICE (REGISTERED POST)

In pursuance of section 7(3) of the Courts Act 1964 the within was served by me on the Defendant, _____ by posting a true copy thereof at _____am/pm on the _____ day of _____ 20__ at _____ Post Office in a registered prepaid envelope addressed to the said Defendant, the said_____ at * _____

Endorsed this _____ day of _____ 20_____

Signed _____

STATUTORY DECLARATION OF SERVICE BY REGISTERED POST

I, _____ of _____, aged eighteen years and upwards, do solemnly and sincerely declare:

1. That I did serve the within _____ dated the _____ day of _____ 20__ on the within named Defendant by posting a true copy thereof at __ am/pm on the _____ day of _____ 20__ at _____ Post Office in a registered prepaid envelope addressed to the Defendant, the said _____ at * _____ (being the last known residence/place of business of the Defendant).

2. That the said envelope has not been returned undelivered to the sender.

And I make this solemn declaration conscientiously believing same to be true and by virtue of the Statutory Declarations Act 1938 and the Courts Act 1964 empowering this Declaration to be used as proof of service of the said †_____ civil bill †_____ (identify other originating document).

Signed _____

Declared before me_____ (name in capitals) a

†notary public

†commissioner for oaths

†peace commissioner

†person authorised by (insert authorising statutory provision) _____ to take and receive statutory declarations

by the said _____

†who is personally known to me,

†who is identified to me by _____ who is personally known to me

†whose identity has been established to me before the taking of this Declaration by the production to me of

††passport no. _____ issued on the _____ day of_____ by the authorities of _____, which is an authority recognised by the Irish Government,

††national identity card no. _____ issued on the _____ day of_____ by the authorities of _____ which is an EU Member State, the Swiss Confederation or a Contracting Party to the EEA Agreement,

††Aliens Passport no. _____ issued on the _____ day of _____ by the authorities of _____ which is an authority recognised by the Irish Government,

††refugee travel document no. _____ issued on the ____day of_____ by the Minister for Justice, Equality and Law Reform,

†† travel document (other than refugee travel document) _____ issued on the ____ day of_____ by the Minister for Justice, Equality and Law Reform,

at ____ this __ day of _____ 20 _____

Signed _____

†notary public

†commissioner for oaths

†peace commissioner

†person authorised by (insert authorising statutory provision) _____
to take and receive statutory declarations

*Postal address in full

†Delete words or clauses which are not applicable.

††Where relevant, provide details of the document by which identity has been established, and delete the remaining alternatives.

Note: In accordance with section 7(6) of the Courts Act 1964, this declaration is to be made not earlier than 10 days after the day on which the envelope is posted.

# CHAPTER TEN

# Occupiers' Liability

## The Landowner and Personal Injury

One of the worrying areas for landowners is their responsibility for personal injury that may happen upon another person whilst visiting or trespassing on their lands. The problem may be even more worrying for members of the farming community who, for example, may have lands that attracts recreational visitors such as hill walkers. Also of concern to landowners may be their responsibility towards neighbouring children who may become injured whilst playing with their own children. Where then does the law stand on such issues and how does one best protect oneself from being sued in relation to a person, adult or child being injured on one's lands?

## The Occupiers' Liability Act 1995

The Occupiers' Liability Act 1995 (the Act) replaced the old common law liability of occupiers with a new scheme and is concerned with the duty of care owed by occupiers of premises or land toward visitors, trespassers and recreational users.

## Definitions Under the Act

### Occupier

The Act provides that an *occupier*[1] is a person exercising control over the state of the premises such that it is reasonable to impose upon that person a duty towards an entrant in respect of a particular danger on the premises. Where there is more than one occupier of the same premises, the extent of the duty of each occupier towards an entrant depends on the degree of control each of them has over the state of the premises and the particular danger.

---

[1] s 1(1).

## Danger

*Danger*[2] in relation to any premises, means a danger due to the *state of the premises*. This means that the occupier is not liable under the Act for loss or injury sustained as a result of any activity in which he or she is engaged on the land. However, if the injury or loss is caused by the condition of the premises then the occupier could face a claim under the Act. If an occupier digs a hole and accidently reverses over an entrant with the digger then the Act will not apply. The entrant must instead proceed with a claim for damages for personal injury under general negligence principles.[3] If, however, there is an existing hole on one's property and the entrant falls into it then the Act will apply. It is interesting to note that the definition of *premises*[4] includes land, water and any fixed or moveable structures thereon.[5]

## Recreational Users and Trespassers

*Recreational user* is defined as an entrant who, with or without the occupier's permission or at the occupier's implied invitation, is present on the premises free of charge (other than a reasonable charge for parking) for the purpose of engaging in a recreational activity.[6] This definition includes an entrant admitted free of charge to a national monument but does not include an entrant who is so present and is:

(a)  a member of the occupier's family who is ordinarily resident on the premises;

(b)  an entrant who is present at the express invitation of the occupier or such a member; or

(c)  an entrant who is present with the permission of the occupier or such a member for social reasons connected with the occupier or such a member.

*Recreational activity* is defined as any recreational activity conducted, whether alone or with others, in the open air (including any sporting activity), scientific research and nature study, exploring caves and visiting sites and buildings of historical, architectural, traditional, artistic,

---

[2] *ibid.*
[3] See chapter 15, p 219.
[4] s 1(1).
[5] Definition also includes vessels, vehicles, trains, aircraft and other means of transport.
[6] *ibid.*

archaeological or scientific importance.[7] Such a definition, therefore, includes hill climbers, ramblers, tourists, huntsmen, fishermen and others. If an occupier charges a recreational user entering his or her premises a fee, there is a danger that the entrant will be categorised as a visitor and owed the higher duty of care, as detailed below.

*Trespassers* are defined as entrants other than a recreational user or visitor.

### Duty of Care

The duty of care owed to recreational users and trespassers is set out in s 4 of the Act. It provides that the occupier has an obligation not to injure the person or damage his or her property intentionally and also not to act with reckless disregard for that person or his or her property.[8] As previously noted, the Act does not define the term *reckless disregard* but s 4(2) offers a number of guidelines to the court in deciding whether an occupier's behaviour could amount to *reckless disregard*.

## Farmers, Recreational Users and Trespassers

Prior to the coming into effect of the Act, farmers were very apprehensive about the level of duty of care, which required them to *take reasonable care*, which they owed to people who were using their land for recreational purposes without their authorisation and consent. There was a growing fear that the countryside was being closed down to recreational users as farmers sought to protect their interests. The fact that the Act changed the duty of care from that of an obligation to take *reasonable care* to that of acting with *reckless disregard* was seen as a strengthening of the position of landowners as against claims for injury arising from recreational users of their land.

### Example of Duty of Care to a Recreational User

This approach is most evident in the Supreme Court decision in *Weir Rodgers v SF Trust*.[9] The facts of the case were that Ms Weir Rodgers had been sitting with friends at the edge of a cliff. As she went to stand up she lost her footing and fell down the cliff face into the sea resulting in a number of injuries.

---

[7] s 1(1).
[8] s 4(1).
[9] [2005] 1 ILRM 471.

She brought an action in the High Court against the defendant for breach of duty under s 4 of the Act. The plaintiff claimed that she was a recreational user as defined and that the defendant occupier had acted with *reckless disregard* for her safety by failing to have the area fenced so as to prevent anyone entering into it and additionally, or alternatively, by failing to erect a warning notice. The High Court agreed with the plaintiff that there should have been a warning notice. It did not agree that the defendant had breached his duty by not having the area fenced off.

The Supreme Court was unanimous in dismissing the plaintiff's claim. Geoghegan J delivered the decision which found that the trial judge had set the level of reckless disregard at a degree which was too favourable to the entrant and adopted the approach of the British House of Lords in *Tomlinson v Congleton B.C.*[10] where it was held that an occupier could not be under a duty to prevent people taking risks inherent in the activities that they undertook.

Geoghegan J put it succinctly when he said:

> "The person sitting down near a cliff must be prepared for oddities in the cliff's structure or in the structure of the ground adjacent to the cliff and he or she assumes the risk associated therewith. There could, of course, be something quite exceptionally unusual and dangerous in the state of a particular piece of ground which would impose a duty on the occupier the effect of which would be that if he did not put up a warning notice he would be treated as having reckless disregard. But this is certainly not such a case."[11]

The use of the term *exceptionally unusual and dangerous* sets a considerable evidential burden for a would-be claimant to discharge in order to succeed under the Act. Farmers, therefore, are not obliged to examine every topographical detail of their lands and erect fences and signs averting people to such low potential hazards, as this would arguably leave the countryside littered with such signs and fencing.

A common sense approach is called for by both the recreational user and the farmer. For example, where there is a dis-used mine shaft on the land this should obviously be flagged and fenced off but a farmer is not

---

[10] [2003] 1 AC 46.
[11] [2005] 1 ILRM 471 at 478.

responsible for a hill walker falling over a boulder as common sense would dictate that the hill walker must take reasonable care for him- or herself and expect that uneven surfaces will occur.[12]

### When a Child Trespasser/Recreational User Suffers Injuries

The Act does not draw a distinction between adults and children. A child who enters onto lands of his or her own volition is owed the same duty of care which would be owed to an adult and no more. However, in the considerations to be taken into account in gauging the standard of *reckless disregard*, the Act makes reference to the conduct of the person, and the care which he or she may reasonably be expected to take for his or her own safety, while on the premises, having regard to the extent of his or her knowledge thereof.[13]

It may be open to the courts[14] to hold that a child could reasonably be expected to take less care for his or her safety than an adult in the same circumstances. Children will not take the time to consider the inherent dangers in their immediate environment and even if they are able to read and understand the full context of warning signs they may simply ignore same in the pursuit of climbing trees or exploring machinery in the farm yard.[15]

As a result, the courts have traditionally afforded more leniency to children[16] given their natural propensity to assume risk and over-estimate their own abilities to navigate dangers. As such the courts may adopt a more lenient approach in favour of the child in terms of determining the standard of *reckless disregard* of the occupier, especially if the occupier is aware of a history of children playing on or near any potential hazards on his or her lands.

### Visitors

As seen above s 1 of the Act defines *visitor* as an entrant who is present on premises at the invitation, or with the permission, of the occupier. The

---

[12] s 4(2)(g).

[13] s 4(2)(g).

[14] Under s 4(2)(g).

[15] Law Reform Commission, LRC 46–1994, *Report on Occupier's Liability* (Law Reform Commission, Dublin, 1994), p 18.

[16] "The notion of implied licence enabled courts, often by a fictitious ascription of permission, to elevate the status of a deserving trespasser – often a child – to that of licensee, with the practical result that liability would be imposed on the occupier." *ibid.*

definition also includes a member of the occupier's family who is ordinarily resident on the premises, an entrant who is present at the express invitation of the occupier or a family member, or an entrant who is present with the permission of the occupier or family member for social reasons.[17]

Section 3 of the Act clarifies the duty that is owed by an occupier towards visitors. This is known as the *common duty of care* and is similar to the standard applied in ordinary negligence law. The *common duty of care* is a duty to take such care as is *reasonable in all the circumstances* to ensure that a visitor to the premises does not suffer injury or damage as a result of any danger existing on the premises.[18]

An injured visitor is obliged to show that an occupier had not taken reasonable care for his or her safety in order to succeed under the Act. What is reasonable in the given circumstances will be determined by the court, which may take into consideration the care which a visitor may reasonably be expected to take for his or her own safety and, if the visitor is in the company of another person, the extent of supervision and control that latter person may reasonably be expected to exercise over the visitor's activities.[19]

This clearly envisages a parent/child situation but it must be noted that this in no way eliminates the duty of care towards the child; it is merely a factor to be taken into consideration when measuring what is reasonable in a particular factual scenario and could in theory give grounds to a defence of *contributory negligence*. In this instance, contributory negligence would mean the amount awarded in compensation for injury may be reduced due to the fact that the child was present with his or her own parent/guardian whom ought to have been able to prevent the accident occurring by exercising due control of the child.

---

[17] A visitor could also be an entrant, other than a recreational user, who is present on premises by virtue of an express or implied term in a contract, or an entrant as of right.

[18] The Act also states in s 4(a) that one must not injure the person or damage the property of the person intentionally; however, the remainder of this chapter will presume that the occupier does not *intentionally* cause harm to any visitor or trespasser but instead focuses on the second leg of the test, being that of acting with reckless disregard for the person or the property of the person.

[19] s 3(2) of the Act.

## What are the Responsibilities Towards Children Whom a Parent's Child Invites Around to Play?

Whilst a child is not classed as an occupier under the Act, a child of the parent occupier does have the capacity to bestow visitor status on friends who he or she invites onto the property, notwithstanding that a child will not be a *person exercising such control over the state of the premises* as is the normal test. This is because paragraph (c) of the definition of *recreational user designates* an entrant who is present with the permission of a member of the occupier's family for social reasons as a visitor.[20]

This means that such children will be deemed to be visitors. The appropriate duty of care will therefore be the higher threshold of care, being the *common duty of care*. As mentioned above, the *common duty of care* is a duty to take such care as is *reasonable in all the circumstances* to ensure that a visitor to the premises does not suffer injury or property damage as a result of being in or around the house.

### Example of Duty of Care to a Visitor

*Heaves v Westmeath Co. Co.*[21] serves as a good example of the care required to discharge the burden of the *common duty of care*. The plaintiff entered the defendant's grounds and paid an entry fee for himself and his two small children. He descended a set of steps and slipped on a moss-covered indentation. The occupier had a cleaning system in place, where on an annual basis he employed an independent contractor to accompany his gardener on a tour of the premises. When potential hazards and trouble spots were identified the contractor was required to take remedial measures. This had been carried out to these particular steps sometime in the recent past.

The plaintiff sued the defendant as occupier of the premises for the injuries he received. He maintained that because he had paid an entrance fee he was to be classified as a visitor and therefore owed that higher duty of care. The Court agreed that he was a visitor within the meaning of the Act

---

[20] Which in turn must be read in conjunction with paragraph (a) of the definition of *visitor* in s 1.

[21] In *Heaves v Westmeath County Council*, (20 ILT (ns) 236 (Circuit Ct, Mullingar, 17 October 2001) Judge McMahon emphasised that the duty is *"to take reasonable care and no more"* and that *"one must be careful, when assessing the [occupier]'s conduct that one is not condemning with the benefit of hindsight"*.

and, as such, the standard of care owed to a visitor under the Act is the common duty of care.[22]

The Court found that the defendant had discharged this duty, holding that the duty of care did not extend to a guarantee that an accident would never occur on the premises; sometimes an accident may occur for which the occupier will not be liable; the occupier is not an insurer. The defendant had personnel appointed to address risks, there was an adequate cleaning system employed and it had worked for several years without incident; the defendant had engaged an outside expert to advise him and implemented that advice.

The plaintiff had approached the steps with his eyes open, fully aware of the nature of the steps that confronted him. The absence of a warning notice did not contribute to the plaintiff's injury. There was no failure on the part of the defendant to discharge its statutory duty to take reasonable care in respect of dangers existing on the premises.

## Reducing One's Liability by Placing a Warning Notice on Lands

Section (5)(2) of the Act provides that an occupier of lands or the landowner may by express agreement or notice restrict or even exclude his or her duty towards visitors. The occupier will be presumed to have taken all reasonable steps if the notice purporting to exclude the standard of care is displayed in a prominent position at the normal point of access to the premises,[23] but any exclusion of the duty of care owed to visitors will only be binding on the visitor if:

(i)   it is reasonable in all the circumstances; and

(ii)  the occupier has taken all reasonable steps to bring the notice to the attention of the visitor.[24] Reasonable steps will mean bringing the notice to the attention of a visitor by displaying it at the normal means of access to the premises.[25]

---

[22] s 3(1) of the Act.
[23] s 5 of the Act.
[24] s 5(2)(b).
[25] s 5(2)(c).

There is no corresponding provision which allows an occupier to restrict his or her liability to recreational users or to trespassers.

It is also worth noting that a warning will not absolve the occupier of liability unless, in the circumstances, the warning went far enough to enable the visitor to avoid injury or loss resulting from the hazard warned of.[26] One cannot, therefore, erect a sign limiting one's duty of care towards a visitor at the entrance to a farm, whilst leaving a mine shaft open and unfenced with no warning notice immediately at the site of that shaft.

A copy of the notice required to limit liability of a visitor to one's property is provided in Appendix 12.

## Limiting Liability Towards Builders

In relation to the builder's employees/contractors who are brought onto the occupier's lands, the situation is somewhat complicated. Section 6 of the Act covers a situation where an occupier is in a contractual relationship with one person who in turn permits another to come on to the premises.[27] In this situation, the occupier will not be entitled, by way of contract, to restrict the duty of care owed to the builder's employees and contractors. Section 6 of the Act makes it clear that an occupier may not restrict liability in this manner; the duty of care is not capable of being modified or excluded by a contract to which the builder's employee/contractor is a stranger. As such, the occupier will be under an obligation to take such care as is *reasonable in all the circumstances* to ensure that a visitor to the premises does not suffer injury or property damage as a result of being on the premises.

### What if the Builder's Employees or Contractors are Injured on Lands at the Fault of their Own Employer?

Section 7 of the Act relieves the occupier of any liability which may be imposed on him or her due to the negligence of an independent builder.[28] So if during the course of building works an employee of the builder falls from a defective scaffold, the occupier may not be liable. This relief is available only if the occupier has taken all reasonable care in the circumstances, including such steps as the occupier ought reasonably to have taken, to satisfy him- or herself that the independent contractor was

---

[26] s 5(5).
[27] Referred to in s 6(2) of the Act as a *stranger to the contract.*
[28] Or contractor as per the Act.

competent to do the work concerned.[29] Therefore, an occupier who is aware or ought to be aware that an independent contractor has carried out sub-standard work or has used unsuitable materials will not be in a position to avail of this exception.

## Responsibility For Builders on Adjoining Lands

If there is an agreement in place with a neighbour to allow his or her builder, along with the builder's employees and contractors onto adjoining lands, consent should only be forthcoming in circumstances where an indemnity is provided. This will effectively mean that if any of those people involved in the carrying out of the works become injured or cause damage to one's property in the carrying out of those works, then that neighbour carrying out the works will ultimately be liable. A form of indemnity is provided at Appendix 2.

As was seen in chapter 2, a works order pursuant to s 45 of the Land and Conveyancing Law Reform Act 2009 allows for an adjoining landowner to seek a court order allowing for entry onto neighbouring lands for the purpose of carrying out works to a party structure where no consent is forthcoming. Section 46 details the various terms and conditions that may be attached to the works order. For example, the building owner may be required to indemnify or give security to the adjoining owner for damage, costs and expenses caused by or arising from the works or likely so to be caused or to arise.[30]

Thereafter, the Act gives a wide discretion to the Judge in the formulation of the works *on such terms and conditions as the court thinks fit*.[31] There is no reason, therefore, why a solicitor, when objecting to the granting of a works order, or seeking certain reassurances from the court, should not seek an indemnity to cover any claims arising pursuant to the Act. As the builder, his or her employees and contractors will be on the adjoining neighbour's lands by *right*, on foot of a court order, they will arguably be treated as visitors and may be afforded a *common duty of care*.

---

[29] s 7 of the Act.
[30] s 46(2)(b).
[31] s 46(1).

## Clearing Snow and Ice

This question needs to be approached on two levels: the first concerns where somebody falls whilst on private property arising out of attempts to clear snow and ice, and the second concerns liability for causing a third party an injury or property damage arising out of efforts to clear a public walkway.

In relation to private property, the usual tests under the Act apply, meaning that the duty of care that is owed to individuals will depend upon whether the person is a visitor, recreational user or trespasser on the lands.

So in terms of a *visitor*, a *common duty of care*, meaning to take such care as is *reasonable in all the circumstances*, is applicable. If, therefore, an attempt is made to clear one's footpath carefully using, for example, a spade and some salt, then a court may very well find the test of being reasonable in all of the circumstances has been discharged. If, on the other hand, the occupier decides to use boiling water to clear his or her footpath only for it to freeze over and render the path more dangerous, and pile cleared snow in a hazardous position, then the courts may find that such actions would not be considered reasonable.

Of course there is also an onus on the visitor to act in a responsible manner even in icy conditions. It may be reasonably be expected that the footpath will obviously be more slippery than on a dry August evening and, as such, the visitor will be expected to adjust his or her behaviour accordingly. *Trespassers* and *recreational users* who may slip and fall, thereby injuring themselves, on a footpath will have an even greater challenge in circumstances where it will be necessary to demonstrate the presence of *reckless disregard* for such persons' safety.

In the course of a Dáil Debate[32] the Attorney General's Office was quoted by the Taoiseach of the day who stated that:

> "… with regard to liability for members of the public when clearing snow from outside residential and business premises. There is clear advice from the Attorney General. The issue of liability does not arise

---

[32] Dáil Éireann, Vol: 723 Col: 642, 01 December 2010, Brian Cowen, then Taoiseach, responding to a question from Enda Kenny TD.

for snow that is cleared in a safe manner. If a pavement is cleared in a manner that disposes of snow so as not to create any obstacle or hazard, there is no issue of liability. I think common sense prevails."

## Clearing Snow and Ice on a Public Footpath

First and foremost, there is no obligation on any individual to clear the footpath outside the home. This will be the responsibility of the local authority. If a private citizen intervenes to clear a public footpath then he or she will find him or herself outside of the scope of the Act and the ordinary rules of negligence arise in terms of the standard of care that he or she must exercise for fellow footpath users. In this instance, the court will adopt the *reasonable person test* in determining if the individual clearing the footpath exercised reasonable care in the circumstances of the particular case. The reasonable person test essentially means that: "a defendant cannot plead accident if, treated as a man of ordinary intelligence and foresight, he ought to have foreseen the danger which caused injury to his plaintiff".[33]

The choice therefore remains with each individual, and although the remarks above from the Attorney General's Office are of some relief, there is no law in this State providing immunity to citizens who may be found on the wrong side of the civil law in trying to act in the common good.

If, however, a public authority fails to clear snow and ice it is not generally liable for any accidents if people slip and fall. This is based on the principle of *non-feasance*, meaning that where it takes no action to clear the footpath it can't be held liable. On the other hand, if maintenance is carried out on the footpath in a negligent manner causing an accident, this is termed *mis-feasance* and then it may be held liable.

## Criminal Entrant

Section 4(3)(a) and (b) of the Act at first glance seem to absolve the occupier of any liability owed to an entrant who, while on the property, commits an offence or attempts to commit an offence or enters the property for the purposes of committing an offence whether on that particular property or elsewhere. This relief is, however, limited as a court may impose a duty of care on an occupier towards a criminal entrant if it considers that it is in the *interests of justice to do so.*

---

[33] *Kirby v Burke* [1944] IR 207 at 214 as per Gavan Duffy J.

## Conclusion

Most landowners will have a policy of insurance in place that will cover any major risks involving third parties, whether they be visitors, trespassers or recreational users. It will, therefore, more often than not be the insurer of the lands who will need to apply the law as it currently stands in relation to occupier's liability. If there is no valid policy of insurance in place then the landowner leaves him or herself open to having to personally defend claims arising out of personal injury and property damage to entrants onto his or her lands.

**Appendix 12**

# NOTICE

## OCCUPIERS LIABILITY ACT 1995

### IF YOU PASS
### BEYOND THIS POINT
### YOU ARE ON A PREMISES

### TAKE NOTICE THAT
### THE OCCUPIER OF THIS PREMISES

GIVEN THE NATURE CHARACTER AND ACTIVITIES OF THESE
PREMISES HEREBY IN ACCORDANCE WITH
SECTION 5(2) OF THE OCCUPIERS LIABILITY ACT 1995

### EXCLUDES THE DUTY OF CARE
### TOWARDS VISITORS

UNDER SECTION 3 OF THE ACT

## WARNING

## UNAUTHORISED ENTRY IS

## PROHIBITED

# Criminal Law (Defence and the Dwelling) Act 2011

The Criminal Law (Defence and the Dwelling) Act 2011 (the 2011 Act) came into effect on Friday, 13 January 2012 and, in summary, provides that a person may use reasonable force to defend him or herself in his or her home. On the coming into law of the 2011 Act the, Department of Justice and Law Reform[1] stated *inter alia* that:

> "It recognises in a very practical manner the special constitutional status of a person's dwelling and makes it clear that a person may use reasonable force to defend themselves in their home. It allows for the use of such force as is reasonable in the circumstances, to protect people in the dwelling from assault, to protect property, to prevent the commission of a crime, or to make a lawful arrest. The Act also extends the protections it contains to the curtilage of the dwelling, it explicitly provides that a person is not under an obligation to retreat from their home when subject to an intrusion in their home and provides that a person who uses reasonable force, as provided for in the Act, cannot be sued for damages by a burglar and will not be guilty of an offence."

The 2011 Act defines *dwelling* as a building or structure, or a vehicle or vessel which has been constructed or adapted for use as a dwelling, or any part of a dwelling. *Curtilage* in relation to a dwelling is defined as an area immediately surrounding or adjacent to the dwelling which is used in conjunction with that dwelling, other than a public place.[2]

## The Main Provisions

Section 2 of the 2011 Act can be seen as the operative section and in essence provides that it shall not be an offence for a person who is in his or her

---

[1] http://www.justice.ie/en/JELR/Pages/PR12000003, press release dated 12 January 2012.
[2] For the purposes of the 2011 Act, *public place* is defined as any place to which the public have access whether as of right or by permission and whether subject to or free of charge.

dwelling, or for a person who is a lawful occupant of that dwelling, to use force, against a person or against the property of that person, in certain defined circumstances.[3] Those circumstances provide that a person may use such force where:

(a) he or she believes that the person has entered or is entering the dwelling as a trespasser and for the purpose of committing a criminal act; and

(b) the force used is only such as is reasonable in the circumstances as he or she believes them to be.[4]

Importantly, a person will be entitled to rely on the provisions of the 2011 Act even in circumstances where he or she may have been presented with an opportunity to retreat from his or her dwelling.[5]

## The Test as to What Constitutes Reasonable Force in the Circumstances

It would appear that a subjective test will be applied when determining whether or not someone acted reasonably in the circumstances. In general terms, a subjective perspective focuses on the state of mind, the intentions and foresight of the defendant, meaning the home owner/occupier. By contrast, an objective perspective, while focusing on the state of mind of the defendant, asks the question whether an ordinary, reasonable person would have behaved in a similar manner. Reasonableness is determined by an objective test: whether a hypothetical ordinary, reasonable person would have responded in the same way.[6] In terms of a defence to a criminal prosecution, therefore, the subjective test is deemed to be a lesser burden to discharge, i.e. it is not a measure of the actions of the accused against what the behaviour of an ordinary, reasonable person would be; it instead focuses on the particular mindset of the person in the particular set of circumstances.

The general subjective test will, however, be tempered by the further considerations as set out at ss 2(b)(i), (ii) and 2(4). In other words, force[7]

---

[3] See s 2(7) where force may include force causing death.
[4] s 2(a) and (b).
[5] See s 2(5) and 3 of the 2011 Act.
[6] Law Reform Commission, LRC-95-2009, *Report on Defences in Criminal Law* (Law Reform Commission, Dublin, 2009), p 16.
[7] *Force* and the circumstances in which force may be used are defined under s 2(6).

used is only such as is reasonable in the circumstances as he or she believes them to be:

(i) in order to protect him- or herself or another person present in the dwelling from injury, assault, detention or death caused by a criminal act;

(ii) in order to protect his or her property or the property of another from appropriation, destruction or damage caused by a criminal act;

(iii) in order to prevent the commission of a crime, or to effect, or to assist in effecting, a lawful arrest.

Section 2(4) provides that the court shall take into consideration the absence or presence of reasonable grounds when determining whether or not somebody honestly believed that he or she used reasonable force.

Section 2(3) of the 2011 Act would appear to prohibit a person from relying on the provisions of the Act in circumstances where he or she has brought about a situation for the purpose of allowing him or her to use force against another. A person may be entitled to rely on the provisions of the 2011 Act in circumstances where he or she was engaged in a lawful act that brought about the situation, but this would concern a consideration of the circumstances of the case. Interestingly, s 2(8) provides that an act will be deemed to be a "criminal act" even in circumstances where the person acted under duress, where the person acted involuntarily or was intoxicated, where the person was insane or where a person under the age of 12 committed the criminal act.

## Civil Liability

Section 5 of the 2011 Act provides as follows, under the heading of *Civil Liability*:

> Notwithstanding the generality of any other enactment or rule of law concerning the civil liability of persons in relation to trespassers, a person who uses such force as is permitted by section 2 in the circumstances referred to in that section shall not be liable in tort in respect of any injury, loss or damage arising from the use of such force.

Accordingly, s 5 of the 2011 Act should be read in accordance with s 4(3)(a) of the Occupiers' Liability Act 1995 which provides that where a trespasser enters onto land for the purpose of committing an offence, or while present on the land commits an offence, the occupier is relieved of the duty not to act with reckless disregard for the person or his or her property.[8]

## Conclusion

The 2011 Act sets a new departure in Irish tort law with s 5 now explicitly providing a defence in relation to claims in tort for personal injury arising out of the individual's right to defend the home. However, caution is still required as any person wishing to avail of the defence will still need to satisfy a court that he or she believes that the person has entered or is entering the dwelling as a trespasser and for the purpose of committing a criminal act; and the force used is only such as is reasonable in the circumstances as he or she believes them to be.[9] That said the test is subjective.

---

[8] See chapter 10, pp 169–174.
[9] s 2(a) and (b).

# CHAPTER TWELVE

# Animals and the Law

In Ireland, most dog biting attacks are rapid single bites and in one study,[1] in 50 per cent of the cases the owner/bite victim was unable to identify any signal of the dog's intention to bite. Fifty per cent of the victims of dog biting attacks required professional medical assistance following the attack, and seven per cent of the owner group and 31 per cent of the non-owner group required hospital A&E admission and major medical treatment. Dog bites and personal injury caused by animals generally are, therefore, a real concern for property owners.

## When a Dog Attacks Causing Injury

In this situation the owner of the dog is held responsible for the actions of his or her dog in causing personal injury to another individual. Section 21 of the Control of Dogs Act 1986 (the 1986 Act) could not be any clearer, stating that *the owner of a dog shall be liable in damages for damage caused in an attack on any person by the dog* and, as such, this piece of legislation is said to impose what is termed in the law as *strict liability* on the owner of the offending dog.

Strict liability in this area of tort law is the imposition of liability on a party without a finding of fault,[2] meaning that the plaintiff need only prove that the *tort* or incident causing the personal injury occurred, and that the defendant's dog was responsible. Therefore the person who suffers the bite and wishes to bring a claim for compensation for personal injury and other associated damages need only prove that he or she was bitten and thereafter prove that the dog is owned by a certain individual.

---

[1] As per Edmond O'Sullivan, a full-time veterinary inspector in Cork County Council and the author of a report completed for his Master of Veterinary Medicine at UCD: see http://www.ucd.ie/news/0710_october/081007_dog_bite.html: for more detail on his findings (21 March 2012).

[2] Fault such as negligence or tortuous intent.

Section 21 of the 1986 Act replaces the common law *scienter principle* as the overriding principle of law in this area. In general terms, the *scienter principle* meant that any individual who suffered a dog bite would have to first prove that the dog in question had a previous *mischievous or vicious propensity*: the rationale being if the owner of the dog was aware of such a character in the dog he or she would be on notice to exert more control over the animal given the increased likelihood of an attack by that dog.

It may be stated with confidence, therefore, that since the enactment of s 21 of the 1986 Act it is a great deal easier for solicitors to achieve compensation for personal injury and associated damages arising out of dog bites as a result of the shift away from the *scienter principle*.

## When a Dog Attacks a Trespasser

Where a person enters onto a dog owner's land without invitation, express or implied, that person is known as a trespasser. Pursuant to s 21(3) of the 1986 Act, a trespasser once bitten and injured by a dog may not rely on the strict liability as afforded by s 21 of the 1986 Act, but must instead resort to the old *scienter principle* and set about discharging the burden of proof in relation to the animal in question having a *mischievous or vicious propensity*.

Householders with dogs would be strongly advised to take out a policy of home insurance that includes insurance covering compensation payable to a third party, i.e. a neighbour's child, in the event that their dog causes personal injury to a person. When discussing the policy with the insurance company, *the proposer*, that is the person taking out the policy of insurance, must be *uberrima fides*, or act with the utmost good faith in answering the questions of the insurer in allowing it to determine if it is willing to insure the risk associated with the animal. The insurance company will have no knowledge of a mischievous or vicious propensity of the dog and instead rely on the owner to be forthcoming in this regard. If the dog is found to have had such a mischievous or vicious propensity in the past, the insurer may seek to set aside the policy of insurance as a result of such non-disclosure in relation to new claims on the policy in this regard.

Similarly, the person taking out the policy of insurance must be aware that even if he or she has a policy that covers the risk associated with keeping a dog, the insurance company may not be obliged to pay out compensation to an injured third party if it is found that the dog owner was under an obligation to keep the pet securely muzzled when in public. It may be the case, for example, that the breed concerned was classified as a dangerous breed by the insurance company. No one policy of insurance will be the same as the next and the proposer must endeavour to read the small print and always act within the confines of the policy especially when bringing the dog out into the public domain.

## Guard Dog Signs

Individuals who keep a sign warning people of the presence of a guard dog or a vicious dog at the entrance to their private residences may in fact be going some way to acknowledging that their own dog is one with a mischievous or vicious propensity as per the *scienter principle*. The presence of these signs, therefore, may make it more difficult for the dog owner to offer a defence in a claim for damages arising out of personal injury caused by his or her dog towards a trespasser to his or her property.

## Dogs and Injury Done to Livestock

Subsections 21(1) and (2) of the 1986 Act provide as follows:

> 21.—(1) The owner of a dog shall be liable in damages for damage caused in an attack on any person by the dog and for injury done by it to any livestock; and it shall not be necessary for the person seeking such damages to show a previous mischievous propensity in the dog, or the owner's knowledge of such previous propensity, or to that such injury or damage was attributable to neglect on the part of the owner.

> (2) Where livestock are injured by a dog on land on to which they had strayed, and either the dog belonged to the occupier of the land or its presence on the land was authorised by the occupier, a person shall not be liable under this section in respect of injury done to the livestock, unless the person caused the dog to attack the livestock.

The above provisions of the 1986 Act appear to afford more protection to livestock than to humans in relation to the capacity to claim an award in damages arising out of injury inflicted by a dog.

For example, as per s 21(1) the dog must cause the injury in an *attack* whilst the threshold for livestock is *for injury done*. This essentially means that if a cow is walking out of a trailer and trips and falls over a dog, breaking a leg which results in it being put down, the owner of the dog is responsible. If, on the other hand, a person walks out of a shop and trips over a dog and breaks his or her leg, the owner of the dog is not liable pursuant to s 21 as the person was not attacked by the dog. As discussed in chapter 15, it is of course still open to the injured party to explore a cause of action in negligence.

## If One's Dog Injures Another's Livestock on One's Own Land

Section 22 of the 1986 Act does not hold a dog owner responsible for the actions of his or her dog where livestock has strayed onto the dog owner's lands and where the owner of the dog does not cause his or her dog to attack the livestock.

## When a Livestock Owner May Shoot a Dog to Kill

Section 23 of the 1986 Act provides farmers with a complete defence to an action for damages if they can show that they had reasonable grounds to shoot the dog as it was about to *worry* or was in the process of *worrying* their livestock and there was no other reasonable means of ending or preventing the worrying. The 1986 Act describes *worry* in relation to livestock as to attack or kill or to chase livestock in such a way as may reasonably be expected *to cause the death of or injury or suffering to the livestock or to result in financial loss to the owner of the livestock*. There is an obligation on the person who has shot the dog to report the shooting to the member in charge at the nearest Garda Station within 48 hours of the shooting. This requirement subsists whether the dog has been shot dead or is merely injured.

## Dangerous Dogs

The Control of Dogs Regulations 1998[3] place controls on 10 breeds of dogs, namely: the American Pit Bull Terrier; English Bull Terrier; Staffordshire Bull Terrier; Bull Mastiff; Doberman Pinscher; German Shepherd (Alsatian); Rhodesian Ridgeback; Rottweiler; Japanese Akita; Japanese Tosa; and on every dog of the type commonly known as a Ban Dog (or Bandog).

The controls, which must be observed when the dog is in a public place, require that these dogs, or strains and crosses thereof, must be kept on a

---

[3] SI No 442 of 1998.

strong short lead (only up to two metres long) by a person over 16 years of age who is capable of controlling them. Such dogs must also be securely muzzled.

## Reporting a Dangerous Dog

Under s 22 of the 1986 Act any interested party may bring a complaint to the District Court in relation to a dangerous dog not being kept under proper control. Where it appears to the court that the dog is dangerous and not kept under proper control, the court may order that the dog be kept under such control or be destroyed. Whenever the court orders the destruction of a dog, it may direct that the dog be delivered to a dog warden or any suitable person to be destroyed, and may even direct that the expenses of the destruction of the dog be borne by the owner of the dog.

Where a dog is proved to have caused damage in an attack on any person, or to have injured livestock, it may be dealt with under this section as a dangerous dog which has not been kept under proper control. If, therefore, a member of the public is seriously worried about the potential of a dog to cause harm and have made such a compliant to the local authority and had no satisfactory response it is open to him or her to bring the case him or herself to the District Court. In order to commence this process, the form in Appendix 13 must be completed and served on the owner of the purportedly dangerous dog.

Furthermore, s 26 of the 1986 Act allows for the issuing of search warrants if a judge of the District Court or a Peace Commissioner is satisfied by the information on oath of a member of the Garda Síochána that there are reasonable grounds for believing that a dog has attacked a person or has worried livestock. A search warrant under this section authorises the member of the Garda Síochána named in the search warrant, along with such other members of the Garda Síochána as may be necessary and presumably the dog warden, to enter the premises specified in the search warrant and search for the dog. The member of the Garda Síochána who is authorised by a search warrant under this section to enter a premises may also use such force as may be reasonably necessary to secure entry into the premises. Any dog which is found during a search pursuant to a search warrant under this section may be removed from the premises and detained by the Garda Síochána for examination.

## Where a Dangerous Dog is Inhibiting Access to Lands

In *Grainger v Finlay*[4] the plaintiff complained that the defendant kept a vicious and dangerous dog upon his land which prevented the plaintiff and his family from using a right of way which passed close to the defendant's land. The plaintiff lost his case on a technical point, as he never stated in the pleadings grounding his case that his fear, and the fear of his family, in using the right of way was a reasonable one. Had he done so and had he been able to satisfy the court of the truth of this claim, then the court it seems would have allowed him to recover.

Despite the plaintiff losing the case, the decision is a precedent for dealing with a dangerous dog causing a nuisance through a civil action in the courts. The case of *Grainger v Finlay* demonstrates that dangerous dog owners leave themselves open to a claim in damages for nuisance and may be compelled to exert due control over their dog by way of an injunction obtained from the courts. Furthermore, the unsuccessful party will, as a matter of course, have to pay the costs of the winning party.

## Stray Dogs

In relation to stray dogs s 11 of the 1986 Act obliges dog wardens to take all reasonable steps to seize and detain any dog that appears to them to be a stray dog. The dog warden may also enter any premises, other than a dwelling, for the purposes of such seizure and detention. Similarly, a member of the Garda Síochána may seize and detain any dog that appears to him or her to be a stray dog and may enter any premises, other than a dwelling, for the purposes of such seizure and detention.

Naturally, in the first instance, if an individual is worried about a stray dog causing a nuisance he or she should contact his or her local authority and report same to the dog warden with responsibility for that administrative area.

## What To Do About Barking Dogs?

Excessively barking dogs are a major source of annoyance for families trying to enjoy the peace of their own homes. Such problems are compounded when families have infant children. The first step in any such situation is to contact one's neighbour to make him or her aware as

---

[4] (1858) 7 ICLR 417, 3 Ir Jur N.S. 175.

to how the barking affects one and one's family in an effort to try and resolve the matter in a mutually convenient fashion. However, not all neighbours are amenable to such an approach and sometimes the aggrieved neighbour is left with little choice but to pursue a more formal course of action to resolve matters.

Under s 25 of the 1986 Act it is open to any person to make a complaint to the District Court where it appears that a nuisance has been created by excessive dog barking.[5] Before any person makes a complaint to the District Court in relation to a nuisance caused by the excessive barking of a dog, he or she must serve a notice in the prescribed form, within such time as may be specified in the notice. The notice must inform the occupier of the premises where the dog is kept of the intention to make such a complaint.

Any person who intends to make a compliant in this regard should first of all refer to chapter 9 on noise orders for advice and guidance on practice and procedure as to how to best to formulate a successful application for a Dog Nuisance Order, as the evidence required will be similar to that for a noise order pursuant to s 108 of the Environmental Protection Agency Act 1992. The relevant noise and nuisance diary sheet that needs to be presented in court to substantiate one's claim may be found at Appendix 15.

If satisfied with the application, the District Court may order the occupier of the premises in which the dog is kept to abate the nuisance by exercising due control over the dog. Alternatively, the court may make an order limiting the number of dogs to be kept by the respondent on his or her premises. In more serious instances of excessive barking the District Court may direct that the dog be delivered to a dog warden to be dealt with as if the dog were an unwanted dog.

Section 12 of the 1986 Act details such provisions in relation to unwanted dogs and empowers the local authority to arrange for the dog's destruction in a humane manner, or alternatively to take the dog and dispose of it by giving it to a new owner. The person to whom the dog is given becomes the new legal owner of the dog and the title of its previous owner is extinguished.

---

[5] The relevant application form is contained in Appendix 14.

It is also open to the local authority to bring such applications. Individuals may wish to first approach their local authority with a copy of their nuisance noise diary sheet in order to determine if the local authority will bring the application pursuant to s 25 of the 1986 Act. A copy of the noise and nuisance diary sheet needs to be provided to the local authority to substantiate the claims made. In the event that the local authority fails to proceed with the application, this should not be interpreted by the complainant as indicating a particular weakness in his or her case but may simply be due to time and resource constraints on the local authority. As such, the complainant should proceed on his or her own or in tandem with other affected neighbours.

There is no difficulty with a group of neighbours coming together to submit one application to the District Court. If this is the chosen course of action then one person need only sign the application form and indicate that he or she is doing so on behalf of and with the consent of the other named concerned individuals.

## Dog Identification and Dog Licences

Dog identification becomes important when one is seeking to have the owner of a dog held responsible for the actions of his or her dog and one must determine the identity of that owner. The Control of Dogs Regulations 1998 (SI No 442 of 1998) do not require a dog owner to microchip his or her dog but does require the owner or other person in charge of a dog to ensure that, at all times, the dog wears a collar having the name and address of the owner on an attached plate, badge or disc. The regulations contain penalties for non-compliance with this requirement and for defacing or rendering illegible the above particulars.

## Dog Fouling

Section 22 of the Litter Pollution Act 1997 makes it an offence for the person in charge of a dog not to clean up when his or her dog fouls in a public place. Failure to clean up one's dog's waste can lead to a €150 "on-the-spot" fine or on summary conviction to a fine of up to €3,000.

Again, one's local authority will have a litter warden who will be able to deal with such complaints and bring the necessary District Court proceedings if deemed appropriate. If the issue arises that the dog is not fouling in a public place but is doing so on private property the matter will be left to the individuals concerned to be resolved as a civil matter. Chapter 15 details possible civil remedies in this regard.

## Horses

Under the Control of Horses Act 1996 (the 1996 Act) all local authorities (city and county councils) are responsible for the control of horses in their areas. The term *horse* under the 1996 Act covers horses, donkeys, mules and hinnies or female mules.

Under s 17 of the 1996 Act, a local authority may, through the implementation of bye-laws, declare all or any part of its functional area to be a *Control Area*. In order to be classified as a *control area* the local authority must be satisfied that horses in that area should be licensed having regard to the need to control the keeping of horses, the need to prevent nuisance, annoyance or injury to persons or damage to property by horses and such other matters as it considers relevant.

The development of this legislation came about in response to problems, particularly in urban areas, with horses straying, roaming, causing danger on roads and being ridden without proper restraint by underage riders. In order to keep a horse in a designated control area, the horse owner must obtain a horse licence,[6] issued by his or her local authority. Failure to have a horse licence in a control area can mean an on-the-spot fine or it could mean that the horse could be seized and impounded. If a horse is owned and kept outside of a control area, there is no obligation to obtain a horse licence.

In order to obtain the horse licence, s 20 the 1996 Act allows for an inspector from the local authority to visit the premises at which it is proposed to stable a horse. The inspector must be satisfied that proper accommodation, food and water and veterinary attention will be provided for the horse.

## Powers to Seize a Horse

Local authorities have the power to appoint authorised persons to deal with any problems relating to the control of horses. Such powers are not reserved for so-called control areas but are applicable in relation to all horses whatever their location. Authorised persons from the local authority have, in accordance with ss 34 and 37 of the 1996 Act, the power

---

[6] s 18 of the 1996 Act.

to seize and impound the horse, impose an on-the-spot fine and take court proceedings against its owner.

Furthermore, members of the Gardaí and authorised persons from the local authority have the right to seize and detain horses in circumstances where they suspect a horse is:

- a stray;
- causing a nuisance;
- being mistreated;
- not under adequate control;
- posing a threat to other people or property;
- posing a threat to the health and welfare of other people and animals;
- not identifiable or capable of being identified;
- in need of veterinary attention and is unlikely to receive this care;
- in an area/kept in an area/being ridden/driven in an area where it is not allowed by the local authority; and/or
- kept in a local authority Control Area without a licence.

Pursuant to s 40 of the 1996 Act, if a horse has been detained on two or more occasions within the previous 12 months, the local authority may decide to dispose of the horse. Any complaint in relation to nuisance horses should be directed to the local authority or the Gardaí and the complainant should require that the appropriate action be taken in accordance with the powers vested in the local authority and the Gardaí under the 1996 Act.

## Livestock on the Roads

The governing piece of legislation in this area is the Animals Act 1985 (the 1985 Act). Prior to the coming into force of this piece of legislation, the law in Ireland was similar to the law in England,[7] which was particularly indulgent to the owners of animals which stray onto the highway. Prior to the enactment of s 2 of the 1985 Act, the rule was very much *driver beware*, in that livestock holders enjoyed immunity from liability for property damage and injury caused by stray animals on public roads.

This section has since been interpreted by a decision of the High Court in the case of *O'Reilly v Lavelle*[8] as raising the presumption of a legal doctrine

---

[7] *Searle v Wallbank* [1947] AC 341.
[8] [1990] 2 IR 372.

known as *res ipsa loquitur* or *the facts speak for themselves*. Normally in a case where one is being sued for property damage or personal injury arising out of the collision of a car with a farm animal, it would be for the plaintiff, the person bringing the claim, to prove on the balance of probabilities that the livestock owner was negligent in allowing the livestock wander onto the road to cause the accident.

The effect of s 2 of the 1985 Act allows for the doctrine of *res ipsa loquitur* to apply meaning that the normal rules of evidence in relation to the burden of proof are reversed and it is the livestock owner who must prove, in the first instance, that he or she was not negligent in allowing the livestock wander onto the road. All the person bringing the claim need show is that the collision with the animal occurred and that the particular animal belongs to the owner.

However, a Supreme Court decision in 2005, *O'Shea v Anhold*,[9] expanded on the applicable principle further. In that case a Mr Patrick O'Shea sued a Horse Holiday farm and a Mr Tilman Anhold for damages for personal injuries and loss which he sustained as a result of a car collision with a horse owned by Horse Holiday Farm Ltd, the second-named defendant.

The High Court found in favour of the plaintiff as against the second-named defendant, the company operated by the first-named defendant, Mr Tilman Anhold. The court surmised that "[t]he situation was that either the fencing on the laneway or field was inadequate or someone had opened the gate, let out one horse and closed the gate again. On balance the first possibility was much more likely than the second".

In the course of the Supreme Court appeal, the plaintiff argued that he had done everything in his power to prevent the animal from breaking from the field in which it was grazing. Mr Anhold stated that on the evening of the accident, at 4.30 pm, he fed the horses. The horses were in a concrete portion between two gates when they were fed. The gate leading to a field was open. He left the horses on the concrete portion and walked through to the spring loaded roadside gate and closed it. He was sure that the gate was closed as it had to be lifted so that the bolt could be moved slowly.

---

[9] Unreported, Supreme Court, 23 October 1996.

Expert witnesses called on behalf of Mr Anhold testified that the fencing was adequate for ordinary commercial purposes. They were satisfied that the only way a horse could have escaped was if somebody had opened the gate. This evidence was not disputed by Mr O'Shea.

Keane CJ, in summing up the case, said that if the defendants had taken all the precautions which a reasonable person in their position ought to have taken to prevent a horse escaping, then the fact that the horse succeeded in getting onto the road was not a result of any negligence on their part.

The former Chief Justice went on to say that s 2 of the 1985 Act had abolished the somewhat anomalous immunity from the ordinary law of negligence which the owners of land from which animals strayed on to the highway previously enjoyed. It had not, however, imposed any form of absolute liability on such persons. He said:

> ". . . to hold the defendants liable for negligence in the circumstances of this case where the admitted evidence was that they had taken all reasonable precautions which a reasonable person would take to prevent the particular animals, a herd of horses, from straying onto the road, would be to impose a higher duty than "to take such reasonable care" recognised by the Oireachtas as applying to such persons."

Therefore, any individual holding livestock on his or her lands needs to take all reasonable precautions; that is to say that each person holding livestock on his or her lands, and especially livestock on lands near to or adjoining the highway, owes a duty to behave as a reasonable person would under the same or similar circumstances. Best practice therefore would dictate that such livestock holders should have a documented procedure in place for the routine checking of fencing and gates on their lands in an effort to prove, if ever the need arises, that they have taken all reasonable steps to ensure that the fences and gates to their lands are well maintained and regularly checked for defects. Better again if the livestock owner adopts a policy of pad locking gates that lead onto the public highway.

## Conclusion

Many of the fears of animal and property owners will be assuaged by having in place a satisfactory policy of home and/or farm insurance which will normally cover the risks of animals causing injury to other animals or indeed individuals. As with all policies of insurance the onus is on the person taking out the policy to be fully forthcoming with the insurance company in relation to any perceived risks associated with a particular animal. If for example the home owner knows that their dog has a vicious propensity then this should be made clear to the insurance coming so as the associated risk may be insured accordingly. To hold back such vital information from the insurance company could well result in the insurance company refusing to cover any loss arising out of the actions of the animal concerned.

For farmers much of the worry regards the straying of livestock causing property damage and or personal injury will be assuaged by simply adopting a policy of pad locking gates that adjoin the public highway.

## Appendix 13

No. 91.1

O.91, r.3(3)

### CONTROL OF DOGS ACT 1986

Section 22(1)(a)

### NOTICE OF INTENTION TO MAKE COMPLAINT THAT A DOG IS DANGEROUS

District Court Area of District No.

_____Complainant

_____Defendant

WHEREAS the above-named complainant, of _____ is an interested person within the meaning of section 22(1)(a) of the above Act, AND

the above-named defendant, whose premises is at _____ in court *(area and) district aforesaid, is *(the owner) *(the person in charge) of a dog.

TAKE NOTICE that the complainant intends to make complaint to the District Court sitting at _____ on the day of 19 at a.m./p.m. pursuant to the said section 22(1)(a) that the said dog is dangerous and not kept under proper control, by reason of the following:-

† that on the \_\_\_\_\_ day of \_\_\_\_\_ 20 at Dated this \_\_\_\_\_ day of \_\_\_\_ 20.

Signed _____

Complainant/Solicitor for Complainant

To

of

(Owner of the dog)

*(to

of

Person in charge of the dog).


* Delete words inapplicable
† State cause of complaint

## Appendix 14

**NOTICE OF INTENTION TO MAKE A COMPLAINT TO THE DISTRICT COURT IN RELATION TO NUISANCE ALLEGED TO BE CAUSED BY THE EXCESSIVE BARKING OF A DOG**

District Court Area of _____ District No_____

To _____

(Occupier)

of_____

_____

_____

(the premises in which the dog is kept)

Notice is hereby given, in pursuance of section 25 (2) of the Control of Dogs Act 1986, that I _____ of _____ intend to make a complaint to the District Court sitting at _____ on the _____ day of _____, at ____ am/pm, being a date within seven days from the date hereof, in respect of the nuisance which I allege to have been caused by the excessive barking of a dog kept in the above-named premises, situated in the said court area and district.

Where it appears to the District Court that a nuisance has been created as a result of excessive barking, the Court may:—

(a) order you to abate the nuisance by exercising due control over the dog;

(b) make an order limiting for such period as may be specified in the order the number of dogs to be kept by you on your premises;

(c) direct that the dog be delivered to a dog warden to be dealt with by him, as if the dog were an unwanted dog, in accordance with the provisions of the Control of Dogs Act 1986.

Dated this _____ day of _____

Signed _____

# Appendix 15

Noise Diary Sheet – Control of Dogs Act 1986

Application Pursuant to Section 25

Nuisance By Barking Dogs

YOUR DETAILS:

Name: _____

Address: _____

_____

_____

Source of Noise Problem: _____

| Date | Start Time | Finish Time | Type of Noise/ Nuisance | How it affects me |
|------|-----------|-------------|-------------------------|-------------------|
|      |           |             |                         |                   |
|      |           |             |                         |                   |
|      |           |             |                         |                   |
|      |           |             |                         |                   |
|      |           |             |                         |                   |

I certify that the above record is a true statement of the nuisance/noise complained of

Signed: _____

Date: _____

# CHAPTER THIRTEEN

# Backyard Burning of Waste

The term *backyard burning* is applied to the uncontrolled burning of waste which is frequently carried out in backyards and in gardens, but the term also refers to the burning of any waste in open fires, ranges and other solid fuel appliances or in the open generally and includes the burning of waste on building sites. The Environmental Protection Agency (EPA) highlighted backyard burning as a significant issue in its 2005 report on "The Nature and Extent of Unauthorised Waste Activity in Ireland".[1] In that report the EPA indicated that 80 per cent of local authorities had identified backyard burning as being a significant problem. Uncontrolled burning of this nature is estimated to account for approximately 50 per cent of dioxins[2] released into the Irish environment.

## The Problems

Whereas before neighbours were concerned about the nuisance aspect of smoke billowing across their gardens, and ruining their washing, the problem in modern times has been compounded with the application of chemicals to preserve and enhance products and the widespread use of metals and plastic in most manufacturing items. As a result of the changes in manufacturing processes, burning is far more harmful to our health than previously thought as the dioxins released by incineration can increase the risk of heart disease, can aggravate respiratory ailments such as asthma and emphysema, and can cause rashes, nausea, or headaches.

---

[1] http://www.epa.ie/downloads/pubs/waste/unauthorisedwaste/name,13695,en.html (22 March 2012).

[2] Dioxins are a group of chemicals known to increase the likelihood of cancer. An unwanted by-product of many manufacturing methods, they are formed when heating processes involve the use or production of certain chemicals, particularly chlorine. But they are also produced during many man-made events which involve combustion such as waste incineration.

Burning rubbish in barrels produces significantly higher levels of dioxins as the barrel receives limited oxygen, and thus burns at fairly low temperatures, producing not only dioxins, but a great deal of smoke and other pollutants.

## The Law

There are two laws which prevent the burning of waste, even when waste is being burned as an alternative fuel. The Air Pollution Act 1987 prohibits the discharge of emissions in such a quantity, or in such a manner, as to be a nuisance.[3]

Part IV of the Waste Management Act 1996 states that there is a general duty on people to dispose of their waste in an environmentally friendly manner and, more specifically, s 32 of the Waste Management Acts 1996 to 2011 states that a *person shall not hold, transport, recover or dispose of waste in a manner that causes or is likely to cause environmental pollution.* Section 4 of the Air Pollution Act 1987 defines air pollution as *a condition of the atmosphere in which a pollutant is present in such a quantity as to be liable to:*

(i)   *be injurious to public health; or*

(ii)   *have a deleterious effect on flora or fauna or damage property; or*

(iii)   *impair or interfere with amenities or with the environment.*

## The Waste Management (Prohibition of Waste Disposal by Burning) Regulations 2009[4]

In 2009, the then Minister for the Environment, Heritage and Local Government, in exercising the powers conferred on him by ss 7, 18 and 39 of the then Waste Management Acts 1996 to 2008 and s 53 of the Air Pollution Act 1987 banned outright the disposal of waste by burning. The Waste Management (Prohibition of Waste Disposal by Burning) Regulations 2009 (the 2009 Regulations), make more explicit the offence of the disposal of waste by uncontrolled burning and various actions are prohibited by the 2009 Regulations, including such *disposal within the curtilage of a dwelling.* Failure to comply with the new regulations is an offence and fines of up to €3,000 are applicable for summary offences brought to court.

---

[3] s 24(2) of the Air Pollution Act 1987.
[4] SI No 286 of 2009.

The following provisions now apply as a result of the coming into force of the 2009 Regulations:

- It is an offence to burn any type of waste[5] including garden waste[6];
- The use of devices to burn waste, such as "domestic waste incinerators" which are often advertised for sale, is an offence;
- It is an offence to burn household waste by use of stoves or open fires[7]; and
- Untreated or uncontaminated wood waste and other similar materials can be used in barbeques for the purpose of cooking food.[8]

## Hallowe'en and Celebratory Bonfires

Hallowe'en and celebratory bonfires are only permissible at events determined by the local authority for the area concerned. If the bonfire is to be sanctioned by the local authority, the waste to be burned must only consist of untreated or uncontaminated wood waste or similar materials.[9] If an individual is concerned about a particular fire being organised, he or she needs to make contact with his or her local authority's environment section and enquire as to whether the fire being organised has been sanctioned by the local authority and if not, the complainant should deliver a letter of complaint to the local authority.

Should any sporting club wish to organise a celebratory bonfire an application should be made to the local authority for permission. It would be expected that the organisers would need to undertake to the local authority to use untreated or uncontaminated wood waste or similar materials.

## Farmers and the Law on Burning Vegetative Waste

The 2009 Regulations[10] do provide an exemption, which applies until 1 January 2014, to allow farmers to dispose by burning of untreated/ uncontaminated wood, trees, trimmings, leaves, bushes or similar materials[11] generated by agricultural practices as a *final measure*. A final

---

[5] Reg 4(1).
[6] Reg 5(1)(a).
[7] Regs 3 and 4.
[8] Reg 5(1)(d).
[9] Reg 5(1)(e).
[10] Reg 5.
[11] This exemption does not apply unless the waste is generated by agricultural practices so it would not apply to leaves, grass and bushes in a domestic garden for example.

measure means that farmers must declare that such burning will be done, following the application of the waste hierarchy, as follows:

i.   reduction of waste produced in accordance with best agricultural practice;
ii.  re-use of waste where practicable;
iii. recycling of waste through shredding and use as compost or wood chippings, where practicable;
iv.  salvage of waste for use as fuel, where practicable; and
v.   disposal, where none of the options at (i) to (iv) above are practicable or economically viable, but subject to the following conditions:
  a.  adequate measures will be taken to limit the overall nuisance or possibilities for endangering human health or causing environmental pollution; and
  b.  no accelerants will be used when undertaking the disposal activity.

This essentially means that the farmer or holder of the waste must, prior to disposal by burning, explore all other more environmentally friendly methods of treatment of his or her green waste starting with reduction, recycling by shredding, composting or wood chipping before proceeding to disposal by burning. Thereafter, where none of these methods are deemed by the farmer concerned or the holder of the waste to be practicable or economically viable, he or she must notify the local authority by way of a statutory notice, a copy of which is found in Appendix 16, of his or her intention to burn such waste. There are no mandatory notification. In the absence of any follow up a complaint may be made to the Ombudsman as detailed in chapter 15.

## Conclusion

As seen above backyard burning is obviously a significant environmental hazard due to the dioxins released from the burning of waste. The Waste Management (Prohibition of Waste Disposal by Burning) Regulations 2009 and in particular the €3,000 fine on summary conviction should act as a necessary deterrent in controlling the problem. Any party concerned about a breach of the regulation should report same to their local authority who should have their environment section follow up on the complaint.

# Appendix 16

## Schedule
Statutory Notice

Checklist of advance information to be provided by a person to a local authority concerning the proposed burning of agricultural waste in accordance with the provisions of Regulation 5(1)(*a*).

Name:

Address: (correspondence address)

Telephone:

Local authority administrative area:

I hereby give notice to (give the name of the local authority) of my intention to burn waste solely consisting of uncontaminated (free of dangerous substances, preservatives or other artificial impregnation or coating) wood, trees, tree trimmings, leaves, or brush, or other similar waste generated by agricultural practices (but excluding garden and park wastes and cemetery wastes and waste arising from infrastructural development works)

on (give the proposed date of the burning) at (location where proposed burning will take place).

Declaration of suitability: I declare that such burning will be done as a final measure following the application of the following waste hierarchy:

i.   reduction of waste arisings in accordance with best agricultural practice,

ii.  reuse of waste where practicable,

iii. recycling of waste through shredding and use as compost or wood chippings, where practicable,

iv.  salvage of waste for use as fuel, where practicable,

v.   disposal, where none of the options at (i) to (iv) above are practicable or economically viable but subject to the following conditions—

(I)   adequate measures will be taken to limit the overall nuisance or possibilities for endangering human health or causing environmental pollution, and

(II)  no accelerants will be used when undertaking the disposal activity.

_____ Name (block capitals)

Date _____

WARNING. A person who gives false or misleading information for the purpose of this notice may be guilty of an offence.

# CHAPTER FOURTEEN

# Low Flying Aircraft

A s strange as it may seem, this is and was a real source of annoyance and nuisance for a great number of Irish householders in the recent past. It was more of a problem during the economic boom when Ireland had at one time the greatest numbers of helicopters per capita in the world.[1] Helicopters and low flying fixed wing aircraft can be a cause of great annoyance in terms of noise and invasion of privacy. They may also give rise to safety concerns so much so that their use could constitute an attack on an individual's right to the peaceful enjoyment of their home.

The Irish Aviation Authority[2] is the body responsible for the regulation and enforcement of the laws in this area and derives its powers from the Irish Aviation Authority Act 1993 (as amended).[3] The Aviation Authority is a State-owned company responsible for the regulation of safety aspects of air travel. It is also responsible for providing Air Traffic Control (ATC) services to Ireland's three main airports, namely Dublin, Shannon and Cork. The Authority regulates the safety standards of Irish civil aviation and provides air traffic management and aeronautical communications services in Irish-controlled airspace.

However, as detailed below, it is not the work of the Aviation Authority to investigate noise complaints but to ensure adherence to the so-called rules of the air, which include restrictions on the height at which aircraft may fly.

---

[1] www.guardian.co.uk/business/ireland-business-blog-with-lisa-ocarroll/2010/nov/12/lisa-o-carroll-ireland-business-Blog (3 May 2012).

[2] Not to be confused with the Commission for Aviation Regulation which is responsible for regulation of the economic aspects of air travel in the State.

[3] As amended by the Air Navigation and Transport (Amendment) Act 1998 (No 24 of 1998), the Aviation Regulation Act 2001 (No 1 of 2001) and the Aviation Act 2006 (No 7 2006).

## Rules of the Air — Flight Restrictions

The actual detail in relation to what constitutes negligent or reckless operation of an aircraft is to be found in the Irish Aviation Authority (Rules of the Air) Order 2004, known as the *rules of the air*.[4]

## Flying Over a House and People

Rule 3 of the rules of the air states that, except as permitted by the appropriate authority, aircraft shall not be flown over congested areas of cities, towns or settlements or over an assembly of persons, at less than a height of 450 metres (1,500 ft) above the ground or water, or a height of 300 metres (1,000 ft) above the highest obstacle within a radius of 600 metres from the aircraft, or such other height as would permit, in the event of the failure of a power unit, a safe forced landing to be made. In relation to flying an aircraft in other areas, an aircraft may not be flown closer than 150 metres (500 ft) to any person, vehicle, vessel or structure, or at a height less than 150 metres (500 ft) above the ground or water.

## Power of the Aviation Authority to Prosecute

Under s 74(2) of the Irish Aviation Authority Act 1993, the Aviation Authority has the capacity to prosecute the operator of an aircraft and the pilot in command in relation to a contravention of a provision of the Act or any of the Rules of the Air made pursuant to the Act. Any such person shall be guilty of an offence.[5] This provision does not apply to aircraft controlled by agencies of the state such as Customs and An Garda Síochána.[6]

A person found guilty of an offence under the Act is liable on summary conviction to a fine not exceeding €5,000 or to imprisonment for a term not exceeding six months or to both.[7] Under s 74(6) it shall be a defence for the person to prove that the contravention concerned was due to what is termed as *stress of weather* or other unavoidable difficulties.

---

[4] SI No 72 of 2004 — Irish Aviation Authority (Rules of the Air) Order 2004.
[5] Interestingly, s 74(3) states, notwithstanding s 10(4) of the Petty Sessions (Ireland) Act 1851, summary proceedings for an offence under this Act may be instituted within 12 months from the date of the offence.
[6] s 3 of the Irish Aviation Act 1993
[7] s 2 (c)(i) of the Aviation Act 2006.

## Complaints Procedure

Would be complainants are referred to the complaints submission form[8] in Appendix 17, which should be completed as accurately and as with as much of the required detail as is possible in order to allow for the Irish Aviation Authority to carry out effective enquiries.

Without the aircraft registration details it is difficult to determine the identity of the aircraft in question. The registration markings on a fixed wing aircraft will normally be displayed on the underside of the wings and on both sides of the aircraft. In respect of helicopters, the registration markings are normally displayed on both sides of the tail of the helicopter. The registration details may be important as a large number of helicopters and light aircraft operate in what is known as uncontrolled airspace. In such instances, pilots operate on a *see and be seen* basis and the pilot is not required to file a flight plan or to contact air traffic control.

That said, it will not necessarily be fatal to any application for an investigation if the registration markings of the particular aircraft are not provided to the Aviation Authority as it may still be able to trace same with details of the location, date, time and details of the incident(s) of low flying. It may also be able to extract information from radar installations based in Cork, Dublin and Shannon, and obviously if a helicopter is habitually stationed at a particular address, the Aviation Authority should be able to locate it.

The pilot/owner of any aircraft allegedly involved in a breach of the rules of the air will be required to co-operate fully with the investigation by the Aviation Authority and any non-co-operation may be deemed to be an offence in accordance with s 74(5) of the Irish Aviation Authority Act 1993. In certain instances of helicopters causing annoyance to neighbours, matters may be resolved by the Aviation Authority prescribing a particular route to the helicopter operator in order to minimise any disturbance to an adjoining landowner.[9]

Complaints forms should be forwarded to:

Low Flying Aircraft Reports,

---

[8] This is not a statutory requirement pursuant to any of the Aviation Acts, but is designed to provide the Irish Aviation Authority investigating officer with as much detail as is possible.

[9] Rule 3(2)(b) of the Irish Aviation Authority (Rules of the Air) Order 2004.

Flight Operations Department,

Irish Aviation Authority,

The Times Building,

11-12 D'Olier Street,

Dublin 2.

## Planning Law and Helicopters

Chapter 6 deals in detail with the *exempted development*, meaning a development for which planning permission is not required. Such class of development constituting exempted development has been laid out in detail in the Planning and Development Regulations 2001. There is no exemption from an obligation to obtain planning permission for a heliport[10] or a private aerodrome in any context.

If a neighbour is suffering an annoyance or nuisance from a helicopter being kept at a heliport that does not have the benefit of planning permission, the aggrieved party needs to complete the unauthorised development complaints form[11] and submit same to his or her local authority who are then obliged to investigate the matter as a breach of the planning code.

## Noise Disturbance and Low Flying Aircraft

Chapter 9 deals in detail with applications to the District Court for noise orders pursuant to s 108 of the Environmental Protection Agency Act 1992, and advises in relation to the maintenance of a noise diary form[12] and the necessary practice and procedural requirements for bringing such applications to the District Court. While the law does not specifically mention an exact level or standard of noise that is illegal, the frequent operation of a helicopter on adjoining lands may satisfy the necessary test as a noise that is of *such duration or pitch or occurring at such times as to give reasonable cause for annoyance to a person in any premises in the neighbourhood.*[13]

---

[10] Official aviation term for a helicopter pad.

[11] See Appendix 4.

[12] See Appendix 7.

[13] Definition as per s 108 of the Environmental Protection Agency Act 1992.

A local authority has the power to investigate complaints about neighbourhood noise, and failing a satisfactory response from one's local authority, it is open to any concerned individual to bring the application for a noise order in the District Court.

## Conclusion

The Aviation Authority regulates the safety standards of Irish civil aviation and provides air traffic management and aeronautical communications services in Irish controlled airspace. However, it has no remit in law to investigate complaints in relation to noise disturbance from low flying aircraft. That said, it is possible to simultaneously initiate the complaints procedure in respect of a low flying aircraft with the Aviation Authority, bring an action against the owner and/or pilot for noise disturbance in the District Court and complain the owner of the lands upon which the helicopter or fixed wing aircraft lands to the local authority for breach of the planning code.

## Appendix 17

### COMPLAINT IN RELATION TO LOW FLYING AIRCRAFT

PURSUANT TO THE IRISH AVIATION AUTHORITY ACT 1993
(AS AMENDED)
AND
THE IRISH AVIATION AUTHORITY (RULES OF THE AIR) ORDER 2004

<u>**YOUR DETAILS**</u>:

Name: _____

Address: _____

_____

_____

Telephone Number: _____

*TO:*

*Low Flying Aircraft Reports,*
*Flight Operations Department,*
*Irish Aviation Authority,*
*The Times Building,*
*11-12 D'Olier Street,*
*Dublin 2.*

Source of Problem: _____

Name of Pilot or Aircraft Operator (if known): _____

If appropriate provide address of location of where the aircraft landed:

_____

_____

_____

Type of Aircraft: Helicopter _____ Fixed Wing _____

Registration Details of the Aircraft[14] (if known): _____

---

[14] The registration markings on a fixed wing aircraft will normally be displayed on the underside of the wings and on both sides of the aircraft. In respect of helicopters, the registration markings are normally displayed on both sides of the tail of the helicopter.

**Description of the aircraft (size, colour and other distinguishing characteristics):**

_____

_____

_____

| Date | Start Time | Finish Time | Approximate Height of the Aircraft | How it affects me |
|------|-----------|-------------|-----------------------------------|-------------------|
|      |           |             |                                   |                   |
|      |           |             |                                   |                   |
|      |           |             |                                   |                   |

I certify that the above record is a true statement of the instance(s) of the low flying aircraft complained of:

Signed:_____

Date:_____

# CHAPTER FIFTEEN

# Civil Remedies

## Private Nuisance

The law of nuisance was created to stop such bothersome activities or conduct when they unreasonably interfered either with the rights of other private landowners. The Irish courts have defined private nuisance as consisting of any interference without lawful justification with a person's use and enjoyment of that person's property.[1] A person's use and enjoyment of his or her land might be interfered with by dust, noise, vibration, tree roots, sewerage or odours.

In terms of assessing whether a nuisance has been suffered, the courts adopt an objective test stating that an owner of land is entitled to, as against a neighbour, the comfortable and healthy enjoyment of the land to the degree that would be expected by an ordinary person whose requirements are objectively reasonable in all the particular circumstances.[2] So, for example, in the case of *Robinson v Kilvert*[3] the plaintiff's claim was for damage to abnormally sensitive paper stored in a cellar which was affected by heat from adjoining premises. The claim failed because ordinary paper would not have been affected by the temperature, the logic being that a neighbour could not from an objective perspective be reasonably expected to foresee that the adjoining premises may have been storing unusually sensitive paper.

Following this objective test it would be difficult for a rural dweller to bring a successful action against a farming neighbour for offensive odours during slurry spreading on nearby pasture lands as the reasonable objective onlooker may state that putting up with such offensive smells from time to time is part and parcel of living in the countryside. Nuisance, therefore, also implies a geographical consideration, as what may not

---

[1] *Royal Dublin Society v Yates* [1997] IEHC 144 (Shanley J).
[2] *Hanrahan v Merck Sharp and Dohme (Ireland) Ltd* [1988] IESC 1; [1988] ILRM 629.
[3] (1889) 41 Ch D 88.

constitute a nuisance in the countryside may be deemed to be a nuisance in a built-up residential neighbourhood or, as the court stated in *Sturges v Bridgman*,[4] "[w]hat would be a nuisance in Belgravia Square would not necessarily be so in Bermondsey".

To determine whether the interference is unreasonable from an objective perspective, the court will consider factors such as the locality and standard of comfort that a person living in the area where the property is situated might reasonably expect, the duration, frequency or extent of the interference or the time of day. As was seen in chapter 9, this is particularly true for noise nuisance. In the case of *Christie v Davey*[5] the plaintiff had been giving music lessons in his semi-detached house for several years. The defendant, irritated by the noise, banged on the walls, shouted, blew whistles and beat tin trays with the malicious intention of annoying his neighbour and spoiling the music lessons. The defendant was found to have been causing a nuisance and an injunction was granted to restrain the defendant's behaviour.

Where a person has a cause of action in private nuisance, that person may be able to enter the property from where the nuisance[6] is emanating to abate[7] the source of the nuisance. Notice should be given to the person causing the nuisance before entering the land. Caution must always be exercised, however, in relation to the abatement of nuisance as, if the matter goes to court and the court determines that there was no nuisance in the first instance, there will have been no right to abatement meaning a trespass will have been committed. As was seen in chapter 2, in the absence of consent to abate the nuisance from the adjoining landowner it is always advisable to seek legal advice before abating a nuisance.

As seen above the remedies for nuisance are injunctions, abatement and also damages. In order to recover compensation in relation to a nuisance it will need to be shown that damage was suffered as a result of the nuisance. This may seem like an obvious statement but in some causes of action for an award in damages, such as will be seen below in relation to the law on trespass to property, there is only a requirement to show that the act constituting the wrong has occurred.

---

[4] (1879) 11 Ch D 852 at 865 per Thesiger LJ.

[5] [1893] 1 Ch D 316.

[6] Other than noise nuisance.

[7] The legal term for *stopping* the nuisance.

## Trespass to Real Property (Land)

Trespass to land consists of any unjustifiable intrusion by one person upon land in the possession of another. The intrusion may be intentional or it may be negligent: in either case, it is actionable in the absence of lawful justification.[8] In this way, trespass is said to be actionable *per se*, meaning that a plaintiff only needs to show that the trespass happened and does not have to show that he or she has suffered or will suffer any actual damage. However, for any meaningful award to be made payable, the courts will need to see that the trespass has given rise to substantial damage to the lands upon which the trespass has occurred.

Trespass may also be actionable if it occurs above or below the ground. In relation to trespass of airspace this may occur, for example, if an adjoining landowner were to construct an advertising hoarding overhanging the adjoining landowner's property.[9] A similar situation may occur if roof tiles/guttering/eaves overhang an adjoining property. A trespass may also be actionable if it occurs in the subsoil, accordingly, a mining company cannot mine beyond the boundary of its lands, thereby trespassing into the subsoil of the adjoining landowner.[10]

## Negligence

In negligence, a plaintiff is required to prove that the defendant was in breach of a duty of care imposed under law. Fault will be attributed where there has been a failure to take reasonable care in circumstances where the injuries were reasonably foreseeable. Lord Atkin first stated the test in *Donoghue v Stevenson*,[11] emphasising that "you must take reasonable care to avoid acts or omissions which you can reasonably foresee would be likely to injure your neighbour".

In terms of what constitutes *reasonableness*, Lord Macmillan expanded upon this concept, stating that:

> "[t]he standard of foresight of the reasonable man eliminates the personal equation and is independent of the idiosyncrasies of the particular person whose conduct is in question. Some persons are by nature unduly timorous and imagine every path beset by lions. Others,

---

[8] *Royal Dublin Society v Yates* [1997] IEHC 144.
[9] *Kelsen v Imperial Tobacco Co* [1957] 2 QB 334.
[10] *Bulli Coal Mining Co v Osborne* [1899] AC 351.
[11] [1932] AC 562 at 580.

of more robust temperament, fail to see or nonchalantly disregard even the most obvious dangers. The reasonable man is presumed to be free both from over-apprehension and over-confidence".[12]

The courts have applied this broad test to a wide range of circumstances, including road accidents, medical treatment, accidents in the workplace and on private premises. In general terms, the courts apply a four-point test for a plaintiff to succeed in a case where negligence is pleaded: on the balance of probabilities, there must be found to exist:

- a duty of care;
- a breach of this duty of care;
- a loss or damage; and
- a causal link between the breach of the duty of care and the loss or damage suffered.

However, in the case of *Glencar Explorations v Mayo County Council*,[13] the court arguably rendered it more difficult to succeed in a claim for negligence, creating another dimension to the test by stating that the court must then take a further step of considering whether *in all the circumstances, it is just and reasonable* to impose liability in negligence on the defendant.

In *Glencar Explorations v Mayo County Council* the applicants were two publicly quoted mining companies engaged in prospecting for and mining ores and minerals. In 1968, they were granted ten prospecting licences by the then Minister for Energy for the purpose of exploring for gold in an area south of Westport in County Mayo. They entered into a joint venture agreement with a company called Newcrest Mining Ltd, one of the largest Australian gold producers (hereafter 'Newcrest') in November 1991. Under that agreement, Newcrest was to spend at least IR£1.6 million on further exploration and, in return, was to be given a 51 per cent interest in the venture.

In February 1992, however, Newcrest withdrew from the joint venture as a direct result, the applicants alleged, of the inclusion in the county development plan of a mining ban. The applicants then applied for and were granted leave to institute the proceedings by way of judicial

---

[12] *Glasgow Corporation v Muir* [1943] 2 All ER 44 at 48.
[13] [2002] 1 ILRM 481 (SC).

review in the High Court, in which they claimed, *inter alia*, damages for negligence and breach of duty, including breach of statutory duty.

The High Court agreed with the applicants that Mayo County Council had been negligent in adopting the mining ban, but held that this negligence did not give rise to any right to damages. The companies appealed that decision to the Supreme Court which in turn rejected the appeal, with Keane CJ stating:

> "It seems to me that no injustice will be done if the courts are required to take the further step of considering whether, in all the circumstances, it is just and reasonable that the law should impose a duty of a given scope on the defendant for the benefit of the plaintiff."[14]

## The Rule in *Rylands v Fletcher*

There is not a great deal of reported case law on the rule in *Rylands v Fletcher*[15] in the Irish context and in other jurisdictions, such as Australia, the rule in *Rylands v Fletcher* is simply considered to be a restatement of the principles of ordinary negligence.[16]

In *Rylands v Fletcher* the defendants employed independent contractors to construct a reservoir on their land. The contractors found disused mines when digging but failed to seal them properly. They filled the reservoir with water. As a result, water flooded through the mineshafts into the plaintiff's mines on the adjoining property. The House of Lords found for the plaintiff notwithstanding that the defendant was not found to be negligent as the work was done by independent contractors, or guilty of nuisance as the damage was caused by a *one off* escape and not by reason of a continuing state of affairs that caused the damage over a drawn out period of time. Importantly, therefore, the rule in *Rylands v Fletcher* is seen as imposing a form of *strict liability*[17] on the defendants that cause damage to adjoining lands.

---

[14] [2002] 1 ILRM 481 (SC) at para 102.
[15] (1866) LR 1 Ex 265.
[16] *Burnie Port Authority v General Jones Pty Ltd* [1996] 4 LRC 605 at 607 per Mason CJ, Deana, Dawson, Toohey and Gaudron JJ.
[17] Strict liability is the legal responsibility for damages, or injury, even if the person found strictly liable was not at fault or negligent. It is enough to simply prove that the damage occurred.

The salient features of the rule are easily identified: the self-interest of the landowner, his or her conduct in bringing or keeping on his or her land something dangerous which involves a risk of damaging his or her neighbours' property, the avoidance of such damage by ensuring that the danger is confined to his or her own property and liability to his or her neighbours if he or she fails to do so.[18] The rule in *Rylands v Fletcher* is concerned with allowing the owner of the adversely affected lands to bring a claim in the courts to restore the lands to their original state. The claim cannot include a claim for death or personal injury, since such a claim does not relate to any right in or enjoyment of land.

In England, the House of Lords in *Cambridge Water Co v Eastern Counties Leather plc*,[19] decided that *Rylands v Fletcher* is a special form of nuisance. The law of private nuisance recognises that the risk must be borne by the person responsible for creating it and failing to control it. The user of one piece of land is always liable to affect the users or owners of other pieces of land. An escape of water originating on the former, or an explosion, may devastate not only the land on which it originates but also adjoining and more distant properties. The damage caused may be very serious indeed both in physical and financial terms. There may be a serious risk that if the user of the land, the use of which creates the risk, does not take active and adequate steps to prevent escape, an escape may occur.[20]

Again in *Cambridge Water Co v Eastern Counties Leather plc* the House of Lords conducted an in-depth review of *Rylands v Fletcher*, and re-stated the principle, holding, in effect, that *Rylands v Fletcher* had not introduced any radical new departure from the well settled principles of nuisance, but was an extension of the law of nuisance to deal with "one off escapes".

As mentioned above it is difficult to determine the strength of the rule in the Irish instance with the dearth of reported cases in the area, and furthermore it is difficult as a result to gain any insight into the likelihood of the Irish courts following the Australian approach of abandoning the rule in favour of the principles of negligence or whether the rule will be maintained as per the more recent decisions in *Cambridge Water Co Ltd v*

---

[18] *Transco v Stockport MBC* [2004] 4 LRC 314 at 338 per Lord Hobhouse.
[19] [1994] AC 264.
[20] *Transco v Stockport MBC* [2004] 4 LRC 314 at 338 per Lord Hobhouse

*Eastern Counties Leather plc* and *Transco plc v Stockport Metropolitan Borough Council.*

## Judicial Review

Judicial review is the procedure whereby the High Court (and, on appeal, the Supreme Court) is asked to scrutinise or review a decision by a Government Minister, the District or Circuit Court, a semi-state body, a local authority, An Bord Pleanála or a statutory tribunal.[21] As was discussed in relation to judicial review concerning planning matters,[22] the High Court is concerned not so much with the merits of the decision itself but more with how the decision was made and the manner in which the decision-making person or body has exercised the relevant power in making the decision. A major factor in the judicial review may be a complaint by a citizen that the particular arm of the State acted outside of the powers granted to it under a particular piece of legislation. In such an instance that arm of the State may be said to be acting *ultra vires.*

There are two stages in proceedings for judicial review: first, an application for *leave* or permission of the court to initiate a full judicial review hearing must be made.[23] At the leave stage the applicant's legal team will have to apply in court to seek to challenge the legality of the decision at a full hearing. At this, the *ex parte* stage, meaning that the decision-making body will not be present, there is an obligation on the applicant's legal team to disclose all of the pertinent matters surrounding the case to the court. The purpose of the leave application is to prevent the time of the court being wasted with misguided or trivial complaints of administrative error.[24] The initial appeal stage, therefore, weeds out those matters that are not of such importance as to warrant progression to stage two of the judicial review process. In this regard, many decisions, for example a minor decision of a local authority, may be more properly dealt with by the Ombudsman than by the High Court which will be concerned with matters of some substance.

---

[21] The rules governing conventional judicial review proceedings in this jurisdiction are to be found in Rules of the Superior Courts, Ord 84, rr 18-27.

[22] See chapter 7, p 131.

[23] RSC, Ord 84, r 20(1) provides that no application for judicial review shall be made unless the leave of the court has been obtained.

[24] *R v Inland Revenue Commissioners, Ex parte National Federation of Self Employed and Small Businesses Ltd* [1982] AC 617 at 642-643 *per* Lord Diplock.

Once the first hurdle of the leave stage has been successfully negotiated, the applicant's legal team is then obliged to formulate their complaint in detail and serve the grounds upon which they are seeking the judicial review on the decision-making body. That body will in turn draft its own written response defending the merits and lawfulness of the decision the subject matter of the proceedings. Once the exchange of papers has been finalised, the case is listed for court hearing in the High Court. The outcome of a successful judicial review is usually that the decision giving rise to the original injustice is set aside. That decision may be appealed to the Supreme Court.

## Timeframes

The application for judicial review must be made promptly and varying cut off times apply depending on the kind of decision that one wishes to review. Generally speaking, applications for leave must be made within three months.[25] In certain circumstances, where the court is satisfied that there is a good reason for extending the time limit, it may do so at its discretion. The timeframe may be extended, for example, in instances perhaps where the applicant was suffering under a disability and was unable to instruct his or her legal team to initiate the judicial review within the prescribed timeframe. In other instances, such as in the area of planning and environmental matters, the timeframes are even more restricted.[26]

Any individual contemplating a judicial review must immediately contact his or her solicitor in order to protect his or her claim and not fall foul of the judicial review clock.

## What are Injunctions?

An injunction is a court order which orders a person to stop (called a *prohibitory injunction*) or to do (a *mandatory injunction*) a particular act or thing. A breach of an injunction is generally punishable as a contempt of court and in some circumstances can lead to imprisonment until the contempt of court has been purged. The injunction is arguably the strongest weaponry in any legal practitioner's armoury and it is to be deployed only after much careful consideration of the issues at hand.

---

[25] RSC, Ord 84, r 21(1), as amended by the Rules of the Superior Courts (Judicial Review) 2011 (SI No 691 of 2011) states that an application for leave to apply for judicial review shall be made within three months from the date when grounds for the application first arose.
[26] See chapter 7, p 134.

## Types of Injunction

Injunctions are normally classified in terms of their duration and in this way the first type of injunction in terms of shortness of duration is known as the *interim injunction*. An interim injunction is normally applied for in the most urgent of situations where time is of the essence. For example, a local authority may bring an interim injunction application to the courts at extremely short notice where a developer may be in the process of demolishing a protected structure.

In this instance, interim injunctions are either obtained *on notice* or *ex parte*, meaning without notice[27] or representation of the alleged wrongdoer. As with the above example, the courts may allow the application for the interim injunction to proceed without the other side being present. There is little point in trying to put the alleged rogue developer on notice of the application if, by the time the notice has been served, the protected structure will be reduced to rubble, or indeed where giving notice would lead to a serious risk of the alleged rogue developer speeding up his or her demolition wrongly believing that he or she may escape sanction if the structure is demolished prior to the injunction being granted. It must be reiterated that only in the most extreme and urgent of cases will an application proceed on an *ex parte* basis before the courts.

If the court grants an interim injunction it will have the effect of preserving the situation in the immediate term and the court will then usually fix a date for a further hearing with all parties present. Understandably, if an injunction is granted on an *ex parte* basis it will only be fair that the alleged wrongdoer be afforded the earliest opportunity to put his or her version of events before the court. As such, the *ex parte* interim injunction will be made returnable before the court at the earliest opportunity for this purpose. If, at this stage, the court is still satisfied that the injunction should continue to freeze the status quo until a full hearing is prepared and heard, the interim injunction will become an *interlocutory injunction*. Finally, if at the hearing of the action the court decides that the person bringing the application was correct in bringing the application in the first instance, it may convert the interlocutory injunction into a *perpetual injunction*, meaning that the order will continue indefinitely.

---

[27] Or without the other side being present as it will be possible for the respondent to be on notice but not to appear allowing the application to be then made *ex parte*.

Prior to the granting of any injunction the court relies on a set of determining principles as detailed in the case of *Campus Oil Ltd v Minister for Energy (No 2)*.[28] In accordance with these criteria the court will consider:

- whether the plaintiff has established the existence of a *fair issue* or *serious question* for determination by the court at the trial;
- whether, in the circumstances of the claim, the nature of the acts or conduct sought to be restrained and the losses which have been or will be incurred depending upon whether the injunction is granted or refused, damages will be an adequate remedy[29]; and
- depending on the assessment of the above consideration, whether the balance of convenience lies in favour of granting or refusing the injunction.

## Land Disputes in an Urban and Rural Context, Injunctions and Financial Penalties When the Applicant is Unsuccessful

An injunction will only be granted by the court if the party seeking the injunctive relief provides a legally binding undertaking to the court granting an interim injunction. This undertaking requires the party applying for an injunction to give the respondent an undertaking as to damages, i.e. an undertaking to pay financial compensation to the other party for any harm that the injunction may cause if the court should decide at a later date for whatever reason that the injunction should not have been applied for in the first instance.

### Injunctive Relief in the Rural Setting

Take, for example, a land dispute between farmers A and B. Farmer A obtains an injunction stopping farmer B from trespassing onto what farmer A believes is his lands. After a full court hearing of the matter it later transpires that the court decides that farmer B is the rightful owner of the lands in question. Farmer B will then be able to rely on the undertaking of farmer A to bring a claim for damages as a result of the original interim and interlocutory injunctions keeping him off his lands until the court gave its decision re-installing him on his lands. In this way farmer B will be entitled to ascertain how much his loss is in terms of not being able to work the lands the subject of the dispute. Losses could be

---

[28] [1983] IEHC 4.

[29] The Court will not grant an injunction if damages would be an adequate remedy, i.e. if the party applying for the injunction can be redressed in full simply by an award of damages.

incurred, for example, as a result of farmer's B inability to tend to his land and derive an income therefrom. It may also be the case that farmer A will be responsible for all of the associated legal fees of legal teams A and B.

## Injunctive Relief in the Urban Setting

In this instance, homeowner A finds that when he commences building an extension to the side of his dwelling house, his neighbour, homeowner B believes that the extension constitutes an authorised trespass on his lands and seeks an injunction freezing the development until such time as the matter may be dealt by way of a full court hearing. When the court gives judgment, it finds that homeowner A is the actual owner of the lands being built on and, as such, homeowner B's claims of trespass are without merit. In order to obtain the injunction in the first instance, homeowner B will have given the court an undertaking as to damages in order to allow the Judge to grant the injunction at the *ex parte* or interim stage. It will therefore now be open to homeowner A to apply to the court in order to have homeowner B honour the undertaking. As can be imagined, if homeowner A has contracted a team of builders, an architect and an engineer for a specified amount of time and they are still demanding payments as per the contract, the financial impact may be extremely serious for homeowner B.

## Injunctions are a Discretionary Remedy

Injunctions are a discretionary remedy meaning that the court is never obliged to grant an injunction and will use its discretion to only grant an injunction where it appears to be just and convenient to do so. Furthermore, an injunction is what is termed in law as an *equitable remedy*[30] which means any delay in applying for an injunction can seriously damage the prospects of obtaining an injunction. The party applying for the injunction must also come to court *with clean hands*, meaning that he or she must have acted properly in the course of events leading up to the granting of the injunction.

## Damages

The usual remedy for common law causes of action is damages. The purpose of the award of damages is to compensate the plaintiff for loss and injury suffered as a result of the negligent or wrongful conduct

---

[30] Equitable remedies are judicial remedies developed and granted by courts of equity, as opposed to courts of common law. In Ireland, legal and equitable remedies have been merged and a single court can issue either or both remedies.

of the defendant. The sum of damages awarded will be calculated based on the estimated cost of returning the plaintiff to the same position he or she would be in if the defendant had not engaged in that conduct causing the damage or loss. An award of damages can only be made in the form of a lump sum.

The fact that awards for damages are made only in the form of a lump sum means that an assessment as to all losses, both past and future, must be made at the trial. The plaintiff cannot re-commence proceedings if his or her condition deteriorates at some point post-trial. Similarly, if one's case settles prior to going to trial, then the settlement will invariably be in *full and final settlement*. This means that once the agreement, he or she has been concluded and the award of compensation paid the plaintiff will be unable to re-visit the terms of the settlement at a future point in time, notwithstanding that the damage and loss may continue beyond the time of entering into the settlement.

## The Ombudsman

The Office of the Ombudsman was set up under the terms of the Ombudsman Act 1980 (the 1980 Act). The Ombudsman is appointed by the President of Ireland upon the nomination of both Houses of the Oireachtas, and is a civil servant of the State. The Office of the Ombudsman deals with complaints from members of the public who believe they have suffered injustice as a result of maladministration by government departments and public bodies such as local authorities. The Ombudsman is not a political office and he or she must remain independent in the performance of the functions of Ombudsman.[31]

Before contacting the Office of the Ombudsman, attempts should be made to resolve any issue with the public body concerned. As a precursor to lodging a complaint with the Ombudsman, the internal complaints procedure of the body in question should be invoked. Where the complaint is not resolved it may be brought to the Ombudsman. However, the Ombudsman cannot examine a decision to grant or refuse planning permission (see section under Planning below) or decisions and activities called *reserved functions*.

---

[31] s 7(1)(a).

The time limit for making a complaint about a decision or action of a body is 12 months. However, the Ombudsman may extend this timeframe if special circumstances make it proper for the Ombudsman to investigate the complaint.[32] The Ombudsman is barred from investigating the matter complained of if the action is also the subject of any civil legal proceedings.[33]

## The Complaints Procedure

The Ombudsman generally looks at complaints[34] about things that have gone wrong in the process of State administration at the local level such as the powers as carried out by local authorities. Most commonly, complaints are raised where the local authority may have taken a decision:

    (i)   without proper authority;

   (ii)   on irrelevant grounds;

  (iii)   as the result of negligence or carelessness;

  (iv)   based on erroneous or incomplete information;

   (v)   that is improperly discriminatory;

  (vi)   based on an undesirable administrative practice; or

 (vii)   otherwise contrary to fair or sound administration.

## How Complaints to the Ombudsman are Investigated

There are two stages in relation to processing a complaint with the Ombudsman. If a complaint is made to the Ombudsman, he or she will carry out a preliminary examination.[35] The preliminary examination is a quick and informal way of deciding whether a formal investigation is warranted. In any case where a complaint is made to the Ombudsman, and after a preliminary examination in relation to the action, the Ombudsman decides not to carry out an investigation into the complaint or to discontinue such an investigation, he or she shall send to the person who made the complaint a statement in writing of his or her reasons for the decision.[36]

---

[32] s 5(f) and (g).

[33] s 5.

[34] s 4(2)(b).

[35] s 5.

[36] s 6(1).

The next step in the process is for the Ombudsman to carry out a formal investigation where he or she finds that there may be merit in the complaint. The Ombudsman will draft a statement of complaint in consultation with the aggrieved party. The investigation will be carried out in private. The Ombudsman may require any person who, in the opinion of the Ombudsman, is in possession of information, or has a document or thing in his or her power or control, that is relevant to the examination or investigation, to furnish that information, document or thing to the Ombudsman and, where appropriate, may require the person to attend before him or her for that purpose and the person must comply with the requirements.[37]

If a complaint is upheld and if the Ombudsman finds that the aggrieved party has suffered due to maladministration, and if the local authority has not taken steps to remedy this, a recommendation may issue suggesting that appropriate steps be taken. In that recommendation, the local authority may be asked to review what it has done, to change its decision or offer an appropriate remedy, including an explanation, an apology and/or financial compensation. At the end of the investigation process, the Ombudsman must inform parties of the decision.

## How to Apply

A complaint to the Ombudsman[38] must be made as soon as possible. The time limit for making a complaint about a decision or action of a body is 12 months and time starts to run from the date the decision is made, or action is taken or from the date the party becomes aware that the decision or action occurred. A complaint may be in writing, by telephone or by e-mail. All relevant documentation or correspondence should be included with the complaint.

Once the complaint is examined, the local authority will be asked to submit a report. If necessary, the Ombudsman may also examine the files and records and may question people involved with the complaint. It can

---

[37] s 7(1)(a).

[38] The Office of the Ombudsman is open from 9.15 am to 5.30 pm, Monday to Friday. The Ombudsman also maintains monthly regional offices and organises an annual programme of regional visits. Its contact details are: 18 Lower Leeson Street, Dublin 2, Tel: (01)1 639 5600, http://www.ombudsman.gov.ie.

take time to gather the information required. There is no charge for making a complaint to the Ombudsman.

## Example of Action by Ombudsman in Relation to a Complaint Against a Local Authority

The following is a brief synopsis of a complaint lodged with the Ombudsman. The subject of the complaint concerns non-adherence to the planning administration procedures.[39]

*Year Concluded: 2006*

*Name of Body: Dublin City Council*

*Subject of Complaint: Faulty Planning Administration*

*Complaint Details:*

*One of the requirements of the Planning & Development Act, 2000 is that a third party can only appeal a planning decision if he/she has made a submission or objection in relation to the development. Any such appeal must be made within four weeks from the date of the decision of the planning authority. In this case, the complainant, lodged her objection and, as a consequence, was entitled to be informed of the decision on the application within three working days of the planning decision. The development in question consisted of an extension to her next door neighbour's house and she was concerned that it would infringe on her privacy. However, Dublin City Council failed to inform her of its decision and as a result the four week appeal period had passed before she became aware that a decision had been made. When she complained to the Council she was given an apology, but was not offered any form of redress. As a consequence, she felt that she had been unfairly treated and should be compensated financially for the loss of her statutory right of appeal.*

*In the past, I have highlighted my concerns directly to the Council and in previous Annual Reports in relation to cases where a statutory right is denied through an error on the part of a local authority. I regard it as maladministration and it should normally lead to the payment of compensation. I would like to see local authorities take the initiative by offering redress rather than wait for my Office to prompt them following the receipt of a complaint of this type.*

---

[39] http://www.ombudsman.gov.ie/en/SampleCases/Name,7420,en.htm ( 22nd March 2012).

*Following my intervention, the Council decided to pay €1,000 in compensation and revised its procedures to ensure that the same problem does not arise in the future.*

## Conclusion

The civil remedies available to individuals in a neighbourhood disputes are broad and varied. That said, the decision to make use of remedies such as injunctions and judicial review should never be taken lightly and certainly not without first considering a process of alternative dispute resolution such are the financial risks in terms of legal costs for the unsuccessful applicant[40].

---

[40] See Appendix 18 which contains an ADR/ Mediation referral form for Mediation Chambers Ireland.

# CHAPTER SIXTEEN

# Alternative Dispute Resolution

L itigation or going to court should be the last resort in any dispute between neighbours. On judgment day, the court can only pronounce itself in favour of one of the opposing parties to a dispute no matter how compelling and astute the arguments from both sides. Inevitably a decision must be made. In that moment one party will leave the court having lost the case, and may have to pay an award in damages together with the fees of his or her own legal representatives and those of the winning side. It is little wonder that people are turning away from the courts and litigation and the end game scenario that it represents and instead turning towards the various forms of alternative dispute resolution in an attempt to seek a resolution prior to having redress to the courts. Indeed, in relation to neighbourhood disputes many judges, in the first instance, will direct that both parties first attempt mediation in an effort to resolve the matter in the most amicable fashion possible.

The courts are cognisant of the fact that individuals will find it more difficult to continue to live in harmony in a residential setting where one party leaves the court the victor. Clarke J, in the case of *Charleton v Kenny*[1] which involved a retired solicitor and broadcaster, both neighbours in Dalkey, County Dublin, captured the end game nature of neighbourhood disputes and advised both parties to engage in a process of Alternative Dispute Resolution in order to steer them away from the court-delivered decision that was only going to please one side.

However, alternative dispute resolution is not just for disputes in relation to valuable parcels of land and may be used for all manner and size of disputes between neighbours. From noise disturbance complaints to

---

[1] (2006) No 4266P, High Court, 8 to 11 April 2008 (hearing of action) and 15 April 2008 (settlement after mediation). See Law Reform Commission, Alternative Dispute Resolution Consultation Paper, LRC CP 50-2008, Dublin 2008 at para 3.27.

disputed claims for land running into the millions, there is an alternative dispute resolution facilitator for every manner of neighbourhood dispute.[2]

## What Is Alternative Dispute Resolution (ADR)?

Dispute resolution is a term that refers to a number of processes that can be used to resolve a conflict, dispute or claim. Dispute resolution may also be referred to as alternative dispute resolution or ADR for short. Dispute resolution processes are alternatives to having a court decide the dispute in a trial. Dispute resolution processes can be used to resolve any type of dispute including neighbourhood, family, employment, business, housing, personal injury, consumer, environmental disputes and defamation.

## Why Use Alternative Dispute Resolution?

Dispute resolution processes have several advantages. For instance, many ADR processes are far more cost effective than standard litigation in the courts. A 2001 Report by the Department of Justice in the US State of Oregon estimated that, in a typical case, the cost of mediation was 85 per cent lower compared to the cost of a full hearing in court or other adjudicated procedure.[3]

The processes are voluntary, non-confrontational and entirely confidential. Certain processes of ADR can provide the parties involved with greater participation in reaching a solution, as well as more control over the outcome of the dispute. In addition, dispute resolution processes are less formal and have more flexible rules than a full court hearing. ADR also avoids the situation where the winner takes it all as exists in a litigation process in the courts where a Judge may only pronounce him or herself in favour of one party with the losing side having to pick up their own costs plus their adversaries' costs which does little for the fostering of positive neighbourhood living.

## What Are the Different Types of Dispute Resolution Processes?

Dispute resolution takes a number of different forms. The most common dispute resolution processes include the following:

---

[2] See Appendix 18 which contains an ADR/ Mediation referral form for Mediation Chambers Ireland.
[3] See Law Reform Commission, LRC 98-2010, *Alternative Dispute Resolution: Mediation and Conciliation* (Law Reform Commission, Dublin, 2010), paras 3.115–3.116.

## Mediation

Mediation[4] is a private process where a neutral third person called a mediator helps the parties discuss and try to resolve the dispute. The parties have the opportunity to describe the issues, discuss their interests, understandings and feelings; provide each other with information and explore ideas for the resolution of the dispute. The mediator does not have the power to make a decision for the parties, but can help the parties find a resolution that is mutually acceptable, the important point being that the only people who can resolve the dispute in mediation are the parties themselves.[5]

## Conciliation

Conciliation[6] is a process in which the parties to a dispute, with the assistance of a dispute resolution practitioner (the conciliator), identify the issues in dispute, develop options, consider alternatives and endeavour to reach an agreement. Unlike mediation, in conciliation the conciliator may be actively seen to advise and may make suggestions for terms of settlement, give expert advice on likely settlement terms, and may actively encourage the participants to reach an agreement. The conciliator will, however, always remain neutral and impartial to both parties in dispute. Due to the advisory role of the conciliator on the content of the dispute, and in the context of neighbourhood disputes, it is recommended that the conciliator be a solicitor.

Like mediation the process is completely voluntary and each of the disputing parties may leave the conciliation talks as he or she so wishes and revert to letting the matter in dispute go before the court. If the parties reach an agreement, the conciliator may help reduce the agreement to a

---

[4] The Law Reform Commission report LRC 98-2010 makes 100 reform recommendations and includes a draft Mediation and Conciliation Bill: see http://www.lawreform.ie/_fileupload/Reports/r98ADR.pdf. (22 March 2012).

[5] s 4(1) of the Draft Mediation and Consolidation Bill 2010, as contained in the Law Reform Commission report LRC 98-2010, defines mediation as "a facilitative and confidential structured process in which the parties attempt by themselves, on a voluntary basis, to reach a mutually acceptable agreement to resolve their dispute with the assistance of an independent third party, called a mediator".

[6] s 4(2) of the Draft Mediation and Consolidation Bill 2010, as contained in the Law Reform Commission report LRC 98-2010, defines conciliation as "a means a facilitative and confidential structured process in which an independent third party, called a conciliator, actively assists the parties in their attempt to reach, on a voluntary basis, a mutually acceptable agreement to resolve their dispute".

written contract, which may be enforceable in court. As with mediation the cost is usually shared equally by the parties.

## How Does Mediation and Conciliation Work in Practice?

The mediation/conciliation will take place where there is one room where everyone can meet and also a separate room for each party to use as his or her home base. Normally the facilitator[7] will welcome the parties and settle them into their respective rooms and answer any questions before the mediation/conciliation starts.

Most mediations/conciliations start with an open meeting where everyone meets in the same room. The facilitator asks everyone to agree to some basic rules, such as listening without interrupting and not using offensive remarks. Each person then has a chance to talk about the problem as it affects him or her. The facilitator checks that everyone understands what each person has said and allows them to respond. The facilitator helps both parties to identify the issues that need to be sorted out and to understand why the other person feels strongly about his or her case. If either party does not wish to take part in the joint opening session then the facilitator will go straight to what are termed as the *separate sessions.*

At an appropriate time the parties go to their separate rooms for separate sessions with the facilitator. The facilitator then holds private meetings, moving between the parties and gathering information in confidence. In this way the facilitator builds a unique picture of the dispute and of each party's needs, and so can help the parties move towards a solution. The facilitator seeks to earn the trust of each party that nothing disclosed confidentially will be disclosed to any other party, creating a safe environment for exploration and problem-solving.

The facilitator ensures that everyone knows what is going on and that they stay committed to the mediation/conciliation, even when the facilitator is spending time with the other party. The overall aim is to give the parties the best chance of achieving a settlement and the facilitator manages the process to ensure that the parties are kept focused on this outcome. If the parties are able to reach a solution, then a document is

---

[7] Facilitator meaning the person chairing the mediation and/or conciliation.

drawn up by the parties and signed by both of them. Otherwise, everything said at the meeting remains confidential.

## Mediation/Conciliation and Neighbourhood Disputes

### Property Disputes

In relation to property disputes between neighbours, Mummery LJ perhaps summed it up best in the English Court of Appeal decision in *Pennock v Hodgson*,[8] where he stated that:

> "The unfortunate consequences of a case like this are that, in the absence of any compromise, someone wins, someone loses, it always costs a lot of money and usually generates a lot of ill-feeling that does not end with the litigation. None of those things are good for neighbours."

As discussed in chapter 1, very often the boundary dispute is perhaps only one aspect of a more deep-rooted personality clash between adjoining landowners that may have been festering for some time. Most property disputes are well suited to mediation, either as an alternative to court proceedings or at an earlier stage. Speed, cost effectiveness and the maintenance of neighbourly relationships are all advantages in the area of property disputes generally.[9] Mediation and/or conciliation are seen to be more appropriate forums for the resolution of such disputes as the parties have an opportunity to resolve the matter themselves in a confidential and voluntary process which they themselves control, with the assistance of a mediator or a conciliator.

The alternative is stark as a full-blown court hearing in relation to a property dispute may last for days, and be an emotionally draining and stressful experience for the litigants. Any underlying personality clashes may be further aggravated by the fact that the vanquished party to the dispute will end up having to bear the cost of his or her victorious neighbour's legal team and expert witnesses along with his or her own costs. Very often the legal costs may be worth more than the actual piece of land the subject matter of the dispute. Little wonder, therefore, that ADR is seen as a viable alternative in the realm of boundary disputes between neighbours.

---

[8] [2010] EWCA Civ 873, para 46.
[9] E Callanan, *Neutralising Property Disputes: The Role of Mediation* (2009) 14(4) CPLJ 98.

The Law Reform Commission also provisionally recommended that property boundary disputes are appropriate for resolution through mediation and conciliation and those parties should be advised by their legal representatives to consider and attempt mediation or conciliation in such disputes prior to the commencement of litigation.[10]

In terms of both a mediation and a conciliation where the independent conciliator may actively engage in trying to assist parties reach and formulate an agreement in relation to a property dispute, the disputing parties would be strongly advised to have a solicitor act as the independent facilitator in such disputes given the nature and complexity of land law in Ireland. For example, there is little point in parties reaching an agreement in relation to a disputed piece of land only to discover that neither party had a right to the lands in the first instance.[11]

### Noise Disturbance, Anti-Social Behaviour and Mediation

In chapter 9, it was seen that it is possible for individuals to go to the District Court in an effort to obtain a noise order against a neighbour. It was also seen that, in the first instance in such cases, the Judge of the District Court may often adjourn the matter and direct that both parties explore the possibility of arriving at a resolution with the assistance of a mediator.

In such circumstances, Community Law Centres[12] provide a free service where community-based mediators assist in the resolution of neighbourhood disputes typically involving noise, boisterous children and harassment. As with any mediation the mediators provide a neutral, non-confrontational, non-adversarial methodology to resolving conflicts.

These specialised mediators will sit down with both parties in an effort to resolve such disputes whilst paying particular attention to the need to maintain a positive, ongoing neighbourhood relationship as the

---

[10] See Law Reform Commission consultation paper LRC CP 50-2008 at 9.25.

[11] For example, see chapter 4 on squatter's rights: there is not much point in two parties reaching an agreement on a piece of land only to discover that neither may hold the title adversely to the State's interest as the 30-year rule applies for the necessary accrual of proprietary rights as opposed to 12 years for non-State lands.

[12] Interested parties should contact their District Court Civil Office or the Free Legal Aid Advice Service who will provide the necessary contact details for the growing network of Community Law Centres around the country.

individuals involved will often have to continue to live in close proximity and share local amenities.

It should be noted that in the context of neighbourhood disputes involving threatening and abusive behaviour that threaten the physical or mental health, safety or security of individuals, the Garda Síochána should always be contacted in the first instance.

## If One Participates in Dispute Resolution, Can One Later Go to Court?

If there is a failure to reach a resolution of a dispute then either party is free to pursue his or her particular claim through the courts if he or she so wishes. In many respects, this increases the attractiveness of ADR in that parties to a dispute may in the first instance attempt to resolve the matter in a cost effective and confidential setting and failing any resolution at the mediation or conciliation, may return to the courts to have the matter adjudicated upon by a Judge.

## ADR and Confidentiality

It is common for parties entering into a mediation or conciliation to sign an agreement with the facilitator. Maintaining confidentiality is an integral component of any successful ADR process[13] and, as such, prior to any ADR process taking place both parties will be required to sign confidentiality agreements in relation to any matters discussed during the process. This will enable parties to ADR proceedings to be forthcoming and candid with their facilitator.

Standard mediation and conciliation agreements in Ireland frequently contain confidentiality provisions where the parties agree that as a condition of being present or participating in the mediation or conciliation, they will, unless otherwise compelled by law,[14] preserve confidentiality in relation to the course of ADR proceedings. In other words, ADR takes place on what is legally termed a *without prejudice*

---

[13] s 7 of the Draft Mediation and Consolidation Bill 2010, as contained in the Law Reform Commission report LRC 98-2010, (16 Nov 2010) proposes a statutory footing for such confidentiality clauses, stating that *"A party involved in mediation or conciliation may refuse to disclose, and may prevent any other person from disclosing, a mediation or conciliation communication."*

[14] The confidentiality privilege that arises in mediation and conciliation may not apply where the mediation or conciliation communication is used to attempt to commit a crime, or to commit a crime, or to conceal a crime.

basis. This essentially means that no statements or comments, whether written or oral, made or used by the parties or their representatives in preparation for or in the course of the mediation or conciliation may be relied upon during future court proceedings.

Similarly the parties will agree not to call upon or seek to subpoena the mediator or conciliator to give evidence in any subsequent court hearing in relation to the dispute.

## Some Other Forms of ADR

### Early Neutral Evaluation

Early neutral evaluation is a non-binding ADR process in which a neutral professional (the Evaluator), usually a solicitor requests both sides to the dispute to submit a summary of their case and thereafter gives a non-binding confidential opinion as to the likely outcome if the matter was to proceed to trial. This opinion may then be used as a basis for settlement or for further negotiation.

### Expert Determination

Expert Determination is a process in which the parties to a dispute present arguments and evidence to a dispute resolution practitioner, who is chosen on the basis of his or her specialist qualification or experience in the subject matter of the dispute (the expert) and who makes a determination. Agreements for expert determination typically provide for the decision of the expert to be final and binding with no appeal. A party to a dispute should not sign up to an expert determination process without the assistance of his or her solicitor due to the fact that there will usually be no appeal of the expert determination.

### Arbitration

Arbitration in Ireland is governed by the Arbitration Act 2010 which became operative on 8 June 2010.[15] Arbitration is a private process where disputing parties agree that one or several individuals can make a decision about the dispute after receiving evidence and hearing arguments. The

---

[15] It repeals all previous arbitration legislation in Ireland (including the Arbitration Act 1954, Arbitration Act 1980 and Arbitration (International Commercial) Act 1998). The new legislation will apply to all arbitrations which commence in Ireland after 8 June 2010, thereby being retrospectively applicable to arbitration agreements already in existence. The 2010 Act applies the Model Law (as adopted by the United Nations Commission on International Trade Law on 21 June 1985) to all arbitrations in Ireland.

arbitration process is similar to a trial in that the parties make opening statements and present evidence to the arbitrator.

Compared to traditional trials, arbitration can usually be completed more quickly and is less formal. After the hearing, the arbitrator issues an award giving reasons for his or her decision. An arbitrator's decision is final and binding. There is no appeal against an arbitrator's award. A party may, however, apply to set aside an arbitrator's award in certain circumstances; however, this rarely occurs in practice. If an application is made to set aside the arbitrator's award, and that application is refused by the High Court, there is no appeal against that decision to the Supreme Court. Given the binding nature of an arbitrator's decision and its quasi-judicial status individuals will not enter into an arbitration process without being represented by their solicitor and perhaps even a barrister with a particular expertise for the dispute involved.

In the neighbourhood context, arbitration may be useful in terms of a contractual dispute in relation to a contract for the sale of lands or perhaps a determination in relation to an adverse possession case for a valuable parcel of lands. In most situations involving neighbourhood disputes, the first option will be a process of mediation or conciliation.

## Conclusion

One of the core strengths of ADR is that people are offered the opportunity to come together to resolve their disputes in a less adversarial way. The process is completely voluntary and is more cost effective and quicker than going to a court. In particular, ADR is well suited to the resolution of neighbourhood disputes given that the ADR process allows both parties to pull back from the brink and save face which is sometimes all that is needed in the context of a dispute that may often be more of a personality clash than a legal dispute.

The Draft General Scheme of Mediation Bill 2012,[16] building on the The Law Reform Commission[17] reaffirms this position and seeks as a

---

[16] Published on the 1 March 2012 by Minister for Minister for Justice, Equality & Defence see http://www.inis.gov.ie/en/JELR/MedBillGSFinal.pdf/Files/MedBillGSFinal.pdf for the full text of the Bill (2 April 2012).

[17] Law Reform Commission, LRC 98-2010, *Alternative Dispute Resolution: Mediation and Conciliation* (Law Reform Commission, Dublin, 2010).

primary objective to promote mediation as a viable, effective and efficient alternative to court proceedings thereby reducing legal costs, speeding up the resolution of disputes and relieving the stress involved in court proceedings. The Mediation Bill 2012, if enacted in its current format, will see mediation become a standard practice in litigious matters as the Bill proposes the imposition of a statutory requirement on solicitors to inform their clients about the possibility of using mediation as an alternative means of resolving disputes prior to commencing court proceedings.[18]

---

[18] Head Four of the Draft General Scheme of Mediation Bill 2012.

# Appendix 18

## MEDIATION CHAMBERS IRELAND
### Initial Mediation Referral Form
### Civil And Commercial Department

| | |
|---|---|
| Administrative Address: | MCI, 24 -26 Upper Ormond Quay, Dublin 7 |
| Telephone Number: | 01 - 8722013 |
| Fax Number: | 01 - 8736229 |
| Email Address: | info@mediationchambers.ie |

| | |
|---|---|
| Has either party been referred to us previously? | Yes    No |
| Is the second Party aware of the referral? | Yes    No |
| If yes are they willing to attend Mediation? | Yes    No    Not known |
| Preferred Location for Mediation | |

| Party 1 | | | Party 2 | | |
|---|---|---|---|---|---|
| Name | | | Name | | |
| Address | | | Address | | |
| Post Code | | | Post Code | | |
| Telephone | | | Telephone | | |
| Email | | | Email | | |
| Date of Birth | | Age | Date of Birth | | Age |
| Occupation | | | Occupation | | |
| Special Needs | Yes | No | Special Needs | Yes | No |
| Disability's | Yes | No | Disability's | Yes | No |
| Are separate waiting rooms required? | Yes | No | Are separate waiting rooms required? | Yes | No |
| Solicitor (if acting) | | | Solicitor (if acting) | | |
| Firm | | | Firm | | |
| Address | | | Address | | |
| Telephone | | | Telephone | | |
| Email | | | Email | | |

| Type of Mediation | o   Please outline the dispute (use separate pages if necessary) |
|---|---|
| | _____ |
| | _____ |
| | _____ |
| | _____ |

# Index

## A

Abatement
  definition of 59
Adverse possession *see* Squatters'
  rights
Alternative Dispute Resolution
  (ADR) 3, 150, 233
  benefits of 235, 239
    core strength 241–2
  confidentiality and 239–40
  definition of 234
  different types
    conciliation 235–6
    mediation 235–6
      referral form 243
    noise nuisance and 238–9
    others
      arbitration 240–1
      early neutral evaluation
        240
      expert determination 240
  property disputes, between
    neighbours, and 237
Amenity
  definition of 122
An Bord Pleanála 89, 125
  appealing to 125–7
    Board's timeframe 129
    rejection 131–2
  dangerous place and 141
  derelict sites and 135–6
  determines *de nova* 127
  dismissing appeals 130–1
  oral hearings 129–30

An Garda Síochána 70
  dangerous dogs and 189
  noise orders and 151–2
  nuisance horses and 194
  stray dogs and 190
Anhold, Tilman 195
Animals causing nuisance
  dangerous dogs
    inhibiting access to lands 190
    notice to complain about
      198–9
    regulations regarding 188–9
    reporting 189
  dealing with barking
    dogs 190–2
    Dog Nuisance Order 191
    notice to complain
      about 200–1
  dog attacks 185–6
    on livestock 187–8
    on trespassers 186–7
  dog fouling 192–3
  dog identification/licences 192
  farmers shooting to kill 188
  guard dog signs 187
  horses 193
    can be seized by local
      authority 193–4
  livestock on the roads 194
    Chief Justice Keane on 196
    in High Court case 194–5
    in Supreme Court case 195–6
  stray dogs 190
Atkin, Lord 219

# B

Backyard burning (of waste)
  Air Pollution Act 1987 204
  definition of 203
  farmers burning vegetative
    waste 205–6
      statutory notice required
        207–8
  Hallowe'en/celebratory
    bonfires 205
  problems caused by 203–4
  regulations regarding 204–5
  Waste Management Act 1996
    204
Barr, Justice 55
Bland, Peter
  *Easements* 53n
Boundary disputes 2–3
  courts and 4–5
  Lord Hoffman on 2
  solicitor required 3
    to consider relative points 3–4
  timeframes for 5–6
Boundary trees
  *see also* Electricity Supply Board
    (ESB)
  causing a nuisance 82
    definition of 80
  dangerous 84–5
    causes damage/personal
      injury 85
    Justice Hanlon on 86–7
    Lord Oaksey on 87
  fruit/leaves from next door 83
    appeal court on 84
  hedges, law on 92
    exemptions 92–3

in English law 79–80
  overhanging branches/
    encroaching roots 80
    Lord MacNaghten on 81
  poisonous, liability for 87–9
  tree felling, 10-year rule 89–90
  Tree Preservation Order
    (TPO) 89
  work orders 82–3
Boundary works
  Dublin-centric approach to 35
Boundary, Shared
  *see also* Works order
  carrying out work, without
    consent discussing terms
    with neighbour 23–4
  legal issues 21–2
    cost 22
    nuisance/negligence 22
    trespass/injunctions 22
  party structures 82
    definitions 25–6
    types of work permitted 26–7
  planning permission 23
  works order 24–5
Building owner
  financial obligations regarding
    works order 31–2
  ignoring demand for
    compensation 32–3

# C

Civil remedies 218
  injunctions
    a discretionary remedy 227
    damages 227–8
    definition of 224

types of 225–6
　　relief in rural setting 226–7
　　in urban setting 227
　unsuccessful application 226
Office of the Ombudsman 228–9
　complaints procedure 229
　　applying for 230–1
　　example of 231–2
　　investigation 229–30
proving negligence 220
　Chief Justice Keane on 221
　judicial review
　　definition of 223
　　timeframe 224
　　two stages 223–4
　*Rylands v Fletcher rule* 221–2
reasonable care to be taken
　Lord Atkin on 219
　Lord Macmillan on 219–20
regarding noise nuisance 218
trespassing to land 219
Clarke, Justice 233
Coras Iompair Éireann (CIE) 72
Corporeal hereditament 10n
Courts
　defining private nuisance 217–8
　determining boundaries and 17
　　Rules of Construction of a
　　　Deed 17
　　using Old Deeds and Maps
　　　15–17
　District Court and works order
　　24–6
　　barking dogs and 191
　　dangerous dogs and 189
　　granting limited injunctive-
　　　type reliefs 33

regarding noise/nuisance
　applications 149–50
　adjourning for mediation
　　150
　mediation fails 150–1
High Court and squatters'
　rights 72
　judicial review and 223
Supreme Court and recreational
　users 170
Criminal Law (Defence and the
　Dwelling) Act 2011 181
　civil liability 183–4
　main provisions 181–2
　reasonable force test 182–3
Curtilage
　definition of 181

**D**

Dangerous place 141
　definition of 140
Dangerous sites *see* Derelict sites
Dangerous structure
　definition of 140
Declaration of Ownership
　*see also* Ownership
　planning permission is not 23
Deed
　of Assurance 70
　Rules of Construction 17
Demand for compensation *see*
　　Building owner
Department of Justice and Law
　　Reform
　on Criminal Law (Defence and
　　the Dwelling) Act 2011 181

Derelict sites 142
  Act 1990 133
  annual levy on 139
  compensation for acquisition
    of 136–7
  definition of 133–4
  failing to improve 135
    criminal sanctions for 141
  local authority and 135–6
    approaching 143
  Local Government (Sanitary
    Services) Act 1964 140–1
Dioxins 203n
District Court *see* Courts
Dog Nuisance Order *see* Animals
  causing nuisance
Dublin Corporation Act 1890 33–5
Dwelling
  definition of 181

**E**

Easements
  *see also Profit-à-prendre*
  acquiring, transitional
    framework for 66–7
    prior to 2009 Act 67
  created by express grant/
    registration 68
  definition of 53
  extinguishing 68
  in Irish law 54–5
    car-parking 61–2
    right of way 55
      preventing 68–9
    turning a vehicle 62–3
  of necessity 68

  requirements for claiming 64
    lost modern grant 65
    prescription at common
      law 65
Electricity Supply Board (ESB) 90
  felling trees on private lands
    90–1
Enforcement notices 101–3
Environmental Protection Agency
  (EPA)
  noise nuisance and 156–7
  'The Nature and Extent of
    Unauthorised Waste Activity
    in Ireland) 203
European Convention of Human
  Rights 73
European Court of Human Rights
  (ECHR)
  squatters' rights and 72–3
Exempted development *see*
  Planning permission

**F**

Fishing rights 58–9

**G**

Ghost estates 137–8
  local authority and 138–9
Geoghegan, Justice 170
Government Legislation
    Programme
  noise nuisance offences and 152

**H**

Hanlon, Justice 86
High Court *see* Courts

Hoffman, Lord 2
House of Lords 30, 57, 170
    on Rylands v Fletcher rule 221–2

## I

Iarnród Éireann 154
Injunctions *see* Civil remedies
Irish Aviation Authority 209
    *see also* Low flying aircraft
    power to prosecute 210
    rules of the air 210
Irish Institution of Surveyors 14
Irish land register
    definition of 12

## J

Judicial review *see* Civil remedies

## K

Keane, Chief Justice 62, 196, 221

## L

Landowner
    *see also* Occupier
    must assert legal title 75
    ordinary/prudent 85–6
    personal injury and 167
Land Registry 12
    *see also* Registry of Deeds
    mapping 13
        *see also* Maps
    non-conclusive boundary
        system 13–14
    squatters and 6
Law Reform Commission 238,
    241–2

Lindley, Lord 57
Litigation
    rule in 4
Local authority
    ghost estates and 138–9
    power to seize horses 193–4
Lost Modern Grant, Doctrine
    of *see* Easements
Low flying aircraft
    *see also* Irish Aviation Authority
    complaints procedure 211–2
        complaint form 214–5
    flight restrictions 210
    helicoptors 212
    noise disturbance 212–3

## M

Macmillan, Lord
    on reasonableness 219
Macnaghten, Lord 81
Maps
    role of, in determining
        boundaries 17–18
Mediation *see* Civil remedy
Minister for Communications,
    Energy and Natural
    Resources 90
Minister for Industry and
    Commerce 91
Minister for Lands *see* Minister for
    Communications, Energy
    and Natural Resources
Minister for the Environment,
    Community and Local
    Government 96, 134, 140, 204
Mummery, Lord Justice 237

# N

National Asset Management
    Agency 137
National Parks and Wildlife
    Service 93
National Roads Authority 154
Negligence *see* Civil remedies
New York
    Department of Environmental
        Protection 145
Newcrest Mining Ltd 220
Noise nuisance
    *see also* Civil remedies; Courts;
        Low flying aircraft
    An Garda Síochána and 151–2
    appeal, letters regarding 161–5
    barking dogs 153, 190–2
    civil remedies for 153
    decibel levels 147
    enforcement problems 151
    Environmental Protection
        Agency 156–7
    external intruder alarms 148
    in Irish law 145–6
    keep diary 146, 158
    mediation and 238–9
    Planning and Development
        Act 2000 155–6
    Private Residential Tenancies
        Board and 152
    reforming law on 152
    resolving 148
        apartment block of
            multi-unit development
            149–50
        letter of warning 159–60
        rented property 148
    serious matter 157

traffic: aircraft, road and rail
    153–5
Non-conclusive boundary system
    *see* Land Registry

# O

O'Shea, Patrick 195
Oaksey, Lord 87
Occupier
    *see also* Recreational user
    clearing snow/ice
        Dáil debate on 177–8
        on public footpath 178
    criminal entrant 179
    definition of 167
    injury on premises 168
        to visitors 171–2
            children 173
            duty of care 173–4
    Liability Act 167
    liability towards builders 175
        as employer 175–6
        on adjoining lands 176
    warning notice, to reduce
        liability 174–5
        example of 180
Office of the Ombudsman *see* Civil
    remedies
Ordinance Survey Ireland (OSI) 12,
    23, 125
    definition of 13
Ouster principle 61
Overstint 61
Ownership
    types of 6–11
        divided 8–9
            with Mutual Rights of
                Support 9

hedge and ditch presumption
10
of river bed 10
outright 6
presumed, as tenants in
common 7–8

**P**

Party structures *see* Boundary,
Shared
Planning and development
regulations 107–14
Planning permission
*see also* An Bord Pleanála
exempted development 95–6
common types of 98
aerials/satellite dishes
99–100
boiler houses 99
certain house extensions
98–9
front porches 99
garage conversions 99
walls and fences 99
declarations/certificates of 96
applying for 97–8
work orders and 96–7
helicopters and 212
is not a declaration of ownership
23
laws governing 95
objecting to 119
appealing after not 127–8
group 121
objection fails 124–5
observation 129

preparing to object 121
checking property history 122
irrelevant issues 124
Local Development Plan 122
wording 122–3
procedure for 120–1
required when 95
unauthorised development
applying for retention of 118
complaining about 100, 115
anonymously 100
enforcement notices 101–3
timeframe involved 106
warning letters 100–01
penalties for 103
planning injunctions 103–4
retention planning permission
105–6
urgent cases 103
Prescription Act 1832 66
Private Residential Tenancies
Board (PRTB) 148
resolution function of 152
Tenancy Tribunal 152
*Profit-à-prendre* 10n
*see also* Easements
definition of 54
in Irish law 54–5
right of drainage 59
right of eavesdrop and water
from overhanging roofs
59–60
right of estovers 60
right of pasturage 60–1
right of turbary 60
right of way 55
right to light 56–8

right to structural support
from adjoining building 56
right to water 58–9
not in Irish law
right of a structure
to protection against
weather 63
right to a view 63
coniferous trees and 82–3
repeal of prescription law 63–4
requirements for claiming 64
Property Registration Authority
(PRA) 11, 23, 67, 125
squatted lands and 76–7
Propertypoint 62–3

Right of eavesdrop and water from
overhanging roofs 59–60
Right of estovers 60
Right of pasturage 60–1
Right of turbary 60
Right of way
Justice Barr on 55
Right to light
coniferous trees and 82–3
House of Lords on 30
Lord Lindley on 57
Right to park 61–2
Right to water (Riparian Rights)
58–9
Riparian Rights see Right to water
Rodgers, Ms Weir
as recreational user 169–70

# R

Railway Procurement Agency 154
Reasonable force, test for 182–3
Recreational activity
definition of 168–9
Recreational user
children, injured as 171
definition of 168
duty of care to 169
in Supreme Court 169–71
farmers, trespassers and 169
Registry of Deeds
Application Form 15
primary function of 14
Res ipsa loquitur, doctrine of 195
Residential amenity
definition of 122
loss of 119
Richard I (Richard the Lionheart)
65n
Right of drainage 59

# S

Scienter principle
regarding attacking dogs 186
Shakespeare, William
Hamlet 2
Shared Boundary see Boundary,
Shared
Slander of title 1–2
definition of 1
Society of Chartered Surveyors 14
Squatters' rights (Adverse
possession) 5, 77
affirming ownership of squatted
lands 75–6
appealing 76–7
on leasehold titles 77
definition of 71
disabled individuals 73–4
fraudulent claims 73
in urban context 74

preventing squatters from
    acquiring title 75
requirement for 72
timeframe for 71–2
Statute barred 72
Supreme Court *see* Courts

## T

Telecom
    felling trees on private lands 91–2
Tenants in common 22
    definition of 7
Time immemorial 65n
Title documents
definition of 11–12
Tree Preservation Order (TPO)
    *see* Boundary trees
Trespassers
    *see also* Recreational users
    as nuisance 219
    attacked by dogs 186–7

## W

Works order 46–7
    abandoned property, taking
        possession of 49–52
    discharge/modification of 33,
        43, 48
    District Court and 24–5, 39–40
    exempted development and 96
    financial obligations 31–2
    issues of trespass and 28–9
    notice of application for 42
    order that damage be made
        good 45
    procedure 25–7
    right of support and 29
    right to light amongst others
        29–31, 97
    solicitor required for 35
    stopping, pending registration
        of easement 31
    terms and conditions 27–8

Notes